Within the Inscribed

ALSO BY MICHAEL HELLER:

POETRY
Two Poems
Accidental Center
Knowledge
Figures of Speaking
In the Builded Place
Marginalia in a Desperate Hand
Wordflow
Exigent Futures: New and Selected Poems
A Look at the Door With the Hinges Off
Eschaton
Beckmann Variations & other poems *
This Constellation Is A Name: Collected Poems 1965–2010
Dianoia
Constellations of Waking
Telescope: Selected Poems

PROSE
Earth and Cave
Living Root: A Memoir
Two Novellas: Marble Snows & The Study

ESSAYS
Conviction's Net of Branches: Essays on the Objectivist Poets and Poetry
Speaking the Estranged — Essays on the Work of George Oppen *
Uncertain Poetries: Essays on Poets, Poetry and Poetics *

EDITOR
Carl Rakosi: Man and Poet
Poets Poems #21

ON MICHAEL HELLER'S WORK
The Poetry and Poetics of Michael Heller: A Nomad Memory

indicates a title published by Shearsman Books.

Within the Inscribed

Selected Prose & Conversations

MICHAEL HELLER

with a foreword by Xavier Kalck

Shearsman Books

First published in the United Kingdom in 2021 by
Shearsman Books Ltd
PO Box 4239
Swindon
SN3 9FN

Shearsman Books Ltd Registered Office
30–31 St. James Place, Mangotsfield, Bristol BS16 9JB
(this address not for correspondence)

ISBN 978-1-84861-751-3

CONTENTS

Acknowledgments

Many of the writings and interviews in this collection have been previously published and/or presented as indicated below. I would like to thank the publishers, editors and organizations who gave me both permission and space for these works. I also want to thank the many writers and scholars who conversed, counseled, made suggestions, corrected and offered directions in the creation of this collection. Among these, I especially need to thank Xavier Kalck for his Foreword to this book and Norman Finkelstein for letting me publish his side of our conversation in 'On the Poetics of the Jewish Godhead,' part of a long and fruitful dialogue on poetry and poetics we have been engaged in for nearly thirty years. My deepest gratitude also to Burt Kimmelman and Jon Curley whose continuing collaborations and advice have been essential to my writing and thinking.

'On The Way To "The Sacred",' originally presented under the title 'Sacred Encounters: The Poetics of Uncertainty and Disclosure,' was the plenary address at the conference *Tools of the Sacred, Techniques of the Secular: Awakening, Epiphany, Apocalypse, and Doubt in Contemporary English-Language Verse at the* Université Libre de Bruxelles, 4–7 May 2010.

'Buddhadharma and Poetry Without Credentials' published in *The Emergence of Buddhist American Literature*, SUNY Press, 2009.

'From the Notes' published in *Beneath A Single Moon: Buddhism in Contemporary American Poetry.* Shambhala Books (2001)

'Remains of the Diaspora' was presented as the annual Duffy Lecture at Notre Dame University, 2007 and published in *Radical Poetics and Secular Jewish Culture*, University of Alabama Press (2010).

'On the Poetics of the Jewish Godhead' Norman Finkelstein and Michael Heller. *Imagining the Jewish God.* Edited by Leonard Kaplan and Ken Koltun-Fromm. Lexington Books, 2016.

'The Cloud: Exodus 35:1–40:38' published in *The Jewish Daily Forward*.

'Letter for *Archae*' published in *Archae* magazine.

'*Now-Time* Poetics: Under the Sign of Benjamin' was presented at the University of Marail, Toulouse conference, 'Tailor-Made Traditions: Contemporary American Experimental Poetry from H. D. to Michael Heller' and published in

Tailor-Made Traditions: Contemporary American Experimental Poetry from H. D. to Michael Heller (2013).

'A Conversation With Fiona McMahon' published in *Tailor-Made Traditions: Contemporary American Experimental Poetry from H. D. to Michael Heller* (2013).

'Oppen's Thematics [what are poets for?]' presented at The Kelly Writers House and published online in *Jacket2*.

'Glad you've initiated this correspondence' published in *The Oppens Remembered*. Edited by Rachel Blau Duplessis. University of New Mexico (2015).

'Dantean Reznikoff' published in *Talisman*.

'Fight for an Illusion: H.D.s *Helen In Egypt*, Pound's *Cantos* and the Masques of Myth and History' was presented at the 'H.D. and Modernity' conference at the Ecole normale supérieure in 2013 and published in *H.D. and Modernity*.

'The *War* of Poetry: Duncan's Heresies' was presented at the 2018 Louisville Conference on Modern Literature and Culture.

'Norman Finkelstein: Notes on the Scribal Poet' published in *Colorado Review*.

'In What Sense...' published in *Paideuma*

'An Interview with Michael Heller' published in the online section of *Rain Taxi*: http://www.raintaxi.com/an-interview-with-michael-heller/.

for Jane

Foreword

Xavier Kalck

The essays in this book, *Within the Inscribed: Selected Prose and Conversations*, describe a poet's attempts at a definition of poetry that would do justice to its practice as a quest. They are therefore decidedly tentative, inasmuch as the quest itself is endless. In that, they recall Heller's earlier book of essays entitled *Uncertain Poetries* (2005). Yet if that book explored the ways a poet might transform his and his own literary environment's skepticism toward language into a powerful exploratory poetics, this new endeavor bases that search in the specific notion of the sacred, as being inscribed in language.

These essays tell of a search for the sacred, a term that is at the core of this book. Here is one of Heller's central tenets when it comes to this most misleading and slippery word: "I would define the sacred as that which has been made intelligible and in the process made the world intelligible." Heller is interested in the sacred as a sense of striving for that renewed intelligibility, which does not belong to any single doctrine, which is why he always evokes the idea of the sacred through a complex prism of perspectives, some complementary, some at odds with one another. They must all be brought to bear if one is to fully appreciate this poet's concerns and ongoing journey. Heller typically does not present his reader with a single direction to pursue but offers every time a careful articulation of the tensions that make up each of these perspectives, which are always entwined. The book is divided into two large sections: the first focuses on key theological and philosophical issues relating to the nature of language and of the sacred, and on the possibility of achieving a poetics of mindfulness, while the essays in the second section take the form of dialogues with the works of single poets such as George Oppen, Charles Reznikoff, Allen Grossman, H.D., Ezra Pound, Robert Duncan and Norman Finkelstein. The reader will nevertheless be moved to constantly go back and forth from one essay to another as within a chamber of echoes. To understand why Heller proceeds in this fashion is to understand the deeply dialectic nature of his thinking, which this book demonstrates better than any of his previous collections of essays.

From a theological standpoint, Heller roots his thinking in Judaism, but from an outlook that has been deeply influenced by Buddhist teachings, training and spiritual explorations. Heller never quite speaks of, much less advocates, a turn from one tradition toward the other: what interests him is the displacement of tradition that takes place, the building of "a bridge work between the traditions," a kind of theological wandering, a diaspora of one's own faith. As Heller puts it in 'From the Notes,' "I am not after something syncretic, however; no real interest in the resonatings of terminologies, in the re-mirrorings of systems, all the false paths of *this* being like *that*. Rather, I find myself ripe for rubrics and mottoes, for pressures and instructions on how to proceed … to break through the seductive constellations of human ordering." Hence the fact that the questions Heller battles, difficult though they might be, are not put forth as abstract problems, but experienced through a richly hesitant conversation. As a result, the curious reader will find many biographical lifelines in these pages, from well-known thinkers such as Gershom Scholem or Martin Heidegger, to potentially much less familiar figures like Chögyam Trungpa, Herbert V. Guenther, or Gampopa, which the reader may choose to pull at, eager for the promise of a transformative encounter with such important texts as *The Jewel Ornament of Liberation* or *The Royal Song of Saraha*, as well as key texts from the Judaic and Western philosophic tradition such as Gershom Scholem's *On the Mystical Shape of the Godhead*, Heidegger's writings on language or Benjamin's essays.

Most importantly, Heller's concern with the sacred is with a function of language and as an objective in his poetics. From the "scribal poetics" Heller identifies in Norman Finkelstein's work in connection with William Bronk's legacy, to Heller's many insights into George Oppen's poetry's "generative moments[s] in consciousness," which he proceeds to contrast with Duncan's proliferating heresies of meaning. Still, this one central guideline does not help bring peace to Heller's anxious spiritual considerations. Rather, it drives Heller to display a profound skepticism as he contemplates the synonymies between several belief systems and spiritual horizons since, as he writes of Oppen, he is engaged in a "search for a poetics free of dogma and *a priori* views of poetry." This is not as contradictory as might be imagined. In fact, I would argue it describes very adequately Heller's dialectics of concealment and revelation, to borrow the words Heller himself quotes from poet Haim Nahman Bialik, and which can be summarized in the idea that, "the fullness of language must remind us of the void it conceals." Such complementary thinking leads Heller's dual search both for that fullness of expression and for the means to draw as near to that void as possible. By keeping this sort of balance, Heller navigates between a freedom of thought verging on the chaotic and a thoughtfully organized disorder, knowing that this very chaos is rich with many beacons of light, even though he will not be satisfied with a single one.

A similar case can be made regarding Heller's philosophical outlook. His chief focus is on phenomenology—German and French—with a slant on aesthetics. However, if Heller discusses notions of presence and the concept of Being, from a European perspective rather than an Emerson or Thoreau-based American standpoint, he is not concerned with Merleau-Ponty's essay on Cézanne per se, or with Walter Benjamin's essays as such. The phenomenal world, along with humanity's aesthetic accomplishments or philosophical doctrines are envisaged here as so many stepping-stones and, I would venture, subsumed under a single heading—that of language, though I should be careful to point out that Heller is certainly not suggesting any hierarchical superiority of poetry over any other human endeavor. Accordingly, what is particularly refreshing in these essays is that the accumulation of reference points does not compose a web of allusions but punctuates the book with moments in a continued dialogue.

The reason for this is that "language" does not evoke for Heller the poet's command over it; on the contrary, his preoccupation with language sends the poet back to his struggle, "to produce an articulation of that which was previously inarticulate," bearing in mind that that which is inarticulate will never be thoroughly expressed. Heller's poetic faith lies in "linguistic attempts" to enact larger issues which may be approached, not settled, in language. The poet's hope is for "momentary" revelations; a point which, in circular fashion, leads one back to theological matters and to a notion of the sacred as what may be revealed by language and named but only aimed at—not captured in any static representational sense. One will have recognized, in Heller's emphasis on the limits of naming, and as he himself explains, traces of Scholem's thinking on the Kabbalah, of Benjamin's writings on language, and also of Lionel Kochan's profoundly stimulating study of Judaism and iconoclasm, *Beyond the Graven Image: A Jewish View* (1997). Heller also locates his thinking firmly within the American Whitmanian tradition of crisscrossed de-sanctification and re-sanctification of the world, where Buddhism, Western philosophy and the sense of a secular holiness within

U.S. poetry merge into a new sense of awe. His is a similar quest for the spiritual within the secular world, by way of an apophatic theology, a *via negativa* defined as a way through a pared-down language toward the physicality of the world accessed through words provided they are treated, to quote George Oppen, "as enemies." The paradox of a palpable word is defined by Heller thus: "Somewhere in every act of perception, one is reduced to a word. This is not a word that stands for oneself; nor does it represent oneself. This word (the poem) *is* oneself." Heller's goal may seem unattainable, until one is reminded of the path followed by objectivist poets all along the twentieth century, which Heller has been so instrumental in championing. Many of the most resonant essays in this book are indeed those devoted to George Oppen and Charles Reznikoff, in which Heller's idea of a "poetry without credentials" becomes most fascinatingly enacted.

Uncertainty and the patient disowning of credentials have been paramount in Heller's writing for some time, but what is so striking in this book is the perfect equilibrium he reaches there between the credentials one must unlearn and the search for a workable poetic creed. Again, the contradictory character of this logic is what drives it forward. In a sense, it may be compared with the key use of language in a poetics of disclosure that is aimed at showing what lies precisely beyond language's abilities to show. The paradoxical nature of this thinking could be problematic if it were circular to the point of frustration, but it is not. It relies on a passion for continued explorations which Heller calls "midrashic," when he writes that "[t]he midrashic condition for the poet amounts to a situation in which no issue of language is finally settled. Caught at every point in language's endlessness, […] he finds his environment cocoon-like, ever-circling into self-referentiality." Such a cocoon could easily be construed as exceedingly restrictive, although the idea of a self-interpreting text is a foundational element in Midrash. Why it is never the case here is the reason the book makes for such a compelling read: Heller's writing may at times be quite personal and even intimate, he never ceases to share this endlessness of language so that it becomes conversational and eventually relational.

Take for instance the remarks assembled under the heading, 'On the Poetics of the Jewish Godhead,' initially collected as part of a dialogue between Heller and fellow poet Norman Finkelstein, published in a collection of essays entitled *Imagining the Jewish God* (2016). I am thinking, in particular, of the moment when Heller refers to his recent poem, the first in his 2016 collection *Dianoia*, entitled 'Mappah,' the

Hebrew word for the cloth that binds together and protects the scrolls of the Torah. The *mappah* is meant to shield the text from the light of the world, but Heller expands that light to include the dark light of the flames that would destroy it. Used as a title and therefore as an image of the text itself, the word *mappah* suggests that the poem wraps itself around the sacred—its protective embroidery a tactile threshold for our access to a revelation which must be kept out of sight, thus testifying to the dialectics of the sacred as that which can only be shown when it is hidden. *Mappah* is also another word for a wimple, the piece of cloth used during ritual circumcision, among German Jews particularly, to swaddle the child (it is literally cocoon-like), which would be decorated with the child's name and date of birth along with wishes for future prosperity. If one takes this other meaning into consideration, the poem may then be said to open up an elaborate dialogue between tradition and individual life, the sacred text and the mortal body, in which the protective (and coercive) parchment-like linen cloth binds together very different levels of reality and of language use.

"Someone lifts and folds the cloth, someone follows the Hebrew with / the *yod*, the sculpted finger cast in gold. *Davar* and *davar*," writes Heller in this poem. Despite the use of specific terms—the *yod*, a pointer used to read the Torah (which resembles a hand, *yad* in Hebrew) and to keep from touching the sacred text with one's hand, or the word *davar* (speech, words or utterance in Hebrew, but also in the plural God's commandments)—the sense of a loss of ritual and of belonging seems to be suggested in the vague mention of an unidentified "someone" who is performing these gestures and tasks, a choice which contributes to the reader's impression that words and writing are located by Heller in a kind of in-between or half-way between the sacred and the secular, and between the communal and the singular. One might even say that Heller's poetics of uncertainty advocates against the use of such a tool as a *yod*, in that the poet should point directly to the phenomenal word as well as to the written testaments of what that world is or was and must not act as if his were the hand of a god. The word "someone" in Heller's poem, in that sense, means anyone, be they sanctified and authorized or not. However, Heller's poetics shares in the special condition of the *yod* on another level, as the smallest of signs with which God's name nonetheless begins. This particular position of the *yod* is well known. It is the smallest letter in the Hebrew alphabet, yet it is the initial letter of the tetragram. Much has been written about it, namely from the perspective of these oddly paradoxical features, but also because it has been used as an alphabetical allegory of the Jewish people due to its proximity with the Yiddish word *yid* (a Jew, without any of the offensive connotations of that term in English). As an allegory, critics have noted, the *yod* also exemplifies the duality of Yiddish as a secular tongue made up of several vernacular languages and yet written in the Hebrew alphabet which, when modern Hebrew was but a dream, stood out as a sacred tongue.

Heller's poetry, like much of his thinking such as it is recorded in these pages, enacts the function of that *yod*—it takes the reader by the hand over that gap between the sacred and the real and into the inscribed. Charles Reznikoff once wrote of the Hanukkah lights that they were lit "not to see by but to look at." Heller's relationship to language echoes this kind of displacement inasmuch as, illuminated by the sacred, language becomes for him something not only to speak with but to look at. This book stands as Heller's invitation to enter with him in that dialogue about language which dives into the most distant and ancient past while it remains most urgent.

Xavier Kalck is an associate professor at Sorbonne University (Paris). He is the author of several books on twentieth-century poetry in English and French, among them, *George Oppen's Poetics of the Commonplace*, 2017; *Pluralism, Poetry, and Literacy: A Test of Reading and Interpretive Techniques*, 2021, "We said Objectivist": Lire les poètes *Lorine Niedecker, George Oppen, Carl Rakosi, Charles Reznikoff, Louis Zukofsky*, 2019; *La poésie américaine entre chant et parole: l'héritage objectiviste*, 2020), as well as many articles on poetics.

"the sacred has so inscribed itself in language that while it must be interpreted, it cannot be removed
—Geoffrey Hartman

Author's Note

That the *logos* is divine, that it embodies the aura of the sacred, an aura that infuses *poesis*—this is ancient lore and contemporary practice. These are the thematics that I develop in the first section of this collection of writings, conversations, notes and reviews. *The Princeton Encyclopedia of Poetry and Poetics* directs those searching for the meaning of *logos* to look in the entries for "ethos" and "pathos." Ethos centers in the speaker and pathos concerns the listening or reading audience's response. Rhetoric, in its largest sense as the movement of language, becomes bridgework. *Poesis* is shaped by *logos*, by making. But also, especially in the present, as older traditions lose their hold, there is a reverse movement, in which *poesis* remakes *logos*. These are the terms across which we speak and with which I approach the question of divinity and the sacred in the activity of making poems. I think of poetry here as a particular kind of awareness of the world, of its languages, its specificities and tonalities, as enlargements of our sense of what is divine, what is sacred. Further, I seek a ground which through the act of poetry invests these terms with a secular dimension, independent of received religions, which is why, in a number of essays, I draw on the non-theistic aspects of Western philosophy and Buddhist thought.

Such explorations can be seen as already implicit in my previous writings, not only in the work on the Objectivist poets and George Oppen in *Conviction's Net of Branches* and in *Speaking The Estranged: Essays on the Work of George Oppen* but also underlying the writings in *Uncertain Poetries* that focused on poets as diverse as Robert Duncan, Lorine Niedecker, Armand Schwerner, Montale, Stevens and on the instabilities of poetic language, especially in the light of modernism, post-modernism, the Jewish Diaspora and the Shoah. My aim as a practicing poet has been to explore these deeply unsettled relationships to culture, religion and spirituality. This gathering of essays and conversations, spanning approximately twenty years and culled out of a larger body of writings, can be regarded as an extension and development of those long-standing concerns.

How did this present gathering of writings come about? A sort of ur-event that led me to organize this book came when, in going through my papers, I found the text of 'On the Way to "The Sacred"' (originally entitled 'Sacred Encounters: The Poetics of Uncertainty and Disclosure,'), a plenary address I had given nearly ten years ago in Brussels after having received and accepted an invitation from Professor Franca Belarsi of the Université Libre de Bruxelles for the 2010 conference, *Tools of the Sacred, Techniques of the Secular: Awakening, Epiphany, Apocalypse and Doubt in Contemporary English-Language Verse*. That somewhat long-winded title resonated with the title of Jerome Rothenberg's ground-breaking anthology, *Technicians of the Sacred*, and Professor Bellarsi readily confessed that Rothenberg's work had been an inspiration to forming the conference. In the spirit of that anthology, what intrigued me most and led me to want to participate was the phrase "tools of the sacred." What were these tools was the question on my mind when I accepted the invitation to speak. One implicit answer, a governing one for me, is given in Geoffrey Hartman's phrase which I have taken as the epigraph for this book: *"the sacred has so inscribed itself in language that while it must be interpreted, it cannot be removed."* This sense of inscription and trace is what I explore here.

This collection is organized into three related sections. The first section, as I have suggested above, ranges over topics such as Gershom Scholem's notion of "secular holiness," Heidegger's connection to Eastern thought and its influence on such poets as Wallace Stevens and George Oppen, the relation of diasporic Judaism to poetics, Buddhist practice and poetry, Walter Benjamin's "now-time" poetics, and the "sacred" as inscribed in language as discussed in my conversation with Norman Finkelstein in 'On the Poetics of the Jewish Godhead.' The second section contains essays and reviews on specific poets, the themes and questions their work provokes. I write about Oppen and Reznikoff making poetry out of, as Oppen called it, "a language ruined," about H.D. and Robert Duncan, and their poetics or way of handling language, history and questions of culture and myth. I also briefly contemplate Finkelstein's "scribal" poetics, a theme of his early book *Scribe*, which strikes me as resonating with many of the themes of this collection. My reflections focus primarily on poetic language among these poets who throughout their work have been concerned with religious and spiritual traditions and on the questions of uncertainty and poetic-truth value that surround these traditions. The third section, or 'Coda,' consists of three works: a short autobiographical sketch on science and "theisms," a response to a question on poetry and our current cultural and political situation, and a recent interview that covers many interwoven phases of my writing and thinking about poetry.

While this collection of work composed over a number of years is not a monograph, it does exhibit some monograph-like, perhaps obsessive qualities. Among the writers referred to again and again are Benjamin, Scholem, Heidegger and Oppen along with numerous references to Merleau-Ponty, Bialik, Stevens, Cavell, Chögyam Trungpa Rinpoche and Herbert V. Guenther. Their work and thought thread through and, in a way, knit together much of the writing and discussion here. I consider whatever I have to offer in relation to their work to be only hesitantly put forward, more homage, more footnote than scholarship.

"Remains"
(An Addendum)

I write this as I send off the manuscript of this collection to its publisher. It is December, 2020, and words other than mine come to mind: "The disaster takes care of everything," writes Maurice Blanchot in *The Writing of Disaster*. Later he exclaims: "ruin of words, demise writing, faintness, faintly murmuring, what remains without remains." I too, faintly murmuring, write down some few words: the pandemic, the Covid 19 virus and the insanity and absurdity in politics that, like the disease, has infected so many. As with the attacks of September 11th, there is now suddenly a sort of hinge in human affairs, the pandemic and the madness of those in political power, on which literature and the arts swing. They form an axis or take-off point from which words have to stray, to intermingle. At first, they make for an occasion in which certain options of expression seemed to be foreclosed, and yet these foreclosures are in no way sets of rules or prohibitions, they only speak to how one now views one's time. They are not felt to be the sort of obiter dictum that Adorno pronounced on poetry after the Holocaust. Perhaps the following anecdote from Giacometti will seem trivial, but he once spoke, actually quite eloquently, if there were a conflagration in his studio, of saving his cat first before his paintings or sculpture. His words—let's take them as sincerely meant—expressed his intention of wanting to set art in balance with the rest of reality, and he was aware not only of the limited responses art could make to a critical situation, but also of the choices one might face in a crisis. He saw the hinge on his studio door quite literally.

The hinge is no mere moment in time, registering a sea-change. If that were so, Adorno would have been right to chastise art and expression.

But it is a fact that poets refused then as now suddenly to be silent. In fact, on disaster, we have become almost voluble. The hinge, then, appears as primarily a focal point upon which all of one's history, personal, political and cultural, is concentrated by powerful external events. No event for the living, for those possessed of memory and consciousness, is a lobotomy. What "remains without remains" is recollection, something the disaster cannot erase unless in the heat of anguish or passion, we permit our own forgetfulness. And such reflections on our past have a kind of spotlessness to them, which is why the phrase "without remains" doesn't strike me as being either nihilistic or defeatist. This spotlessness, however, is something that doesn't automatically exist. In fact, it must be worked toward. If memory is obscured by the passion of present event, if it is colored into distortion, then, indeed, it is not spotless. If, on the other hand, we can remember our past clearly, that we had such and such a liking and such and such a hate, that we loved X and Y and Z and feared A and B, that we got immense pleasure or anger and frustration out of the dailiness of our lives, whether creating or whether experiencing the world, then we are beginning to see spotlessly, without obscurations.

"Thousands of words, myriad interpretations, are only to free you from obstructions," writes Siketo Kisen in *Song of the Grass Roof Hermitage* (700–790 AD). As I write, I'm circling around trying to say something, trying to justify sending this manuscript to my publisher (all of which was written before our current disasters), at a moment when the world cries out in pain and bewilderment, much of which has been self-inflicted. So I try to make a gesture against the suffering, not so much to relieve it—I don't think art can sufficiently console—but to suggest that, no more and no less, any act which attempts to bring understanding and definition is an attempt to see spotlessly, one of those "myriad interpretations" which leads one to clarity. And then there is the question and possibility of the sacred, for us, for us to use, to make, which is at the root of this work.

I

ON THE WAY TO "THE SACRED"

I take as a starting point the words of the German-Jewish philosopher Gershom Scholem who describes Walt Whitman as having "a feeling of the absolute holiness of the completely secular." Scholem may well have had in mind this passage from Whitman's 'Starting From Paumanouk:'

> Was somebody asking to see the soul? See, your shape and
>   countenance, persons, substances,
> beasts, the trees, the running rivers, the rocks and sands

That dream of a secular holiness, of the sacred re-imagined on a new base as the identification of the poem with the real, is, in a sense, one of the major projective themes of modern and contemporary poetry. It is also complementary to the projective theme of the spiritual quest, a deliverance of human life and consciousness into an accurate and even "divine" relationship with the world.

Whitman's vision, one of "a higher naturalistic consciousness," as Scholem defined it, is an ancient vision. Herbert J. Guenther, whose works on Tantric Buddhism this essay draws on, writes that, in the work of the 10th century Sanskrit poet Saraha, "the spiritual is discovered as a path stretched out before our eyes to a distant goal and yet grounded in ourselves; it is not a spurious addition." Saraha insisted that in such matters one must "understand appearance to be the teacher." If the "spiritual" is revealed via the "secular," grounded in ourselves, then poetry—as opposed to ritual or liturgical poems—can be a mode of the sacred's appearance and revelation. These explorations are configured in the spiritual traditions of Western speculative philosophy and in the non-theistic thematics of Buddhist views with their notions of relative and absolute truth. The traditions and thoughts of the poets whom I will discuss involve large and complex subject areas, and all I can hope to do here is provide a sort of red thread of linguistic gestures, ideas, conceptions and poetry that throw light on the dream of that "secular holiness" experienced by Scholem as he read Whitman.

I want to lay a modern ground for my discussion, so I will begin by looking at the speculative thought of Martin Heidegger, but I do so under a number of permissions, that of Heidegger's focus on Western poetry and on his connection to Eastern thought, and more broadly on the relation of that thought to some foundational ideas of the spiritual impulse in American poetry, specifically as found in the work of Wallace Stevens and George Oppen.

The philosopher Stanley Cavell in his essay 'Thinking of Emerson' argues for the similarities between the thought of Emerson (along with Thoreau) and that of Heidegger. He writes, "I am not claiming that Heidegger authenticates the thinking of Emerson and Thoreau; the contrary is, for me, fully as true, that Emerson and Thoreau may authorize our interest in Heidegger." Emerson would normally be the proper person to start with if one has invoked the secular holiness of Whitman or is going to say something about Stevens, but here I follow what Cavell refers to as Emerson's call for "onward thinking, the thing Heidegger means in taking thinking as a matter of getting ourselves "on the way." Part of getting on the way will be looking at the work of Stevens and Oppen, both influenced by Heidegger's thought, both explorers of the polyvalence of linguistic structures, explorations based on their conviction that the uncertainty inherent in the poetic use of language is the key to disclosure of what Stevens intuits as divinity and Oppen calls "the miraculous". Finally, by way of motive here, I want to cite a few words from George Oppen's *Daybook*:

> Eastern thought: necessarily within the Western and in the Christian tradition at least since Plotinus. And in fact much earlier. The Vedantas are not *esoteric* revelation to the Westerner who has read Western philosophy. The point is rather the Heideggerian idea that all people burst into history with these thoughts... And that all people, all persons, reaching any profundity of thought, are aware of these things.

So I am getting underway, reaching for profundity via Heidegger, who writes in 'What is Metaphysics (1929),' an essay that strongly influenced Oppen, that "the Nothing is not just the opposite of beings: it is essential to their very emergence." I cannot pretend to know the precise meaning of "the Nothing" in Heidegger, but if we take the thrust of his statement as a kind of pressure (a "hint" Heidegger would call it), we begin on a path that leads us to the subject under discussion. Heidegger, in his *Introduction to Metaphysics* insists that "nothingness remains inaccessible to science," and can only be glimpsed via philosophy and poetry.

Heidegger's "The Nothing," like the often misunderstood notion of "emptiness" or "śūnyatā" in Eastern thought and in specifically Buddhist spiritual practice, cannot be assigned a clear definition. As with the Buddhist idea of "emptiness", Heidegger's "Nothing" seems more like a marker than an entity, one without attributes, unborn and un-originated. But we can say, even if we can say little else, that "the Nothing" is related to the cause, the ground, the backdrop to uncertainty in Heidegger's thought, an uncertainty that transforms it from a positivist philosophy into a series of speculations that resemble a practice and a poetics.

The resonances between Heidegger's "the Nothing" and "emptiness" strike as uncanny because, as we know, Heidegger's essay, like much of his work, has links with areas of Asian speculative philosophy. Joan Stambaugh, the Heidegger scholar and his former student, in her review of Takeshi Umehara's 'Heidegger and Buddhism,' writes: "perhaps it is astonishing that any Western thinker comes as close to the East as Heidegger does." In her review, she notes both parallels and differences concerning such key areas as the notion of *śūnyatā* and "being," asymptotic convergences of Heidegger and Buddhism. As she notes, "Heidegger's Being and the Buddhist *shunya* have in common the fact that they are nothing specific or deterministic; they are also not merely 'nihilistic' and cannot be directly expressed." She writes that "Heidegger is not concerned with beings and even speaks of nothingness as the veil of Being." Yet "Heidegger's idea of *Austrag*, (perdurance, sustained endurance)" she claims, "bears a striking resemblance to Dōgen's 'sustained exertion, the highest form of exertion, which goes on unceasingly in cycles from the first dawning of religious truth through the test of discipline and practice, to enlightenment and Nirvana'." In short, we find many linkages and resonances to "Eastern thinking" in Heidegger, especially in such later works as 'A Dialogue on Language' with its imagined leisurely stroll together of a Japanese thinker and an "Inquirer" philosopher. And those linkages, as expressed in 'A Dialogue on Language' are both fruitful and poignant and, to my mind, especially relevant to poetry.

In the 'Dialogue,' the two thought-systems, the Japanese and the Western, as expressed by the speakers on their walk, circle around and occasionally entwine each other, no more so than when the Japanese speaker resorts to the poetic terms of his language like "*iki*" and "*koto ba*," terms that, per force, can only be expressed—can only be pointed to in their fullest sense visually and imagistically. "*Iti*," says the Japanese stroller is "the breath of the stillness of luminous delight." The "*koto*" of *koto ba* means that which "gives delight, itself, that which uniquely in each unrepeatable moment comes to radiance in the fullness of grace" while the "*ba*" means "leaves... especially the leaves of a blossom—petals." For both speakers, the subject that they are discussing, *language*, can be approached only so far with words, and at some point—and this is the poignancy—the discussion must move beyond language, must surrender itself or invoke something that arouses the specter of the inarticulate, "nothingness," "grace," "luminous delight."

Heidegger, trying in this dialogue to situate the thinker with respect to the poignancy of that surrender of words, refers to man as "the message-bearer of the two-fold unconcealment," where Heidegger's "unconcealment" (the Greek *alētheia* or "uncovering") gives a dynamic meaning to the word "truth." The subject of that phrase, "message-bearer," is co-extensive with Heidegger's notion of the poet, for he describes the "two-fold unconcealment [as] the simultaneous laying bare of 'Being and beings'." The word "Being" for Heidegger is not a sign of some existing entity, but, like his word "Nothing," functions as a "hint." As with the Buddhist notion of "emptiness," it lies beyond articulate meaning. The message-bearer is the one who walks, who thinks through this space between Being and beings, what Heidegger calls the "boundary of the boundless," a boundary between the intelligibility of the universe, its capacity to be named—this is its "Being"—and the names of things (of beings) themselves.

Along this boundary, this border condition, what I sense as poignant in Heidegger's thought is most fully expressed, for it is here that the message-bearer's search for articulation lies adjacent to the uncertainty of the poetic enterprise, to the act of naming. Naming, while ultimately resting in the unconcealment of Being and beings, arrives, as I understand Heidegger's thought, out of that "Nothing" which is required for them to emerge. Heidegger describes this struggle, as Stambaugh places it in relation to Eastern thought, as "a ground being sought which will explain the emergence of the essent [the being] as an overcoming of nothingness." For Heidegger, the spirit of poetry and philosophy is superior to that of science, and it is "by the virtue of this superiority the poet always speaks as though the essent were being expressed and invoked for the first time." In this sense, Heidegger's thought can be seen as a late flowering of German Romanticism. And, as we know, his work constitutes a major exploration as well as a major post-note to the sort of problems raised in Hölderlin's poetry or in the "thing" poetry of Rilke.

These problems, to give an instance, are clearly expressed in Hugo von Hofmannsthal's 'Lord Chandos Letter' whose narrator, in the midst of explicating a horrifying vision he has had of poisoned rats in a cellar, exclaims that "once again words desert me." In this vision, he finds traces of "burning Carthage" and other historical catastrophes, but goes on to explain, "there was something more divine, more bestial, and it was the Present, the fullest most exalted Present." Hölderlin has anticipated this experience in his notes: "In the state between being and non-being," he writes, "the possible is everywhere real and the actual [is] ideal, and in free artistic imitation this is a frightful and divine dream."

If the "rats" and "burning Carthage" invoke Hofmannsthal's "bestial," what makes this vision also shimmer with the "divine" and with an "exalted Present?" The poet must first be deserted by words, emptied in a sense, in order to find new ones that are adequate, that will deliver him into the fullness of the "Present." It is as if its author were testifying to the act of poetry itself, as if being astonished by something, then seeking after words and casting them into some sort of image-construct were, to echo Hölderlin's words, to partake of divinity itself. The poetic act gives birth to that which did not previously exist, and that, on one level is its "divinity." In *On The Way Toward Language*, Heidegger's thought seems to reflect the dynamics of both Hölderlin's and Hofmannsthal's poetics. "The illumination of Presence," he claims, "makes poetry." In 'The Nature of Language,' he writes that "whatever bestows being, must it not 'be' itself, all the more and before all else?" Isn't Heidegger here referring to Hofmannsthal's "divine," to something that we can label "sacred?" And isn't Heidegger privileging language and poetry as the bearer of this sacredness?

Language then, as Heidegger suggests, becomes the first tool of the sacred, and while its pedigree of divinity from *Logos* to *différance* is long, does there not exist something *a priori*, call it "Being" or "poetry" which shows forth or bears this sacredness? Geoffrey Hartman, in *Criticism in the Wilderness*, writes that "the sacred has so inscribed itself in language that while it [language and the sacredness of it] must be interpreted, it cannot be removed." Language, according to Hartman, already bears the burden of the sacred, and the implication from both Heidegger and Hartmann are that the poet "unconceals" or "discloses" this inscription.

* * *

Guenther, in his introduction to the *The Royal Song of Saraha*, writes that "the image in its immediacy is a moment of original vision full of suggestions rather than comprehension." "Royal Songs" or "*Dohas*" are teaching poems, written in Sanskrit, described by Guenther as pathways into the Buddhist tantric view of life. The poems, he tells us, invoke

> pictorial, emotional, and cognitive meanings, all of which are present in poetry or a song which may said to bring into the open all that we discuss and then deal with in everyday language. Hence poetry never takes language as raw material ready to hand; rather it is poetry which first makes language possible.

This formulation, as with Hartman's, suggests a recasting—or perhaps a prior casting—of the Heideggerian "two-fold unconcealment." "Being" and "poetry" are, respectively, the hinted-at sources of "beings" and words, which enact a generative simultaneity. For Heidegger, appearance embodies the "reality of presence," a reality that is released into divinity by the poet. The Tibetan translators of the *Dohas* from the Sanskrit, Guenther notes, were engaged in "phenomenalistic thinking, which sees the absolute in the phenomenal, not beyond it. The particular of the moment is the total event, not an abstraction from it which is then contrasted with the universal."

Such a "total event" lies at the heart of Wallace Stevens's poetics. As Stevens reminds us, for a poet, the imagination is first a matter of words, of language. It is an article of faith to the poet's calling, as when Stevens, in his *Adagia*, that marvelous collection of his aphorisms concerning poetry, religion and spirituality, insists that "in poetry, you must love the words, the ideas and the images and rhythms with all your capacity to love anything at all." He writes that "a new meaning is the equivalent of a new word," reminding us that poetry has the same inherent dignity and "thingness" as any natural object in the cosmos. He proclaims this dignity, not as supposition but as fact, throughout the entire body of his work, as in these late lines from 'An Ordinary Evening In New Haven:'

> The poem is the cry of its occasion,
> Part of the *res* itself, not about it.
> The poet speaks the poem as it is,

Not as it was: part of the reverberation
Of a windy night as it is, when the marble statues
Are like newspapers blown by the wind. He speaks

By sight and insight as they are...
...said words of the world are the life of the world

As with so much of Stevens's work and thought, it is a matter of the words' atmospherics, a compact by which what appears to be merely the descriptive function of language, a function closely allied to philosophy's instructive bent, is alchemically transformed. It is poetry's "reverberation" that exposes the marble of solidified thought as the windblown transient words of newsprint. For Stevens, then, the life of words and the life of the world are co-joined in "the cry of its occasion," if not in unity, at least, as he puts it elsewhere, in "equilibrium." The poem is not 'about' a world but rather an instancing, "a *res*," of it, a "welling up," to borrow Heidegger's phrase for the function of poetry.

Frank Kermode, in his brilliant essay, 'Dwelling Poetically In Connecticut,' surmises that for Stevens, Heidegger was most likely "more *myth* than reality." Kermode imagines Stevens conjuring an "image" of the philosopher "in his peasant clothes, darkly speculating upon his hero and supreme poet [Hölderlin], precursor of the angel most necessary when, after the failure of the gods, our poverty [imaginative and poetic] is most complete." Most profoundly, Stevens, with what might be called the rumor of the philosopher in mind, ruminates throughout his late poetry the very question Hölderlin forces on Heidegger: "what are poets for in the time of poverty?" Poetic language is the stay, the complementary stay, as Heidegger would call it, "of our being toward death."

As Kermode makes clear, both Heidegger and Stevens, through a process of magical transmittal (perhaps a Heideggerian "hint") sense the sacred character of poetic language, and that it is the sacred's function to enlarge human freedom, to release us from the enmarbled monuments of thought and give us the palpable feeling of our dwelling on the earth.

If, as Stevens writes, the "said words of the world are the life of the world," that life comes from the power of lyric poetry, not as an enticing dance of words but via its "horde of destructions," as Stevens claimed of art itself in *The Necessary Angel*; the disruptive energies break the bounds of previous thought. Stevens throughout his career sets poetry against discourse or rhetoric, against the hardened concepts of rule and "truth" which hem in the imagination. Creation becomes a new articulation, and creative language is no longer the handmaiden of philosophy or rhetoric. It takes its place in the world, possibly as the object of philosophy itself.

Kermode, borrowing a Heideggerian terminology, sees Stevens's poetry as enacting *alētheia*, that act of "unconcealedness," that, as Kermode puts it, "*lets the earth be an earth*" [Kermode's italics]. This is the sacred act, embodied as revealment and articulation. Unowned by any religion or persuasion. Hence "it is the belief and not the god that counts," says Stevens in *Adagia*.

For a poet, this matter of belief is crucial, especially for one like Stevens who "abandoned a belief in god," only to insist that poetry was "that essence which takes its place as life's redemption"—crucial and vexed. Yeats, I think, struck the cautionary note concerning belief when he reminded poets that they "must not make a false faith by hiding from our thoughts the causes of doubt… The poet, because he may not stand within the sacred house but lives amid the whirlwinds that beset its threshold, may find pardon." What Yeats and Stevens seem to warn the poet about is a kind of theism, not only of religion but of poetry as well. The poet has made a vow to unboundedness, to resisting any sort of limit, either one proposed by tradition or theory. The poet takes a pledge to that which remains to be articulated, to respecting meaning and non-meaning as the ultimate events of language.

Poetry's uncertain or outsider status lies in its refusal of any "limiting attitude." Unboundedness, in this sense is not an idea but a recognition of the continual, generative power of the creative mind, what the late Armand Schwerner, in his study of Stevens, refers to as the poet's attention to "the movemented shuttlings of the world" which open up possibility rather than to "add another limiting attitude to those which constrict the possible grandeur of the imagination." Stevens resists the platonic turn, writing in *Adagia* that "the ideal is the actual becoming anemiac," that to move from particulars to a generalization is to lose both meaning and the sacredness of dwelling. Elsewhere, in *The Necessary Angel*, he tells us that "the imagination loses vitality when it ceases to adhere to what is real."

The poet deconstructs the philosophical and the conceptual to bring us back to Stevens's "primary noon," that moment or place where the mind starts up afresh, where thought's shadow is momentarily abolished. Not in naivete but in full knowledge of how thought itself has overlaid the world. In 'Notes Toward a Supreme Fiction,' Stevens writes, "Begin, ephebe [young man, learner]/by perceiving the idea of this invention…

You must become an ignorant man again/and see the sun again with an ignorant eye." This beginning, as he wrote in, 'To an Old Philosopher in Rome,' his poem on the death of George Santayana, reminds us that the sacred as embedded in language is revealed by the power of analogy, where the "figures in the street/Become the figures of Heaven." Stevens's "primary noon" marks the time and place of Heideggerian "unconcealment" in which the world and being stand free. As he wrote concerning 'An Ordinary Evening in New Haven,' his interest was "to try to get as close to the ordinary, the commonplace and the ugly as it is possible for a poet to get. It is not a question of grim reality but of plain reality. The object is of course to purge oneself of anything false."

Stevens remarks in *The Necessary Angel* "that to confront fact in its total bleakness is for any poet a completely baffling experience." As in Heidegger's idea of "earth, which shatters every attempt to penetrate it" and creates the "rift" between language and reality," the "fact" for Stevens is in essence the arena of poetic activity. That very confrontation, in the willingness of the poet to lean into "fact" with all of his or her power, comprises poetry's sublime beauty. Here, for Stevens, is poetry's function writ large: "the need," he writes in *The Necessary Angel*, "which it [poetry] meets and which has to be met in some way in every age that is not decadent or barbarous, is precisely this contact with reality as it impinges upon us from outside, the sense that we can touch and feel a solid reality which does not wholly dissolve itself into the conceptions of our own minds." For Stevens, this contact with reality is where language's power lies and what precisely constitutes language's deliverance.

* * *

Let me recall Hofmannsthal's response to his horrific vision of the rats that is not only "bestial" but in which he finds something of "divinity," a trace of the sacred that can be attributed to the power of poetry in its active creative role. Hölderlin also reminds us that the poet finds a "frightful and divine dream" in the constant transit between "being and non-being."

Hugh Kenner, writing in *The Pound Era* about the Objectivist poets, among them George Oppen, says that the rubric under which they write could be described as "no myths." In section 8 of 'Route,' Oppen narrates a horrific vision of his own, a narration that, while seemingly scrubbed of any myths or theological traces, nevertheless seems to capture Hofmannsthal's "divinity" on secular terms:

Imagine a man in the ditch
The wheels of the overturned wreck
Still spinning—

I don't mean he despairs. I mean if he does not
He sees in the manner of poetry

Can thrall be divinity? To my knowledge, of the two poets I am discussing here, Oppen is the one most influenced by Heidegger, and the least by any Asian thought. He had begun to read Heidegger in earnest after breaking a twenty-year silence during which he abandoned poetry to devote himself to causes of social and economic justice, joining the American Communist Party and fleeing the United States during the McCarthy era. It was Heidegger's thought and that of other "existential" writers like Maritain and Camus who were guides in Oppen's return to poetry in the late 1950s.

Oppen was a tireless compiler of notes and observations on poetry and on his life. They are collected in his *Daybook* where he writes:

I rather think of verse as a tool of thought, perhaps comparable to the tool of mathematics. Admittedly, the comparison suffers strain. But I find that tho I might well write a poem to test the truth of a common assertion, I would no more write simply to give thrilling tongue to a common belief than I would work a sum for the same purpose. *I do not think that poetry is merely a type of creation.*

This desire "to test the truth," places Oppen in a border condition where, as he puts it in his major poem 'Of Being Numerous,' "the known and the unknown touch," a phrase he may well have taken from Hölderlin via Heidegger.

The juncture between knowing and unknowing, a place best characterized by uncertainty and fear, are the arena of Oppen's poetics. In his sequence, 'The Book of Job and a Draft of a Poem to Praise the Paths of the Living,' unknowing becomes the Heideggerian path, the concretion of being that unveils the spatial drama of existence in the world. "Precision of place," he writes, "the rock's place in the fog we suffer/loneliness painlessly now without fear the common breath/here at extremity." The willingness to place himself in doubt and confusion lies at the heart of his poetics, a poetics that is never a settled matter, but, as in his *Daybook*, becomes ruminative and recursive. "Prosody," he writes, "is a language, but it is a language that tests itself."

In Oppen's ruminations over conventions in language and poetic usage, we encounter a Heideggerian thematics of doubt and boredom, one, that in its relationship to what is most Eastern and Buddhistic in Heidegger, sees poetry as a practice in mindfulness and awareness. Oppen chose for the epigraph to his second post-return collection, *This In Which*, Heidegger's phrase "the arduous way of appearance," which reminds us of Heidegger's comment in 'A Dialogue on Language' that "what matters is to see appearance as the reality of presence in its essential origin."

In the *Daybook*, Oppen writes "what concerns the artist is that the thing exists—and he starts with a ruined language *day by day and then by man, destroyed* achieves language." From "ruined language" to "language" is, in a sense, the trajectory of Oppen's poetics. And like Heidegger's thought in 'On the Way to Language,' metaphors of path-making, of routes created and taken, abound in Oppen. They are, as he describes his poetics elsewhere, a "sequence of disclosure," a Heideggerian "matter of road building." Oppen's constant reapproaches to language seem to hew to the line of Stefan George's that Heidegger pondered deeply in *On The Way To Language*, "Where word breaks off no thing may be."

There are over a dozen references to Heidegger in Oppen's *Selected Letters*, statements of the philosopher's effect on his thinking, queries relating to meanings, even suggestions to other poets to read his texts. One of the last mentions of Heidegger comes in a 1974 letter to Robert Duncan. In it, Oppen, responding to comments by Duncan, quotes Heidegger: "the Word comes to existence, and for the last time, as language." In 1975, he again writes to Duncan:

((Mary, reading this, reminds me that you mentioned Heidegger. Yes, I see. I point: it is true, I don't think everything has been named, yes it is true.

If poetry is "naming," the *essent* [being] spoken for, then poetry only has a future if there remain things to name. As these citations from Oppen suggest, it is the quest for articulation, the persistence or enduring which aligns him so powerfully with Heidegger's thought in its most Buddhistic moments. As he writes in the *Daybook*, "OBJECT in the poem: its function is to burst." Then, an entry or two further on

The Godhead
        I would rather say reality, realness instead
of Being The Godhead: realness That there is realness

"Godhead" and "realness" carry us back to where Whitman's "soul" is
to be found, among places and persons. The poem 'Who Shall Doubt,'
(composed around the time he was communicating with Duncan), has,
at its center, "Mary," the presence of Mary Oppen, the poet's wife, the
source for him, in a sense, of joy and grace:

consciousness
       in itself
of itself carrying
    'the principle
        of the actual' being
actual
itself (but maybe this is a love
poem
Mary) nevertheless
         neither
the power
of the self nor the racing
car nor the lily
    is sweet but this

Here, in the repeats of the words "itself" and "actual," we come again
across a kind of spiritual insistence, that sudden, almost unprepared leap
to "Mary", possibly one of those "bursts" that Oppen noted, from the
precincts of thought into the realm of being and love. Into something we
might see as divine or sacred.

* * *

Stanley Cavell, in an interview in *Bookforum* speaks of the "eastern
longings" in Emerson and Thoreau, of what he refers to as their "scriptural
tasks." Nietzsche sensed these longings in Emerson, referring to him
as one of those "poetic men [who] still seek the limits of knowledge,
indeed preferably of skepticism, in order to break free of the spell of
logic." The unaccountable leap out of logic and into—if I my use the

word carefully—lyric, as in Oppen's 'Who Shall Doubt,' describes the movement forward of a poetics which enjoins the transcendental and the Buddhistic. We see in Hofmannsthal, in Stevens and in Oppen, testimony to the simultaneous appearance of both the poetic and the sacred, an instance, to borrow Buddhist terminology, of co-emergent wisdom. Scholars on spirituality and poetry identify this co-emergence as a characteristic of language itself. Hartman, in *Criticism in the Wilderness* writes "One might speculate that what we call the sacred is simply what *must* (my italics) be interpreted or re-interpreted. 'A Presence which is not to be put by...'" Hartman is alluding to the idea of commentary, the idea that poetry, like scripture or any religious writing remains alive by constant rereading and rethinking.

Guenther's idea of the spiritual as a path, Stevens's *passage* between belief and doubt or Oppen's poetics of disclosure embody similar dynamics. They can be imagined spatially as a movement, as a series of forward movements and regressions between a text and a new understanding or impression of it. I see the poet as walking the boundary of this boundlessness, Heidegger's "message bearer" constantly in transit between the poles of the poetic enterprise. Here the path lies in poetic uncertainty, in the simultaneous experience of lostness and capture, characterizing the languages of our "inner" life, in the rehearsals and operations of memory, in the dictates of dream, fantasy and reality where distinctions are blurred in the symbolic languages of consciousness.

This is the contemporary *locus classicus* experienced and examined by the poets and thinkers we have been discussing, who see in the realm of the psyche, that words, which were once the self-testimonies of objects, no longer present an inventory of the world. The sign-function of the word gives up insisting on the masquerade by which it called itself reality and instead proffers itself as intermediary between the idea of poetry and the idea of language.

In the same paragraph in which he refers to Whitman, Gershom Scholem begins with a question: "who knows the limits of sanctity? ... Perhaps a double way is possible, secular and holy, toward which we are evolving? Perhaps this holiness will be revealed at the heart of the secular..." For Hartman, the "sacred" has been inscribed in language, and as I suggest here, poetry becomes the instrument by which it reveals the sacred to us and by which it sacralizes.

FROM THE NOTES

For Wordsworth's reader, the poem (and sometimes the world itself) is a created set of hermetic signs. For Tu Fu's reader, meaning is subtly infused in the particular forms of the world perceived and uncertain, perhaps, even to the poet; the poem raises up portentous forms, and in doing so, tells you about both the world and the inner concerns of the poet.
    —Steven Owen, *Traditional Chinese Poetry and Poetics*

"Understand appearance to be the teacher."—Saraha. This statement by the great Indian poet-philosopher continues to have great attraction for me. It is connected with my own thinking on the Objectivist poets, on Maurice Merleau-Ponty's phenomenology, on forms of thought or art that point to the "outside," that open up the petty envelope of self and self-anguish. Herbert Guenther's book, *The Tantric View of Life*, with its curious terms and academic jargon, with its abstraction qualifying abstraction, rings certain chords in my head. Occasionally, I find passages that, word for word, could have been lifted from Merleau-Ponty's *The Visible and the Invisible*. I am not after something syncretic, however, and have no real interest in the resonatings of terminologies, in the re-mirrorings of systems, all the false paths of *this* being like *that*. Rather, I find myself ripe for rubrics and mottoes, for pressures and instructions on how to proceed ... to break through the seductive constellations of human ordering. The other side of that breakthrough would be outer space, something unpredictable, the scrim off or at least exposed. Ultimately these will lead me to a teacher (as far as I understand what it means to find a teacher).

Saraha's statement becomes for me a kind of germ, a linguistic spore of my everyday life, a thought that clings to me and to which I cling like a barnacle to a rock.

Appearance, whatever else it might be, is not union. The word proclaims space, distance, separation, perspective, a litany of outsider terms that have deep psychic appeal. Saraha's thought is, first of all, about otherness and loneliness, a comment on one's precious interiority and, above all, self-ignorance. It is also a salve, a balm, a thing to be recited against one's demons of fear and depression. Perhaps it is also a form of quietism as well.

Which suggests the need for a teacher. One wants to know the world, to live accurately in it, not for some mystical purpose but to go about one's life, to work with others. The teacher steps in and disabuses you of your version of the world, not to supplant it with his but to enable a clearer sense of what is. This is what I take to be the meaning of Chögyam Trungpa's remark that "the function of the teacher is to insult the student."

Saraha's small wedge of words, in the context of practice, could become a personal mantra of sorts, driving words into open space, into the gap that lies between self and world. It suggests not only "knowledge" but connection, a way out of the self or a flow of the self across the magical bridge of words into the world. It leads one as reader to poetry again, to words. And as a writer it leads me, not to make worlds, but to wanting to be touched and wounded by worlds. Poems as the possibility of the world's carnality, the body of the world as a word in one's mouth, its savor.

Desire to write an inscriptive language, as though, through words, I were first of all trying to haunt my own body, and then perhaps other bodies. To create a form of invitation, "a willingness" as Trungpa said, "to open oneself to the phenomenal world rather than being involved with a strategy of how to relate to it." To enter the space for poetry unarmed, to not want to control any possibility save the following out of the impulse. Isn't this close to the notion of taking refuge, of being a refugee, essentially homeless, without shelter of manner or technique?

Here the usual notions of craft are turned upside down. Normally, craft is containment, mastery, objectification. But what if one had in mind the opposites, dispersal, vulnerability, objectification still, but in the sense that it was the path to the reader and not a distancing device? George Oppen's "the poet suffers the things of the world and speaks them out." Or the painter Arikha's remark that "style is a way of protecting oneself from that which is untrue." "Suffering the world" and "protecting" from untruth: these could easily allude to why the Buddhist outlook is called protecting the mind.

Minor point: such remarks constitute part of the critique of purely formalist notions of art. Witold Gombrowicz writes: *The artist who realizes himself inside art will never be creative.* And isn't it the desire that in art, one wants to "treat" an experience so as to receive it back untreated? One recognizes the truth that everything is constructed, but some constructions, just as they come to completion, may be a total surprise to their makers.

Mimesis transformed (in its forms) into language. Walter Benjamin's concept of the mimetic faculty as nonsensuous similarity. Here an idea in language rings faintly of *mahamudra*, as with poetry, seeking to create the self-existing symbol. This is the sphere of imagination where the view of the "unconditioned" may be glimpsed. Hence through language, the world, its cities, its lives can be read as sacred, in the sense that everything can be, actually is, under the aspect of *sünyata* or emptiness. Trungpa writes that the right attitude is to regard the entire world as the floor of a shrine room. To see this regard as a function of an art. This is, in some sense the "outer" teaching.

Which, for the poet as well, is the practice of vulnerability: somewhere in every act of perception, one is reduced to a word. This is not a word that stands for oneself; nor does it represent oneself. This word (the poem) *is* oneself. And this word is not one that can be enjoyed or taken for comfort. Whatever else is contained in it, the pain of one's death is also there.

And later, this same verbal artifact, read back to its author, will have a solidity, a sculptural quality. Reading it again, one would no longer find that peculiar confirmatory power that came with the first enunciation. Rather, this solidity would be in the form of an archaic monument or gate, something one went by and looked at with all the fascination of a tourist.

My experience and the act of writing are by no means synonymous. I can't use meditation to cook up something; indeed, practice seems continually to lead away from the corruptions of use. True, meditation may occasionally throw off the ghostly shadow of non-being, which, like a curious, silver gas, permeates and highlights the world about me. An almost painful brilliance. What is seen or experienced afterward might remind one of non-dualism, not as a concept, but as an instance in one's being, a mere snowflake of the unconditioned, cool and bitter on the tongue.

For the poet as a practitioner, the question of what to write down can never have a doctrinaire answer. Even Allen Ginsberg's use of Trungpa's formulation, "first thought; best thought," is always in danger of becoming an ideology, a self-sanctifying gesture. For literature, one must be exceptionally careful of esoteric terminology, of "borrowings." We delude and endanger ourselves by appropriations and promulgations of lore that is culturally bound, that requires initiates. "If a man learns theology before he learns to be a human being," wrote Ludvig Holberg, "he will never become a human being."

The view from practice and the view from the act of writing poetry: occasional synonymy. Victor Segalen's poem 'The Seal-less Reign' (in his *Steles* of 1914) reads like a Buddhist *via negativa*. Segalen postulates the "reign of no seal," which turns the world from being a theater for projections, a clustering of conception, history, and authority, into a reflective surface off of which all thought runs like rainwater off a stone. Poetry, whether in the zero flick of haiku syntax or in the monstrous alternate worlds of Dante and Milton, works on the edge of theistic/nontheistic relating. Practice as constant awareness of the mind's flip-flops along this boundary. Such awareness is also the birth-bed of compassion … or as Segalen puts it, "the dawning of the day when [one] becomes Regent and Sage upon the throne of his heart".

BUDDHADHARMA AND
POETRY WITHOUT CREDENTIALS

for Nathaniel Tarn

I'm here as a poet and student, writing about the inter-relationship of Buddhist practice and poetry. For me, this practice does not mean an exotic use of Buddhist terms to enlard a poem, nor do I mean to suggest anything of an inspirational nature. And yet, to take up poetry, whether as reader or poet, is, in a sense, to take up a path. What kind of path? Such a question cannot be answered in any doctrinaire or even evaluative way. However, for the practitioner/poet in search of his or her "poetics," both Buddhist and non-Buddhist literary and philosophical traditions, their resonances and pointings, will be seen as directional forces. I want to outline some of these forces. Allen Ginsberg sets the tone for such an exploration with his comment that:

> It's an old tradition in the West among great poets that poetry is rarely thought of as 'just poetry.' Real poetry practitioners are practitioners of mind awareness, or practitioners of reality, expressing their fascination with a phenomenal universe and trying to penetrate to the heart of it. Poetics isn't mere picturesque dilettantism or egotistical expressionism.... Classical poetry is a 'process' or experiment—a probe into the nature of reality and the nature of the mind.

Indeed, said this way, poetry and a Buddhist outlook or perspective seem nearly identical.

My way into Buddhist practice came by circuitous routes, experimental probes, intellectual influences, readings, study and finally a "meeting of the minds" with a teacher. I want to write here neither a personal history nor a how-to manual of involvement. A path is intrinsically "personal," but it can also have a sidereal value as reference point for another. Self-exploration will become exposition, and exposition will inevitably have an ethical side. Shelley's perhaps grandiose proclamation that "poets are the unacknowledged legislators of the world," as well as Ginsberg's sense of poets as "practitioners of mind-awareness, or practitioners of reality," reminds us of poetry's possibly active role in the world, one that, as Plato warned, is almost never neutral and perhaps dangerous. Poetic traditions and the materials of individual poetics, those probes into reality, form an arena of conscious thought to be explored and considered. So this writing is, modestly, only one of a myriad, written in the hope of first freeing myself and maybe other readers from obstruction.

A significant approach to laying out the contours of thinking about art from a Buddhist perspective is contained in Herbert V. Guenther's commentary on the *The Royal Song of Saraha*, a study of the Indian "king *Dohas*," poem-songs written and performed under the influence of Mahayana and Tantric Buddhism. For Guenther, the role of the Buddhist-inflected arts are ethical and moral but also philosophically fundamental to human interaction. His book *The Tantric View of Life*, published shortly after his study of Saraha and deeply influenced by his readings of Saraha's *Dohas*, is a meditation on the near synonymity of art and Vajrayana Buddhism. Guenther's discussion in the book is extremely complex, worthy of close study by artists, Buddhist-oriented or not. What I would emphasize here is that for Guenther, "aesthetic experience" is *the* central aspect of Vajrayana practice, its "ground," "path," and "goal," deeply entwined in the Mahayana aims of compassion and liberation. According to Guenther, the royal song, the *Doha*, is a gateway, an opening onto Buddhahood, "the path by which we see what is otherwise not seen." "The pictorial, emotional and cognitive meanings, all of which of which are present in poetry and song... may be said to bring into the open all that we then discuss and deal within everyday language." In other words, as Guenther describes it, "the poet's expression is the formulation of his knowledge of sensuous, mental, and emotional life, and it is this knowledge that he presents for our contemplation. The image in its immediacy," he says—here, reminiscent of Ezra Pound in his Imagist phase—"is a moment of original vision full of suggestions rather than comprehension... It invites us to explore the depth. Thereby a transition from sensuous concretizations to inner feelings of spirituality is effected."

Guenther worked closely with Chögyam Trungpa Rinpoche (the Tibetan Buddhist teacher with whom I was later to study), especially on their collaborative book, *The Dawn of Tantra*, a work which, like *The Royal Song of Saraha*, emphasizes the aesthetic aspect of the Vajrayana outlook. But it was some years before I encountered Trungpa that I was led to Guenther's writings by my readings in Western phenomenology, in particular, the work of Maurice Merleau-Ponty and his influential studies of perception, as in *The Phenomenology of Perception* and in his writing on art and artists. I was most affected by his great unfinished tone poem of philosophy, *The Visible and the Invisible*, with its meditation on "brute being," an exploration of existence derived from his readings of Husserl, and with it, his conception of what he called "perceptual faith," the need to interrogate the nature of our seeing and witnessing. This "faith," in a sense, has a near-religious dimension. As he writes in his 'Working Notes' to the book, "Husserl: human bodies have an 'other side'—a 'spiritual' side," that can only be "invisible."

By the time I began reading it, Merleau-Ponty's work already had had an impact on American poetry and visual art, especially through the writings and teachings of Charles Olson, whose poetry and influential essay 'Projective Verse' profoundly affected his students and colleagues at Black Mountain College, the small experimental school that became one of the founding homes of mid-century American modernism. Among these were Robert Creeley, Robert Duncan, Merce Cunningham and Robert Rauschenberg. Olson's copy of Merleau-Ponty's *The Visible and the Invisible* was said to be the most marked-up book in his library.

Among the essays of Merleau-Ponty, 'Cézanne's Doubt' stands out as a particularly "Buddhistic" piece of writing, in effect, acting for me, as a bridge work between traditions of art and spiritual practice. Merleau-Ponty describes Cézanne's approach to his own art as a kind of *via negativa*, Cézanne's way of attempting to discover, to borrow from Guenther's words, a "moment of original vision," working back through his perceptions and his understandings of the traditions of art to arrive at a depiction of what is actually before him. It is important to remember that Cézanne is an exemplary figure not only for modern and contemporary painting, but also, in his work and thought, a magnetic force for poets as diverse as Rilke and Stevens.

For Merleau-Ponty, "the painter who conceptualizes and seeks the expression first misses the mystery—renewed every time we look at someone—of a person's appearing in nature." Pre-conceptions are viewed by both painter and philosopher as a kind of "heresy" to the understanding, getting in the way of both intellectual and sensory "truth." Merleau-Ponty quotes Cézanne's remark that "the painter's 'conception' cannot precede 'execution.'" Cézanne's efforts can be understood as a kind of applied phenomenology, at least as it is formulated by Husserl and later Merleau-Ponty, a mode of painting that attempts to see the world unmasked, to see it for what it is. Merleau-Ponty's description of Cézanne as an artist resonates with the Buddhist notions of "mindfulness" and "awareness," of one who refuses the comforts of "conceptualizations" and of any *a priori* understanding of experience. Cézanne sits before a landscape or a face to be painted somewhat as a student on his cushion, without hope or expectation. Thus, unlike other painters who have given themselves over to a style or a pre-existing tradition, Cézanne, according to Merleau-Ponty, formulates his task in a wholly original way, to paint "as if no one had ever painted before." This originality is the product of the painter's effort to discover meaning within the lived opacity of our condition, the "silent and solitary experience," as Merleau-Ponty calls it, of one's own relation to the world. Cézanne, the philosopher insists, lives in the knowledge that "the meaning of what a work of art is going to say *does not exist* anywhere—not in things, which have yet no meaning nor in the artist himself, in his unformulated life."

The connection to poetry (as to other arts) is obvious. Poetry, the conventional formula goes, is a "raid on the inarticulate," an articulation of that which was inarticulate, *i.e.*, to produce something otherwise not previously said. Art, including poetry, is here a kind of Heideggerian "disclosure," not a repository of truths so much as a ground from which the way things are is to be discerned. For an American poet, such thoughts are consonant with Walt Whitman's charge to American poets in his 1855 Preface to *Leaves of Grass* to let "nothing hang in the way, not the richest curtain." Poetic traditions are, in Whitman's thinking, to be de-sanctified and re-examined in the light of present circumstances.

The Buddhist sense of Whitman's aspiration, based in a non-essentialist approach to experience, is both clear and perhaps also a bit more complex, since Buddhist thinking is based on the intuitions and discoveries in practice rather than on the abstracted categories of philosophizing alone. My own decision to begin to practice and study with Trungpa was ultimately sealed by two works, his book *Cutting Through Spiritual Materialism* published in 1973 and his essay also published about the same time, 'Buddhadharma Without Credentials,' words of which have migrated to the title of this writing. Both works were concerned with theisms (even of a non-theistic path), its egoisms and attachments that endangered one's journey on a path to clarity: the sense of doing something special, spiritual aggrandizement, acquiring "merit" through special ceremonies and religious empowerments. The scope of these writings was, of course, much larger, examining not only the teaching of Buddhism but of every possible area of human life for the ways in which the mind held its self-serving views (its "credentials") in all areas of our social, cultural and political lives. To explode this process is what the practice of "emptiness" meant. If Buddhist practice sought anything it was to pull down those "richest curtains" of Whitman, to give a dynamic rather than descriptive dimension to the insights of ethics and philosophy as also in Merleau-Ponty's phenomenological investigations. The poet Nathaniel Tarn, in his essay 'Newly Saying the Already Said,' an homage to the Japanese Buddhist philosopher Keiji Nishitani and his book *Religion and Nothingness*, gives what amounts to a nuanced echo of both Cézanne and Merleau-Ponty, one inflected by Tarn's own years of Buddhist practice and study. "But it has been my habit," he writes, "to think of reality this way: as what is left after everyone else has had his ploy and his play and gone home for the day." The poet's reality stems from the unsaid, from what may remain after conventional language (the "ploys" and "plays" of others) have conventionally used up the world. In this sense, poetry's belatedness after the ploys and plays is a mark not of its primal barbarity but of its ever-difficult sensitivity and sophistication to the traditions which have come before. Tarn here echoes one of Cézanne's most famous remarks, that the way back to nature was "through the Louvre," that the ground of an artist's quest was also the undoing of art's overlay of conventions and styles.

Conventions, styles, old habits: these constitute part of the material that the poet works with and works through. Trungpa states that "in all Buddhist teachings, the mind constantly lives in bewilderment and ignorance. Dharmas are the living teachings of clarity appearing spontaneously in all sorts of life situations." Buddhist "faith," he says, "is the readiness to expose whatever is concealed." Guenther speaks of "Buddha intentionality," of the "evaluative cognition of the factual realm," of Buddha as "felt knowledge." In the poetic transformation enacted by the *Dohas*, "the outward image becomes the symbol for an inward process, not its explanation." Imagine the making of poetry, imagine poem after poem not only as made objects but as a series of unconcealments, as revelatory symbols of the poet's "inward process." Words become the medium in which the poet unmasks self, his or her culture, and, indeed, thereby comes to know and understand both self and culture better. Poetry can be seen as the linguistic attempt over time to enact the Four Dharmas of Gampopa, a ritual chant, here translated by Trungpa, used in meditation to stabilize the mind:

Grant your blessings so that my mind may be one with the dharma.
Grant your blessings so that dharma may progress along the path.
Grant your blessings so that the path may clarify confusion.
Grant your blessings so that confusion may dawn as wisdom.

Gampopa (1079–1153 AD), the most central figure after the Buddha in the Kagyu lineage of Tibetan Buddhism, Trungpa's own lineage, is especially valued for his unifying of the monastic and yogic traditions of Buddhist practice. The Four Dharmas invoke, in extremely condensed form, the path to liberation or enlightenment. Guenther, in another collaborative effort with Trungpa, translated and annotated Gampopa's *The Jewel Ornament of Liberation*, one of Tibetan Buddhism's foundational works.

* * *

I was educated in the sciences and technical subjects, graduating with an engineering degree from Rensselaer Polytechnic Institute. More than anything else, I loved the precise language of scientific and technological discoveries. Such a language it was clear seemed to carve moments of clarity out of formlessness and confusion. On their most elevated horizons, so to speak, the attitudes of both science and poetry coincide in a deeply embedded sense of awe; the poet's reaching for the world through language was not so different from the scientist's with his eye at the telescope's reticule attempting to comprehend the cosmos. Later, when I had decided to try to be a poet, Pound's insistence that poetry was "the science of the emotions" became for me a kind of motto, a deeply appealing rubric. In this regard, Merleau-Ponty's phenomenology and Buddhist tantra as described by Guenther seemed to promise such a "science," a richness and complexity of thought that had a bearing on the kind of poetry I hoped to write.

My early thrashings-about as a young poet were vague attempts at understanding my own states of mind, at objectifying them sufficiently that they might be a kind of teaching for me. These attempts were also cluttered with ideas about form, poetic stance, the role of the poet, all kinds of self-imposed external criteria that modified or obstructed the objectifications I sought. I sense that poetry began for me then, in the awareness of that very confusion Gampopa refers to: an awareness which is primary, the glimpse that one *is* confused. In fact, later, as I began to study and practice in the dharma, I sensed that those early moments in poetry were for me not unlike the first moments of sitting meditation when one realizes if only for an instant—the necessary instant—that he has moved from the impelling current of engrossed thought to the gap that ushers in some distance and clarity.

Clearly, that distance, that clarity is connected to the insight latent in Guenther's notion of how the poetic image provides us with a "moment of original vision," not to mistake meditational insight for poetry, but to recognize that the contemplative model and the poetic model have useful similarities. Trungpa, in *The Myth of Freedom*, speaks of the awareness achieved in meditation in terms of "recognition" and "recollection," implying a glimpse into the nature of things, seeing how the world works and for a poet, translating one's recognitions into a kind of witnessing.

This bearing of witness I take to be something like Trungpa's description of the "Lion's Roar," a willingness to proclaim that "any state of mind, including the emotions, is a workable situation." "Workable" means that bearing witness to the misunderstandings or neurotic aspects of one's mind is the material of the path. Trungpa speaks of "transmutation" as an aspect of the "lion's roar," an affirmation of such workability viewed as an alchemical process. From the point of view of the poem, workability implies communication and transmissibility, a sense that the poet's job is not so much self-expression as it is clarification, making one's experience available to oneself and others via language. Experience and communication, the materials of poetry, suggest from a Buddhist perspective a further characteristic, that communication (and by implication, poetry) has the quality of soliciting a judgment about itself, of opening that judgment to inspection. Along with this willingness to state how things are is an implied outlook—not a heavyhanded judgment against the world, but a suggestion as to why the work of art is closer to reality than the conventional notions of science or of experience.

In my view, then, Buddhist thinking does not dictate a poetics. Rather, it suggests, broadly, an openness to experience, intelligence, and self-awareness. Even Ginsberg's principles of spontaneous composition, his "first thought, best thought," slogan, borrowed from Trungpa's teachings, are always in danger of being turned into hardened doctrinaire attitudes about what constitutes valuable poetry.

* * *

The poet George Oppen spoke of his own poetry as enacting a sequence of disclosure, "a process of thought, [a] process of perception." The words on the page were not meant to simply build a clever or even a beautiful image; for him, the image was investigative, interrogating reality as it went along. In his poetic sequence *Of Being Numerous*, he writes:

> Clarity, clarity, surely clarity is the most beautiful thing in the world,
> A limited, limiting clarity
> I have not and never did have any motive of poetry
> But to achieve clarity

Poetry, according to Oppen, is rooted in recognition and receptivity, an acceptance of our state of mind as it is, rather than in some abstract idea of what we think poetry ought to be or in the notion that poetry is an activity which will get us to some goal. The poet's job was to develop and cultivate such a stance, to be receptive, as he called it, to a "philosophy of the astonished." For me, Oppen's "motive of poetry... clarity," as it embodies a mindfulness toward perception, culture and human psychology, has many of the attributes of a Buddhistic practice.

Trungpa sees such a stance somewhat differently. For him, what is important is "right speech" or "perfect communication," one of the characteristics of the Eightfold Noble Path of traditional Buddhist description. Speech here, taken from the Sanskrit "*vac*," also means "utterance," "word," or "logos," any linguistic expression including that of poetry. The term "right" is not a moralistic or censoring idea but, as Trungpa says in *The Myth of Freedom*, "true speech," "being true."

* * *

After years of self-scrutiny, the poet Bashō, the great Japanese haiku master, wrote:

> What is important is to keep our mind high in the world of
> true understanding, and returning to the world of our daily
> experience, to seek therein the truth of beauty. No matter what
> we may be doing at a given moment, we must not forget that it
> has a bearing upon our everlasting self which is poetry.

Bashō's thought might be paraphrased as follows: there is this mind's life, this actual world I am in, and there are also all the hopes and fears synonymous with that life. There are fantasies generated by it, which comprise my "daily experience" and yet there is still the intention to close the gap between experience and "true understanding." This gap, for Bashō, can only be traversed across the poetic act.

Bashō's most well-known haiku, translated by Kenneth Rexroth, reads:

> An old pond—
> The sound
> Of a diving frog

Reading this poem in a Buddhist context, D. T. Suzuki, in a passage from *Zen and Japanese Culture*, quotes R. H. Blyth, an authority on the study of haiku, as follows: "a haiku is the expression of a temporary enlightenment, in which we see into the life of things." Suzuki then comments:

> Whether 'temporary' or not, Bashō gives in his seventeen syllables a significant intuition into Reality. … This sound coming out of the old pond was heard by Bashō as filling the entire universe. Not only was the totality of the environment absorbed in the sound and vanished into it, but Bashō himself was altogether effaced from his consciousness. Both the subject and the object, *en-soi* and *pour-soi*, ceased to be something confronting an I conditioning each other. And yet this could not be a state of absolute annihilation. Bashō was there, the old pond was there, with all the rest. But Bashō was no more the old Bashō.

For Bashō, then, the identity between an awakened mind and poetry is inescapable: "our everlasting self," the always already, operative condition of being, is "poetry." Bashō is testifying to the sense that from the Buddhist perspective of impermanence, the mind's capacity to momentarily arrest transitory phenomena, to capture it in language or art is at the very core of what it means to be human.

Poetry, then, with all its depth and yet with all its as-if and illusionistic power, is synonymous for Bashō with "true understanding." Obviously, he was thinking of his own discipline, the haiku or his marvelous prose narratives, which capture the transitory beauty of the world with the merest flicker of syntax. Such a discipline emulates, once one begins to practice, how one recognizes the mind and self, thought by thought (those "temporary enlightenments" described by Blyth), moment by moment, at once real and unreal, substantial and insubstantial.

Norman Fischer, a Zen priest and poet, examines this situation in another way: "meditation and poetry are ways of being honest with ourselves…." Fischer's words remind us of the painful revealments and internal confrontations that occur on the meditative path or in the practice of poetry. They are acts of self-exposure, powerful and often unpleasant. Such "unmasking," as Trungpa calls it, "is a violent eruption," at times very much like the strong epiphany or visionary moment of the poem. Probing into the nature of mind, relating to one's emotional state with honesty are synonyms for the openness and mindfulness of practice, and, in the sense that they cultivate an attitude or stance towards one's making art, whether it be painting or music or poetry, they are instances of what Trungpa called "meditation in action." This is what the great teachers have taught. And, often it is what art itself has taught when it is not "just art" or "merely" art.

Which brings us to ask, in a Buddhist context, what is poetry?

In 9th-century China, about the time that Tu Fu and other poets worked in the bureaucracy, the labels "artistic" for poetry and "practical" for prose existed in a particularly dramatic way. The fact was that in China, prose was considered an unfit medium for anything but the transmission of facts or the carrying out of minor business matters. Poetry, on the other hand, was the medium for consideration of the *Tao* of government, for serious thought, for generals to inspire their armies with, for the bureaucrat/poets to inform and persuade the Emperor. In this sense, poetry was not a diversion from the ongoing business of the day, but a way of entering into its deepest levels.

David Hinton, in *The Mind of Classical Chinese Poetry*, writes of Taoist and Ch'an (Zen) Buddhist influences on Chinese Classical poetry (that of Du Fu's era) that transform it into a kind of spiritual practice, where, "in its deepest possibilities, its inner wilds, poetry is the Cosmos awakened to itself." In other words, a poet can see, in his own poetry, "inner concerns" that could not have come to him or her any other way—which is to see poetry's potential as a teaching, not so much for readers as for the poet who has written it. Suzuki, speaking of a Bashō who is "no longer the old Bashō," reminds us of one of the older formulations of poetic dynamics, of the poem's ability to alter consciousness. Guenther, in *The Tantric View of Life*, quotes from Gampopa's writings on Mahayana and Mahamudra doctrines in words that may say it most Buddhistically and most simply: "Understand appearance to be the teacher."

* * *

For an American poet, Gampopa's "understand appearance" has a powerful resonance. It echoes back to Pound's 'Imagist Dos and Don'ts,' specifically Pound's injunction that "the natural object is always the adequate symbol." Pound's "always" strikes with almost as much force as Gampopa's "understand," as though visual perception, by its very undeniability, were the moral outline of Vision with a capital "V." Indeed, one might usefully speculate that any number of American poets in the Pound-Williams lineage have been drawn to Buddhist thought precisely because such an idea as Gampopa's (an idea that richly infuses all sorts of other Buddhist thinking) subliminally reminds them of the Imagist legacy at the root of twentieth-century poetry. Let us recall that Imagism itself is already deeply inflected by Eastern thought beginning with Arthur Waley's translations or with Ernest Fenollosa's treatise on *The Chinese Written Character as a Medium for Poetry* which had such a profound impact on Pound. Pound acquired the manuscript version of this essay from Fenollosa's widow and edited it for eventual publication in the form we now have. In fact, among literary scholars and poets, we mostly know of Fenollosa through Pound's promotion of Fenollosa's work. But thereby hangs a tale.

Rick Fields tells it in *How the Swans Came to the Lake*, his elegant study of Buddhism in America. He reminds us that "it was Buddhism that Fenollosa identified as the new genius of Eastern civilization" but that in the literary sphere, this "Buddhistic" side of Fenollosa has for the most part been neglected due to Pound's sympathies with the Confucian aspect of Chinese culture. "By the time of the *Cantos* [Pound's epic poem, fifty years in the making]," Fields writes, "Pound had turned Fenollosa's version of Chinese history completely around. It was Confucius who represented the highest of Chinese civilization, while Buddhists—now called 'Buddhs' in that slurring ethnic shorthand of the *Cantos*—came to stand for the enemy." Yet this Buddhist outlook pervades Fenollosa's thought in the essay and cannot be disentangled from Pound's use of his work. And thus Pound, with his deep interests in Fenollosa, in Chinese and Japanese poetry, with "hokku" and *Noh* drama and with Vorticism and the ideogrammatic method, can be seen in retrospect as creating a permissive—even deeply inviting—aesthetic atmosphere for Buddhist thought and for Buddhist-inflected poetry. (And there is so much more in the larger story to be thought through, from the Transcendentalists to Rexroth to Lucien Stryk's haikus).

Trungpa's teachings, the Buddhist roots of which go back to the lineages of the Kagyu Karmapas of Tibet and to Gampopa, can be seen as especially magnetic works for American poets: Ginsberg, of course, Anne Waldman, and all the post-Beat poets who taught at the Jack Kerouac School of Disembodied Poetics at Naropa Institute. Among such a gathering I would have to include myself and Armand Schwerner, poets who brought with them into this particular fold, the thought of the Objectivists such as George Oppen, Carl Rakosi and Charles Reznikoff—not Buddhists by any stretch of the imagination, but poets who enacted in their work and thought an ethical re-evaluation of Imagism. In addition, one would want to include as environing influence the work of Cid Corman, poet and early publisher of poets such as Zukofsky and Olson. Corman's translations of Bashō and Buddhist-inclined poets were to be found in the pages of his path-breaking magazine *Origin*. Corman, who spent most of his working life in Kyoto, was a true bridge-figure between East and West. His translation of Bashō's *Back Roads to Far Countries*, published in the early 1970s, remains one of the seminal cross-over works in the dialogue between Buddhist thought and American poetry. All of the above (and many others certainly) can be said to have participated in an indirect confluence of Pound's thought and Buddhist ideas about art and poetry. This history is yet to be fully written, but anthologies such as Kent Johnson's and Craig Paulenich's *Beneath A Single Moon* (Shambala, 1991) offer a useful snapshot of the situation.

Let me briefly illustrate by way of some personal observations. Although Trungpa was my teacher and guide, it was George Oppen, whom I met in the late nineteen-sixties, who was most important to me as a poet. I took Oppen's book of poems *This In Which* on my expatriate *hegira* to Spain in the 1960s. The book had as its epigraph, Heidegger's phrase "the third way: the arduous path of appearance." Oppen read deeply in Heidegger and made use of his thought in developing his own poetics, one that was resistant to dogma and pre-conceived ideas of what poetry ought to be. His example had a powerful impact on me. Heidegger explores Buddhist modes of thinking, especially about art and language, in *On the Way to Thinking*. And it is Oppen, foremost among the Objectivists, who seems to use Heideggerian thought in his critique of Imagism, in the sense that he is seeking a more rigorous and philosophically grounded sense of "appearance" as a way of distinguishing his practice from the more "literary" uses, as Oppen saw it, of Imagism in the work of T. E. Hulme or Amy Lowell.

Further, Oppen, in both his poetry and in his correspondence with me and others, constantly stressed his own search for a poetics free of dogma and *a priori* views of poetry. When I began to study Buddhist thought seriously and was exposed to notions such as *sūnyata*, non-theistic and non-essentialist thinking, I felt then a sense of a poetry without credentials, of the activity of making poetry as a kind of path or at least reinforcing the path I had set out upon, sort of circular, even recursive path of influences, atmospherics and receptivity.

* * *

"The desire of the poet," says the late Louis Zukofsky in his Objectivist manifesto 'An Objective,' "is not to show himself but to show his world." If we are to enter our worlds, *poetry*, as Bashō proclaimed, *i.e.*, as a ground of being, must inevitably arise. To repeat from Bashō's statement above:

> No matter what we may be doing at a given moment,
> we must not forget that it has a bearing upon our everlasting self
>   which is poetry.

There is something movingly unequivocal in this statement, uncompromising in some fundamental way. Our life, Bashō insists, is poetry. He is not talking about some category or class of people who write poems; rather, he is talking about the very basis of our existence. In suggesting that whatever we are doing we *are* in a sense, poetry, he is implying that the label of "poet" with its freight of self-conceptions and imposed criteria (at least as the public conception of poetry has evolved in the present), is unnecessary. Bashō, I think, would want us to regard the poet not as a purely literary figure but rather as someone who essentially works without such credentials, who maintains an awareness towards states of mind and intentions, his own and others. Such a poet would seek an even larger or broader context for poetry, something implicit in Wittgenstein's well-known remark that "the limits of my language are the limits of my world." In this context, the question "what is poetry?" seems like a secondary question. Or it might, with some sense of humor, which is the same thing, become a question one imagines Bashō asking: "what is not poetry?"

The great German Romantic poet Hölderlin, as Heidegger interprets him, comes at Bashō's question from another direction. Heidegger has often referred to Hölderlin as the "poet of poetry," the poet who seeks to understand what it means to write poetry. And indeed, Heidegger has placed Hölderlin at the center of his philosophical meditations. In his essay entitled 'The Nature of Language,' he cites from Hölderlin's hymn, 'Celebration of Peace' this passage: "since we have been a discourse and have heard from one another…." Heidegger sees in these lines that, for the poet, the distinctions between poetry and communication are artificial, that "song is not the opposite of discourse, but rather [has] the most intimate kinship with it; for song, too, is language." Following on Heidegger's thought, I would suggest that the word "since" at the beginning of the fragment, suggests that what we have previously seen as an intention (to write poetry) has about it, as Hölderlin's words imply, the character of necessity, that something we might identify as poetry, is always at the base of language and thought. Heidegger, in his essay '…Poetically Man Dwells…,' also based on some lines of Hölderlin, reflects, like Bashō, on the nature of language. In responding to Hölderlin's lines, the philosopher seeks to place poetic language at the core of human existence. It is not simply that poetry can be something "literary," written about where one dwells, for example, but rather that, as Heidegger insists, "poetry first causes dwelling to be dwelling. Poetry is what really lets us dwell." Heidegger suggests that our being lies in the very ground of expression, of our need to resort to language and hence to poetry: "the responding in which man authentically listens to the appeal of language is that which speaks in the element of poetry." This "responding," Heidegger insists, defines humanity. What Heidegger says, via Hölderlin, seems as unequivocal in meaning as Bashō's words above. The individual is "the one who dwells poetically," who bears witness to being through poetry and language. Bashō and Hölderlin meet in the idea that there is a need to express, to witness, that the ground of our lives *is* poetry, and is, therefore, expressible.

* * *

I want to circle back to an essay I wrote echoing Trungpa's thought, entitled 'Poetry Without Credentials,' about poetry's power to alter consciousness, to lead us away from our habits of mind and our certainties and toward uncertainty and openness and with a friendliness toward ourselves. I wrote it with young, beginning poets in mind because I was concerned with the interference to writing created by the credentialing roles of such terms as "poet" and "poetry," about how our pre-conceptions concerning such terms might actually work against the possibility of making poetry. To understand such things would not lead us toward a Buddhist poetry, indeed, maybe not even lead us to poetry at all. But it would lead us perhaps to being more human, to recognizing our human state. Art influenced by Buddhist practice—perhaps better to say by a practitioner—held the possibility of being a mindful art, an art probing reality, most importantly, an art in honest relation to its maker and perhaps even to its audience. I don't think we can find a formula for this, but rather we can imagine that whatever state of mind achieved in practice can be entwined around or shine forth in one's work. And then a term like "Buddhist art" would be a redundancy.

We come to study and practice with a teacher not because we want to improve our art, but, as the literature puts it, because we are nauseated with samsara, with our neurotic habits and egos, or because we have the hunger for spiritual meaning (it is up to each of us to pick the right words for ourselves). So someone enters on this path of practice and study, and, as he or she so desires, brings the understandings and clarity derived from practice to the making of their art. I repeat here the last section of the essay I wrote because, couched in a non-esoteric language, it nevertheless invokes what I believe to be the teaching power of poetry:

Poetry Without Credentials

If we look closely at the effects strong poems have on us, we may discover something quite strange.

The poem 'alters consciousness' it is said; it shakes up and disrupts our certainties. We could say it introduces uncertainty where perhaps there was none before. New truths, new conceptions of world or life are tendered by the poem. Yet we return again and again to the poem to find ourselves shaken up. What is curious about powerful poetry, what is profound about it, is not the conceptions of truth offered but the disruption, the actual opening and experiencing of what is when the conceptions have been torn away.

In the moment of that happening, everything we are has a bearing – our experience has led us here – and is also beside the point. The only thing which has meaning is the uncertainty; our attempt to maintain a grasp on the solidity of our views has been undermined.

How strange! What is actually true is not the certainty but the uncertainty. If we are willing to recognize that moment, to live

thoroughly in that understanding, we recognize that it is just as
we give up our views and our values, give up ourselves and our
credentials that poetry takes place.

This is what we mean by poetry without credentials.

It strikes me that given the ground prepared by both poetic and spiritual forbearers, American poetry has already moved along a very promising path, that the "circuitous routes" of other poets similar to the ones I have followed are full of both promise and, even more important, openness and workability.

REMAINS OF THE DIASPORA

If the Diaspora is my ground of no-ground, and yet the place where both signification and metaphor operate, then what does a term like "radical poetics" mean to me? If the diaspora is geographic and physical, it is also psychic and emotional, rife with constantly agitated language and even more agitated silence. Scattered, scatterings. I can only speak of it via some indirection, speak of it as remains, as traces left by encounters with others, encounters with my surroundings. My thoughts then are modified by a diaspora that never totally exists for me, and (to place my thought properly) never totally does not exist. Texts and textuality, allegiances and disavowals. Pressures. Every thought, every word should be useful, ripe with both fullness and negations, and depending on context, every word should sputter and decay toward silence. The ground of the diaspora that is not a diaspora is the place where this paradox is given in words, where the pressure on language is at its utmost.

The Hebrew poet Haim Nam Bialik, who saw himself as a creature of endless exile, wrote in his essay 'Revealment and Concealment' that "the most dangerous moment—both in speech and in life—is that between concealments, when the void looms." Let us say this writing, these words, are a concealment, and that the territory and act of the poem are always begun "between concealments." Or, as Bialik puts it: "no reply to the question of essence is ever possible in the process of speech." As soon as a word is deployed as poetry—or, better, and more generally, as soon as a word is or becomes part of a figure, a verbal construct, it has forsaken or supplemented its conventional referentiality to become something other, different, more, or even something less. Bialik ascribes the impossibility of answering the question of "essence" to the perpetual dynamic of language where "a word or system declines and yields to another, not because it has lost the power to reveal, to enlighten, to invalidate the enigma.... but for the very opposite reason—because the word or system has been worn out by being manipulated and used." The word, Bialik says, "can no longer divert mankind momentarily." A "crack" is opened, terror ensues and the "void" looms, a void which must immediately be covered with a new word. Lorca had his *duende*, and the poet who is in touch—allied in some fashion—with Judaism's speculations on language has as his animating creative goad primarily his awareness of the "between," of the space of the diaspora.

This "between" is, in a sense, foundational. It exists in the relational sphere between the law of religious observance and secular life. Robert Alter, commenting on Walter Benjamin's reading of Kafka, sees it as operative in the decay of "traditional" tradition (if I may use an oxymoron), the loss of Halakic Judaism to Aggadic Judaism. What is left, according to Alter, is "lore in quest of Law, yet so painfully estranged from what it seeks that the pursuit can end in a pounce of destruction, the fictional rending the doctrinal." Alter could as well be speaking of the poetic, for Kafka's 'graven' images are imagistic and allegorical constructs, already caught in the "between" of Law and lore, and demanding to be read across the two genres.

Another Israeli thinker, Ari Elon, whose thoughts in *From Jerusalem to the Edge of Heaven* inform my discussion here, writes movingly of what he calls the *ribboni* individual, the secular Jew whose activity he contrasts with the *rabbani,* the follower of the Halakic tradition who sees in Judaism's spiritual literature primarily Law. Elon speaks to the religious/secular crisis in his native country, but that crisis mirrors the conflicting pulls that animate American intellectual life as well. The central question to be asked about this crisis is put by way of a parable of doubleness, in which Elon's narrator performs a kind of mercy killing on a holy man (as Elon makes clear, this is his other self) who has been walking the streets of Jerusalem muttering that "it is Shabbat today... it is forbidden to put on tefillin... it is forbidden to tear the strings that mark the Shabbat boundaries... it is Shabbat today... it is forbidden to throw stones at dogs today." What the holy man fears most is that the dogs will run off to the edge of town and tear the strings of the Shabbat boundaries, "and then Jerusalem will not be marked off from the rest of the world...." Elon's parable concerns the struggle within, the act of near self-murder he must undertake to release himself from a constraining religious orthodoxy.

The *ribboni's* mission, Elon implies, is to "turn the Torah of Israel from a source for authority to a source for inspiration." "Law" into "lore." The *ribboni* must take a walk into or over the void, at which point he or she is suspended between the religious and the secular worlds, but there, according to Elon, the *ribboni* must try to hang in suspension. The "Shabbat" boundary signifies not only the limits of the theocratic dispensation but is also the edge beyond which *labor must continue.* If "shabbat" poetics sanctify rules, strategies, even moments where labor is no longer governed by thought in the sense that it is rule- and precedent-driven, the poetics of the space beyond the Sabbath's broken string boundaries, requires endless questioning and testing. Nothing is established as final. No clean break, no new totalizing embrace. The *ribboni* is not a new person; rather, he must live with Shabbat memory, the time and space of sanctity that, like a mother's embrace, offered answers and comfort. He is governed by this history, by his textual origins. For the poet of the diaspora, then, all yearnings, even those seeking to recover a lostness, involve, even if only *sub rosa*, a sense of felt opposition, of yearning against as well as for. And "innovation," warns Elon, "without tradition creates alienation and sows a short-lived field of rootless symbols doomed from their inception."

But isn't this lack of rootedness a condition of all poem-making? For example, the Syrian-born poet, Adonis, in his *Introduction to Arab Poetics*, a book written while under his own diaspora and exile from his homeland, tells us that "legislation and codification go against the nature of poetic language, for this language, since it is man's expression of his explosive moods, his impetuousness, his difference, is incandescent, constantly renewing itself… always a disrupter of codes." This is not a particularly unconventional view. But he goes on: "It [poetic language] is the search for the self, and the return to the self, but by means of a personal exodus away from the self." Adonis's words entail "exodus" as dynamical, in a sense, always about being in motion, but always about being in some relation between the place of departure and the place of arrival.

With Adonis, we could say that the diaspora only has meaning in terms of the exodus one has made from a homeland, or that homeland only has meaning in terms of an exodus. The poet participates in just such a movement between the capacity of language to render certainties and at the same time to undermine them, to carry a reader of the poem away from the familiar to the unfamiliar.

Whatever I have to say, then, never stands alone, never makes of itself an entity without referencing an elsewhere, an elsewhere that remains invoked and yet undefined. If, like Adonis, I search for the self, I also seek that exodus from it. And this very movement will express a kind of return to the other term, the other side of the in-between. (I would admit here to a resonance with Eliot's doctrine of the impersonal, which he saw as an "escape from personality.") And in fact, mustn't it be true that as soon as I find a border or contour to something I label the self, I am already looking over the perimeter toward the non-self? Thus, I do not see the whiteness of the page or screen on which these words are placed as something neutral but as a part of the Heisenbergian motion of uncertainty, as itself a real fiction, an element in what a Buddhist would call the "as if" illusion of the real. I am not alone, certainly not in this realization.

From the *ribboni's* standpoint—my standpoint—there is little difference between the governed utterances of the *rabbani* and those potentially free-standing ones of the purely secular (if such an utterance could even exist). For the *ribboni*, language is never determined nor free. Rather, he finds it lying between the sacred space of Israel or religion or belief and the purely secularized and mechanical spaces of the outlyings. Bialik, in his essay, constructs the fable of a word's birth, its winning of articulation from fear and confusion, and also how it is at first full, then hollowed out, then filled again (if differently) in the course of usage in time. In the sacred space, the word has already assumed its fullness of meaning; to utter is to partake of the language of God, of scriptural authority. In the outlyings, in its phases of emptiness, it has reduced itself to a husk, even to a manipulable purity: music, *art pour l'art*, a signifier without need of its signified.

Bialik, in his meditations on poetry, seems to continually worry such points. His thoughts lie along the border not only of concealments but of our reifying tendencies. "If the empty word enslaves," he writes, "how much more is this true of the full word?" "No word," he continues, "contains the complete dissolution of any question. What does it contain? The question's concealment." Bialik's thoughts are not only a great defense against literalism but also, in the most curious way, a defense against the autonomy of language. For "concealment" can only occur referentially. That is, something before the poet must be at stake, something like the sacred nature of an object or idea, something—if we follow the kabbalists—containing within itself the Creator's intent. The boundary lines of emptiness and fullness are only the markers of a region where pressure exists for something to fulfill its function in transcendence or to "lapse" toward the profane. The word's existence, by its very nature, is always signifying a signified. But, it is also performing another more mysterious function, as Bialik notes, "by virtue of the process by which it closes up the small aperture of the void—constructing a barrier to prevent the void's darkness from welling up and overflowing its bounds."

Poetry, as I sense it, as I find confirmation in Bialik and in my reading, covers the underlying void and exposes it at the same time. One of my tutors here has been Oppen in his late poetry, which I read not as fragmentary or discontinuous but as a place of *agon* where void and concealment struggle with each other as he strives for a complete utterance, an utterance he is at great points not to have confused with any idea of the Rimbaudian "derangement of the senses." Oppen referred to this desire as "speaking the estranged."

It is true that signifying—pointing at an object, for instance—is one of every word's more complicated strengths. The shifting dynamism of language, of syntax and meaning often make the act of signification a secondary power. Bialik admits as much, remarking that "no reply to the question of essence is ever possible in the practice of speech." Essence, as Oppen notes, is always "estranged," always beyond possession. But from another perspective, to ignore or even eliminate language's signifying function—assuming this could ever be done—is to strip it of all power, to reduce it to mere sound or clever fancy. For at all times, the fullness of language must remind us of the void it conceals.

Concealment, as Bialik suggests, is always related to fear and uncertainty. Our urge to write or speak, our logorrheic disposition, comes, as Bialik points out, from "man's atmosphere of knowledge," an atmosphere that "must never for a single moment be rid of words, crowded and consecutive like the links in a great suit of armor, without so much as a hair's breadth between them."

Long before I had read Bialik, in a gesture of my own, in my memoir *Living Root* and in my poem in the volume, "The American Jewish Clock" I speculate on the fact that my grandfather's Old World European first name Zalman was translated into "Solomon" on his arrival into the United States. What did it mean to have that added extra syllable? The *Book of Genesis* has this passage, which I quote in the memoir, in which God speaks to Abraham at one of the most crucial points in the founding of Judaism: "As for me, behold my covenant is with thee, and thou shalt be a father of many nations. Neither shall thy name anymore be called Abram, but thy name shall be Abraham, for a father of many nations have I made thee."

The onomastic moment, in which the named one is renamed, has struck me as the singular poetic act of the Judaic sensibility, the act that contains all the empowerments of faith, psychology and self-determination. In my speculations on the poem in the memoir, I too, somewhat like Bialik, had imagined that for a Jew, the universe was constructed of an immense brick wall of words and wordings and that the introduction of so much as a new syllable would indeed, like forcing a brick into such a wall, create a shattering and crumbling of what was there. If man's atmosphere of knowledge were a seamless armor of language—and surely this image has a monstrous paranoia about it—a continuous intoning of words, like the mumbled dovening by rote in *shuls* and *yeshivas*, wouldn't it be the poet's task to intervene, to wake one's self and others from the sleep of such "holy" and mechanical verbiage?

My thought here remains speculative, poetic perhaps. What intervenes in the drone of language is the name because the name is surrounded not by more language but by silence. For a name to be a name, it must arise from and fall back into the space of soundlessness. A further speculation, as I hinted at in my book on the Objectivists, *Conviction's Net of Branches*, was that the poem, conceived of as a name, is in effect a stand-in for personage. This idea is ancient, rife with mystical and spiritual aspects. Gershom Scholem, in *On the Mystical Shape of the Godhead*, seems to infer exactly this sense of naming. In the book, he refers us to a key passage from Marcus, one of the early Gnostic teachers, whose work is associated with kabbalah. Marcus writes:

> When, in the beginning, the fatherless father, who is neither grasped by the mind nor has a substance and who is neither man nor woman, wanted to express His ineffable being and make His invisible being visible, He opened his mouth and produced a word that resembled Him. In coming to him, it showed him that it was thereby becoming manifest as the shape of the invisible.

If, to remind ourselves of the Gospel of John, that "in the beginning was the Word," Marcus's scenario is something like the Big Bang of primordial naming. Its physical structure, in Judaic terms, seems to undergird all subsequent acts of naming. Here God's unconcealment, his visibility is made possible by the production of a word that "resembled Him." The word "in coming to Him" seems to be a gathering of His attributes, which function like an empowering toward the word's utterance. They are traceries of powers and qualities. The sounding of the word will not display these attributes but will manifest as the "shape of the invisible." It is as though Bialik's terms, "revealment and concealment," were simply the two sides of the same coin. The name both posits God and preserves His mystery, preserving as well, the invisibility of the "fatherless father."

Walter Benjamin writes, in the spirit of Bialik's "revealment and concealment," that "the theory of proper names is the theory of the frontier between the finite and the infinite," the conditions of his "void," transposed onto something like a mathematical plane. Not only does name reside alongside the use of number (finities and infinities) in a range of poetics, but, like mathematics itself, poetry is very much the carrying of ratios into articulation. I would add that the proper name and the poem point to similar entities, specificities created by language that cannot be reduced solely to genre or class. Benjamin says elsewhere that "a speaker who is poetic in the literal sense of the word—namely a maker whose activity is that of producing a new meaning, a maker who is creative—is someone who at the same time compels language to take on his/her individuality."

Neither "expression" nor "art" seem like adequate terms for this Benjaminian concept of naming. Nor do the workings of a programmatic avant-garde or 'experimental' poetry answer adequately to the challenge of the name. The 'experimental' as it is often conceived, seems to me to remain always in the realm of "art," in the realm of a "consumerist" culture of planned obsolescence and inflated political claims, thus offered no serious challenge to the constructs of language that actually govern and empower individuals, societies and institutions, whereas the activity of naming—always an intervention—returns language to the social realm, to questions of identity and non-identity,

For a poet, then, the "danger" Bialik speaks of, the one that exists between revealment and concealment, can be re-thought as being at the very heart of poetic practice. Bialik continually explores the dynamics of this danger zone: "The profane turns sacred, the sacred profane. Long-established words are constantly being pulled out of their settings, as it were, and exchanging places with one another. Meanwhile, between concealments, the void looms."

How to take Bialik's thought? At points, its dualism is instructive. In his essay, 'The Sacred and the Secular in Language,' he writes that "the whole purpose of Hebrew speech, that is to say, the rule of language over life, is to turn the sacred into the profane. That is the point of secularization—we had a sacred language and we're turning it into a secular language." He is, of course, describing what has been occurring with Hebrew in Israel, but he means something more universal, in that every country has, as he put it, "a sacred and a secular language."

Scholem's commemorative poem on Bialik, translated by Richard Sieburth, brings to the fore in a disguised form some of the troubling ambiguities of the sacred/secular nexus. Here is the poem in full:

BIALIK

So communicative was he that his words
were almost anonymous in their reach
So close was he to the people's world
that each meeting deepened his speech.

His death is but a pause in the conversation
in which, lost in thought, he still perseveres—
Ah, who could break this cursed silence
which carries him off, screaming in our ears.

17 July 1934

The words "communicative" and "anonymous" suggest that in Scholem's reading of the poet, the hieratic and religious nature of Hebrew, its coming from "on high," are brought earthbound, made demotic and secularized to the level of the "people's world." And yet, Bialik's death, the "pause in the conversation," further exposes the void or concealment underlying this newly secularized speech. Steven Wasserstrom, in his Introduction to Scholem's poems, remarks of this poem that "a spare two quatrains, this lament drew its agonizing theme from Bialik's other major essay, 'Revealment and Concealment in Language,' which contains the following lines: "for man shall not look on me and live,' says the void, and every speech, every pulsation of speech, partakes of the nature of a concealment of nothingness, a husk enclosing within itself a dark seed of the eternal enigma."

Scholem, who in *Judaism in Crisis* discusses the dichotomy between a perfunctory use of language and a language of the mysteries, of the enigmas at the heart of the sacred text, echoes Bialik. He maintains that the burden of revealing the mystical is hidden "because it appears in forms which are new to the concepts of tradition." Possibly this is an enabling dichotomy: if poetry is the medium in which tradition is made, only to be unmade, then revealment of the mystical is poetry's task."

* * *

Bialik tells us that "the word receives its full vitality only within its existence in its country, that is, within the work as a whole." Let us assume that the ambiguity between "country" and "work" is either a problem in translation or that Bialik is pointing to a sense in which the categories of residence are subsumed under the larger, more encompassing sense of one's writing. While the ambiguity poses problems, let us shift the discussion and ask, what does "full vitality" mean if one's "country" is the diaspora, if the sensibility of the poet, in this case the "Jewish-American" poet, is always aslant the "America" making up a piece of that hyphenated term. Robert Alter's formula of "lore in quest of Law" seems precisely to define the exilic poet's dilemma and desiring. It suggests, as well, that the attempt to conceive of the diaspora as a new kind of homeland runs against the tensions of the self's poetic "exodus." It would be unfaithful, in other words, to turn diaspora into a new kind of Law.

* * *

The French poet and novelist Marcel Cohen writes "If we have seen the values of a civilization blown to pieces, a corollary of this is that over the same period, in war as in peace, we have seen the 'self' surrender any real grasp on its destiny." "Destiny" is a very loaded word, one that at its "fullness," if I may borrow from Bialik, might very well point toward a heavily nationalistic or theologically based concept of the individual; at its most empty, it may simply mean the inalienable right to "do your own thing." Somewhere, in between the nationalist and the free spirit, is a more common "surrender" of political and social will to forces or pressures of seeming inevitability, cultural, linguistic and intellectual. Surrender of the "self" in this middle place becomes more subtle as the individual allies himself with forms of group-think, with making a bet on the zeitgeist or its ethos. On the surface, such a surrender seems freely chosen. However, in a secular intellectual culture (I use this phrase to distinguish the primarily literary and academic culture in which I live as distinct from the increasingly sectarian saturation of American cultural life), while the old gods are dispensed with, it seems clear to me that new ones in the form of critical ideologies take their hold. I believe that it is part of my work as a poet to try not to occupy such a place, whether in a clique or within a theoretical construct or within a belief structure of how and what poetry ought to be. I still want to grasp my destiny or, as Alon says of the *ribboni*, to be master of myself, "not the master of the world or of other people."

* * *

Daniel Stern, in his essay 'Midrash and Indeterminacy,' describes the spatial aspects of polysemy as conceived in various interpretative traditions. Meaning in traditionalist "logocentric" readings of texts is defined as located "behind" the text; in post-modern or deconstructionist readings, as being "in front" of the text. In the case of Rabbinic Judaism, the divine guarantee of meaning is described as "coming from above." Above, not only from a divine presence but also in the physical sense, as given on a mountain top, from Mount Sinai. In this far from positive description of polysemy, I hear echoes of Scholem's plaint in his poem to Bialik. The secular poet of the diaspora might well sense that meaning comes to him not from any unitary direction, but surrounds and even overwhelms him, and mostly comes to him "through" other texts, entrained by other meanings and surfacings. And, as Scholem reminds us, even the religious poet must acknowledge that the imageless God of the Jews manifests almost exclusively as speech. The texts of the world (and the voice of His-self as text too) arrive as traceries. They are not works, but linguistic representations of works. The ear cannot not hear, and the poet has no dispensation except as a kind of stand-in for the palimpsest on which the traceries do their work. His "place" is, in a sense, to be experimented on by meanings, by culture, tradition, history and personal circumstance. Such a poet may well go in fear of instrumental technique or of any procedures that release him from the burden of meaning's tasks. At least, this is how I took my sense of being a poet, less a maker than a recorder.

This understanding implies a method. Caught between numerous texts and cultures, and as a figure of many cultures, the poet can turn to commentary because commentary is the place of engagement, of both synthesis and confrontation as products of a poetico-rhetorical stance with tradition. Commentary, the practice of *midrash*, or something like it, defined by Daniel Stern as "avoiding the dichotomized opposition of literature versus commentary" is the path that most appeals to me because it is true to the spirit, the "inbetween" of being. To take up midrash, as Stern says, is to live in "the dense shuttle-space between text and interpreter," what I have described as "the surround" of meanings offered by texts. Alon, in speaking about his *ribboni* figure, claims that such activity, because it is always in relation to both its origin and its destination, creates "organic symbols." Such symbols can only be "cultivated" by midrash.

This midrashic condition for the poet amounts to a situation in which no issue of language is finally settled. Caught at every point in language's endlessness, in the web Bialik describes, the poet finds his environment cocoon-like, ever-circling into self-referentiality, a genuine condition but, surely, not yet poetry. What then?

Revault d'Allonnes, in his marvelous book *Musical Variations on Jewish Thought*, gives a clue: "The major artfulness—not to say astuteness—of Jewish thought has been, on this very point, to approach everything by writing, above all, by the names of things." Writing, and its punctuating corollary, naming, are the products of time and are also its consumers. Revault d'Allonnes lays the importance of these practices in the Judaic cultural matrix to the shift in early Jewish religious thinking away from Yahweh, the god of tribal geography and its spatialness, to Elohim, the "God of the nomads... the universal divine principle who is linked neither to a people nor to a land... a god of time" unlike Yahweh "who is 'a god of space,' of territory."

For Revault d'Allonnes, Elohim is the "true Jewish god," and the "entire ideological history of the people of Israel can be presented as dominated by the conflict between Elohim and Yahweh, between the nomadic and the sedentary life... between internal morality represented by time, nomadism, fidelity, and by external power represented by space, sedentarization, the State."

For me, the Ark is portable. Especially if inwardness is central. The Ark's interior place, as Revault d'Allonnes points out, is signified by the Hebrew word *kerev*, the same word for the interior space of the human body, the body cavity which "each person conveys everywhere with him or herself." Indeed, time and nomadism so predominate in those who inhabit the Elohimist ethos, that according to Revault d'Allonnes "writing... constitutes their sole possible monument." The state religion of the avant-garde, with its rule-bound products, its strictures and group demands strikes as foreign to the Elohimist position (or non-position, as I would have it).

The poetics I reach for would be one that was receptive to limit and to closure. The awareness of time made manifest not by its ongoingness but by fits and starts, its stuttering coalescences in naming. Susan Handelman rehearses such a poetics in her discussion of Benjamin, pointing to *The Origin of German Tragedy*, where Benjamin writes that "truth is not a process of exposure which destroys the secret, but a revelation which does justice to it." Such a style will exercise the "art of interruption in contrast to the chain of deduction." Put another way, the aim of such a poetics would be something like Oppen's "limited, limiting clarity."

In Talmudic and midrashic perspectives, clarity is virtually synonymous with truth and revelation. If, for a poet like Oppen, they were the words which "could not not be understood," for the midrashist, they are incitements. In Stern's essay on midrash, we find the following: "The words of the wise," says Rabbi Eleazar Ben Azariah, "are like goads; like nails well-planted are the words of the masters of assemblies; they were given by one shepherd." For Rabbi Ben Azariah, the shepherd may have been God or the intelligible face of creation. Geoffrey Hartman, quoted in Stern, has seen that this process, the love of truth, is close to commentary itself "the taking away, modification, elaboration of previous meanings." Hartman I think is referring to the relational aspect of Jewish thought, the I Thou-ness, within the sacred and the poetic, to the back and forth course of its motions. The temple's question and response, a conversation held under the roof of the *kerev*, the interiority of self and Ark, strikes as the diasporic model of the poetics I seek to describe.

Revelations are the momentary end process of a poetic practice. They are announced through time, to be cognized, to register and to invoke an awe-filled pause in language. They expose the void underneath the very words that construe them. Revelation, as understood in both secular and non-secular Judaic traditions, is bound to the ethical, and therefore to vulnerability. What makes poets and their poetry vulnerable is not so much newness or uniqueness but communicability, an opening to being verified or falsified by experience. Emmanuel Levinas, in Handelman's view, supplies a mild corrective to both Benjamin and Scholem, thinkers who have invoked "the mystery of language beyond meaning" (Benjamin) or "pure language" (Scholem). All thought, even its most theoretical or poetic utterances, is, according to Levinas—as Handelman reminds us—"an address to another, it must be *told*." While communications eventually pass from truth into a kind of falsehood or non-relevance, the revelations stand. "Man," Bialik asserts, "has the ability to declare that any day is a holiday.... This is not merely a matter of will. The power of the day is great because many memories are attached to it that are not attached other days, and this day thus receives, as it were, an extra soul." Day by day, poem by poem, the poet makes and commemorates revelations. As such they constitute the remains of the diaspora I speak of and to which I belong.

ON COUNTER-MEMORY

(working notes for an autobiography)

Where memory and history coincide?

Biale, p. 201 on Scholem's "counterhistory, an account of the productive conjunction of opposites: myth and rationalism, etc. A static picture cannot be objective because it only reflects the constellation of forces at a particular moment, obscuring the hidden level on which future developments are being prepared... Counter-history is history written by the *engagé*."

The idea of "antiquarianism" in Scholem? Wouldn't it first begin with the idea of the antiquarian, that is pertaining to an interest in antiquities. Antiquarianism would be the mode or outlook which treats things in history as antiquities, remote and without presentness. Now one of the things that antiquarianism enables is this distancing and, in a sense, purification of its objects. I grew up in Miami Beach. One of the jobs I took in high school was showing movies to guests in the lobbies of hotels, and now I see, in the decor of these lobbies, this antiquarianism at work. Antiquarianism reduces a cultural object to its decorative aspect and allows anomalies and anachronisms to coexist in the present in such a way as to deny them their original symbolic or spiritual power. [Is this an earlier precursor of postmodern *bricolage*?] What function does this décor serve? To feel oneself in the presence of 'culture' *without* having to do any work for it? *Fin-de-siècle Vienna*? Contemporary yuppism—the consumer's desire for "art" to put on the wall rather than to study or worship at?) Already, then, Miami Beach as a resort, naturally, and, in its specifics, appeared less a place to live than a consumer object.

*

Buber's remark: "The Word formed late..." (Biale, 7986)

*

From a letter (15 March 1991) MH to Larry Fixel:

On a parallel line, I have been working on more autobiographical prose. The question has been how to organize the work, or indeed what lies behind the motive for even doing it. By good fortune, I had been reading David Biale's book on Gershom Scholem. Scholem formulates what he calls "counter-history," history which voices those irrational elements that lie in the depths of tradition yet that the tradition often tries to exclude. And so I asked myself, isn't there also a counterpart on the level of the individual, which one could usefully call "counter-memory," a recalling such as Mandelstam performs in *The Noise of Time* or Leiris in *Manhood*, a recounting which functions to voice the unofficial or irrational of personal history. So, on this I have embarked and though, in a sense, it is nothing new in the world of letters, the term 'counter-memory' gives me hints and hopes of structure against my fears of formlessness and indulgence.

*

Benjamin (Biale, 198): "brushing history against the grain" a means of overturning the oppressive judgments of past historiography.

I would want to brush *personal* story against the grain, forcing the individual bristles (which have been combed to lie a particular way by the sociopolitical cultures in which we live) to stand vertically again, to become turgid (the metaphor is meant to be sexual) with long dead passions, angers and ideas, so as to reenergize lost aspects of the psyche. Not to reclaim a prior time (childhood, primitiveness, etc.) but to restore wholeness, breaking open into fluidity what had become mechanism or forgetting.

*

Exemplum from Biale/Scholem (198): "Where the nineteenth century said [of the mystical tradition] only 'degeneracy and impotent hallucinations,' Scholem finds 'the great living myth'."

*

Is this an attempt to unlearn? That which has been structured becomes the bondage of a reflex. How to feel or tease these out? Fears (examples):

was I a "good" child which meant would I at least succeed in not doing anything which might kill my sick mother? How sensitive was I to my father's wrath, deeply buried, much disguised, which emerged on the rarest of occasions (and then with volcanic dimensions); he only hit me twice, as I remember.

My mother showed her anger more quickly, usually by yanking our hair. Once she hit me with a broom handle because it was in her hand I think when I was having a big fight with my younger sister.

*

Ernst Bloch believed that religious heretics were the most genuine religious figures. (Biale, 199) Bloch's aim: not to 'democratize' religion but to 'de-theocratize' the Bible to save it as a text.

*

Gottfried Arnold: the true history of Christianity is the history of the persecuted, the martyred, the heretical. (Biale, 199)

True Christianity has no external history, since its essence is the recurring inward struggle of the soul and not the fate of world institutions.

Can we not look at individuals in the light of Arnold's formulation, *i.e.*, an autobiography is not so much the story of the fate of an individual in the world as it is the record of the inward struggle of the individual caused by and in interplay with a world. And given expression as part of or show of the world.

So it is about resistance to coercion in many forms, often the most outwardly innocuous having immense force.

To revise Joachim of Fiore, autobiography constitutes a personal "theology of crisis."

*

Biale, 200: "Dogmas arise out of the submission of inward religious experience into worldly institutions: dogma is the consequence of world history."

Hence orthodoxy as the real heresy because it suppresses the freedom necessary for true religion.

*

Scholem insists, however, that the category of "individual inwardness" is foreign to Judaism (as it is foreign to the "objectivist" poetics which nurtured me?) and that "Jewish history unfolds in a public communal tradition, even when its foremost representatives seem to congregate in esoteric sects." (Biale, 201)

Counter-history but also counter-story (as with my concept of "counter-continuities" which I formulated in the 'Avant-Garde Propellants...' essay) would invoke a counter-tradition, the poets of which would exist outside the current orthodoxies.

*

Aside: a proposed poetry anthology: *Stolen Air: The Counter Tradition of Contemporary Poetry.*

*

Reread Biale, 210, 211, for hints on how to proceed.

*

FOR THE AUTOBIOGRAPHY:
—the magical disappearance of the object (?) in the Hudson Arms lobby.
—servants:
    —in NYC, our maids, Belle and Marie.

    —in Miami Beach, Aunt____, Blanche and _____ (who stirred me sexually when I was maybe 12?)

*

Manhood by Leiris, 17,18: the analogy between the confessional writer and the *torero* is linked by adherence to "the rules of the game." The rules work something like this: the prescribed physical gestures of the bullfighter are emulated in the refusals of the confessional writer to indulge in an artifice which would make his "confession" more palatable.

*

Thinking about Blanchot's *The Imagination of the Disaster*: doesn't disaster make individuals childlike, the world suddenly become wrathful like an angry, incomprehensible parent? And then, doesn't the individual go through a number of stages or motifs from frustration to despair, to something like the "Stockholm Syndrome" where one tries to befriend or even emulate the disaster?

*

In Hayden White's *The Content of the Form*, there is a discussion concerning the differences between poetic allegory and historical allegory as filtered through Dante's discussion in the *Convivio* and Singleton's commentary on it:

> The "allegory of poets," which is that of fable, of parable (and hence also to be found in Scriptures), is a mode in which the first and literal sense is one devised, fashioned (*fictio* in its original meaning) in order to conceal, and in concealing to convey, a truth. Not so in the other (scriptural allegorical) mode.... There the first sense is historical, as Dante says it is, and not "fiction." The children of Israel did depart from Egypt in the time of Moses. Whatever the other senses may be, the first sense abides, stands quite on its own, is not devised 'for the sake of.' Indeed it was generally recognized that in Holy Scripture the historical sense might at times be the only sense there. These things have been so; they have happened in time. This is the record of them.

White suggests that the historical "fact" (rather than the *ficto*) of historical narrative conveys the moral or anagogical significance, which is why Singleton interprets Dante's notion of history as being "God's 'poetry.'" Thus, Dante, therefore, thinking that no poet could be as great as God, tried, in the *Commedia*, to imitate God's way of writing.

Also in White, Ricoeur's notion that every historical discourse is a literal representation of humanity at grips with the "experience of temporality. This content, in turn, is nothing other than the moral meaning of humanity's aspiration to redemption from history itself."

*

Miłosz in *Native Realm*: "A three-year-old's love for his aunt or jealousy toward his father take up so much room in autobiographical writings because everything else, for instance the history of a country or a national group, is treated as something 'normal' and, therefore, of little interest to the narrator. But another method is possible. Instead of thrusting the individual into the foreground, one can focus attention on the background, *looking upon oneself as a sociological phenomenon* (my italics). Inner experience, as it is preserved in the memory, will then be evaluated in the perspective of the changes one's milieu has undergone."

*

Benjamin wrote of Baudelaire that he "assembled the days of remembrance into a spiritual year." (*Illuminations*, 185) In his 'Historico-philosophical Theses,' Benjamin suggests that "sparks of hope" are concealed in the past, which modern consciousness of redemption pulls together and fans into a flame.... The "time of the Now" is shot through with "chips of Messianic time." (See discussion by Stephen Moses on Benjamin and Rosenzweig in *The Philosophical Forum*, Vol XV, 12, Fall–Winter 1983, 84, pp 203–204).

*

Notes from Morse's *Word by Word: The Language of Memory*:

This quotation from Carlyle's *On History* which Morse uses as an epigraph: "Our very speech is curiously historical. Most men, you may observe, speak only to narrate, not in imparting what they have thought, which indeed were often of very small matter, *but in exhibiting what they have undergone or seen, which is a quite unlimited one, do talkers dilate* (my italics)."

Being in memory as a kind of physiological state. Isn't it our experience that we are transformed when we call up memories? We are thrown into another mode, as it were, not only more richly textured in emotions, but one in which we are totally seduced by our own language. Interruptions, attempts by others to move us from the discourse we are engaged in only enrage us. (Likewise as in reverie, which I tried to illustrate in my novella, *The Study*.) Naturally, the memory reciter, the raconteur, the man 'lost' in story is also a figure for comedy. His audience senses him as in love with his words, but more often the case, he is enraptured by the significance of the story behind the words. Perhaps there are only degrees, and that any excessive or obsessive love of one's utterance has to do with more than the sound of the words, with the self-narrative that they set up even when no narrative function is present.

A CONVERSATION ABOUT *LIVING ROOT*[1]

(Between Michael Heller and Burt Kimmelman)

BK: A thematic and aesthetic agenda of *Living Root* is the uniting of, a making whole of what has been torn apart, a world of fragments, which is perhaps accomplished through the book's ongoing meditation on ritual. Your own life, especially your early years, was one of dislocation and parental illnesses, which in a way parallels the history of your family's passage across the Atlantic Ocean to America from Poland, which also, the book seems to suggest, is an artistic parallel to, even as it is a historic part of, the Jewish Diaspora. Indeed, this memoir finds ritual taking many forms, in your discussions of poetry, religious heritage, ethnic heritage, and personal relationships, as well as in your contemplation of ritual's nature itself. Was the writing of *Living Root,* which took a number of years, now in hindsight a sort of ritual as well?

MH: Ritual and the undoing of ritual are at the heart of the book. I took ritual to be a kind of protection, like a soul being sheltered, placed under a bell jar, enclosed within the sacred. But I had come into that ritual space by the accidents of birth, upbringing, environment. It was not truly my own; in that sense, the bell jar also stifled. And given the life around me, my mother's non-belief, my father's uneasy relationship with his grandfather, the Rabbi, writ large, I was seeing cracks and flaws in that ritual space, in the conventions and acts of faith that I had not truly made my own. At the same time, the aspects of Jewish tradition which deeply drew my allegiance were those involving writing and rewriting, midrash, commentary upon commentary, all those activities which allowed one to re-imagine the meaning and space of the rituals. And, in truth, as I began and wrote, a kind of Proustian involuntary memory kept taking place, ignited into language, as it were, by the artifacts, the picture albums and letters, the detritus of my parents' lives, which came to me after their deaths. And the parallels which you mention, the large-scale movement of the Diaspora, and the scattering of one Michael Heller outside the house of his received rituals, were part of the substance of that matrix of old yellowed paper, curling photographs and unbidden memories out of my past.

---

[1] *Living Root: A Memoir*. SUNY Press, 2000

BK: In other words, from early on you have been an outsider—not unlike those in the scriptural tradition whose faithful are devoted to words, words that stand apart from things—even to the extent that the most intimate details of your own origins are both within you and apart from you somehow?

MH: As I wrote in the memoir, "I am remembering then, not for the sake of what was, but, in a sense in order to be." As I reflected on the sheer unaccountability of origins, their arbitrariness, their unchosen quality, the "quantum mechanics," as I put it, of autobiography, I sensed also my going out toward much that is in tradition and in the histories I was exposed to of my family and of the Jews and of poetry. The act of reflection on the details of one's life in this sense is dynamic in much the same manner that the literal words of the Bible become dynamic once subjected to the ongoing process of Talmudic or midrashic reflection. The Ba'al Shem Tov says that memory is the secret of redemption, and Yosef Yerushalmi, in *Zakhor*, reminds us that Jews, while not the fathers of history, are "the fathers of meaning in history." I would hope that on a small, personal level, my work is in that tradition.

BK: But doesn't this mean that you, as a Jew, as both a reader and writer, are begging the question implied by your memoir's title: how is there a "living root" if one sees oneself as in some sense an indirect outgrowth of family and heritage?

MH: In the book I speak of "the juncture," the "boundary membrane" of the root where "what is dead and what is alive are indistinguishable." I could not trace myself to the roots alone. What I keep finding is an evolution with respect to those roots, a re-thinking and re-imagining. If nothing else, an elaborate scheme to avoid thinking of myself as pre-destined.

BK: As for the past—setting aside the idea of a destiny—you acknowledge that both family and heritage apparently have been infiltrated by your reflections on them, your explorations, and what is more they have been about the simultaneous removal from, and the one-and-the-sameness of, experience—thus your concern in your memoir for the Kabbalistic *devekuth* or adhesion as well as your professed devotion to Walter Benjamin's life and work, particularly his notion of replication, although this may not be quite the right word.

MH: You are perhaps thinking of Benjamin's essay 'The Work of Art in the Age of Mechanical Reproduction,' but that is not the work which is significant here. Rather, for the purposes of the memoir, such concepts as his "chips of messianic time" and his thinking about the principle of montage deeply influenced me. I can't remember that I actually use the phrase in *Living Root,* but the idea was implicit in the work. (I mention this in an interview published in *Talisman* magazine.) The non-linearity of the book is based on seeking a "spiritual" rather than "temporal" ordering of a life. Benjamin's revelatory "messianic chip" is, like Proust's madeleine, the thing/event/artifact which opens a floodgate of autobiography and the energy associated with it. My method was to let the family albums, the letters, the orts and crumbs of my family history, speak to me in a like manner. Such overhearings have very much to do with the genesis of the book, as in the first pages, begun in thinking about the contrasts between my grandfather and my father performing the Passover service. My grandfather's ease and comfort speaking to his God compared to my father's dis-ease and caution astonished me. My hearing them opened up all sorts of questions in my mind about religion and faith and, of course, about ritual. It was no longer a dead thing to me, but a deep and telling marker of one's commitment and psychology. Thus to my mind, the idea of "writing," which you stress, needs to be related to the larger Jewish concern for commentary and its auditory equivalent, for overhearing, as in Gershom Scholem's observation that "revelation is something overheard."

BK: Benjamin writes, as you quote him in *Living Root,* of the photograph as the "posthumous moment." You contextualize your concern with your ancestry by way of a book of old photos of pre-war Bialystok (in Poland) that you acquired when still a young man. You write, early on in the memoir, of your desire to "compel memory and history to coincide." They may only coincide in this book, which is an act of writing, no?

MH: Writing is THE gathering, the making of connections, transforming the chronicler's bald list of events or the found items in the scrapbook into a life, a presence for the author and the reader. Making those posthumous moments part of one's present life and giving that life a measure of futurity as well as pastness.

BK: And a literary tradition flows through you, Michael Heller, through your entrance into the sensorium of experience that was both literary but also simply visceral? For instance, your boyhood is influenced by your older cousin Arthur who reads to you and your sister Tena from the *Iliad*, and in your awareness as you would drift into sleep you "felt the battle for Troy occurring on the borders of my consciousness, itself a vast dark plain like the one before that ancient city." No mere words here? There is likewise, as you report, the mingling of prayerful incantation with Passover food and wine. Even the subtle ethnic prejudices you encounter directly as a boy in Miami Beach, your recollection of them, mingle with the passed-along documentations of the Shoah in response to which your grief is real albeit it is ultimately mediated by writing. You are, therefore, real as a reader and writer. Is this not, looking at what has come before, a Jewish destiny?

MH: Arthur, my cousin, my adopted brother—his parents had died while he was in his teens and my family took him in—was the first intellectual person I knew. Not only were those nightly readings of poetry immensely important but so were his radical political opinions, although, as I explain in the memoir, the flatness of the often ideological speech he used never came close to the "visceral" power of Homer or any of the other poets he introduced to me. So that was a lesson in itself about levels of speech. And in the late Forties, the Shoah was still rumor, still barely defined. No one, least of all a young self-involved boy in sunny Miami Beach, could imagine its enormities. But there was this atmosphere of something terrible having taken place, like a pall or cloud, which would later surround everything. I reacted to anti-semitism with anger and even some curiosity about who'd dare it on me. Only later, long after I started to write, and on visits to my parents, when I would go through their memorabilia, through the books and photos on Bialystok, did I sense I could use a word like Holocaust or Shoah in my work.

I'm leery of the term "Jewish destiny," unless one means it in a historical sense, from the outside, so to speak. And even then, one can see in reading *Living Root* that much of its writing has been an interrogation of those two words, neither accepting nor rejecting them, but rather making use of them as I try to re-imagine or even re-invent myself. But, of course, someone will say, "that's very Jewish!" So perhaps in spite of my efforts, there is a little Jewish hunchback inside of me, as there was one named "dialectical materialism" in Benjamin's chess-winning puppet in the opening paragraph of his 'Theses on the Philosophy of History.' Unlike Benjamin's hunchback, I'm a lousy chess player.

BK: Well, surely there is for you an operative dialectic inspired by Benjamin, as we have been saying. *Living Root* includes your beautiful poem 'Constellations of Waking' that addresses his suicide in 1940 when on the run from Nazism. And in a note for the poem you speak of his idea that knowledge is external to something essential in us. To be sure, he believed in, as you write, "the allegorical nature of all text and history." Do we see in this the conceptual precursor of your self-realization through the writing of *Living Root?* In your "boundary membrane" metaphor, which admits of an intercourse, there is the intermingling of the dead and the living, of the tradition outside of you, one which you critically embrace.

MH: I refer to that externality, but I don't say that we are missing something essential. Quite the opposite. Benjamin saw our lives happening moment by moment, and language as bonding us to the things of the world as they took place. But he was deeply resistant to the already discredited ideas of innate human nature. Remember, the idea of innateness, Aryan or Jewish, played an important role in the Nazis' racialist theories. The allegories are the multiple meanings, multiple stories, including one's own, which writing and history offer up to us. The idea of a univocal text or literalist reading of even the most spiritual document was anathema to Benjamin. In the book, I refer to Benjamin as "the patron saint" of the work. And you know I've written a libretto for an opera based on his life. So yes, he is central to the book. But he is by no means its only "precursor." He is there with poets like George Oppen, Charles Reznikoff, and Carl Rakosi, not to mention all the writers and thinkers in my rather off-handed 'Works Cited,' those listed and unlisted (indeed, I beg forgiveness from those not mentioned) who must also be acknowledged as co-authors.

BK: Yet in some sense Benjamin seems to be, although he precedes you and can set an example for you, your allegorical Other. Now, I say this because of your final comment in the note to the Benjamin poem— one I hope you might enlarge upon-that "[t]he contemporary notion of the disappearance of the author which he anticipated in word and deed, culminating in death by his own hand as he sought to escape the Nazis, would seem to provide the Jewish-born (as opposed to the Israeli-born) writer with an exemplary if cautionary tale."

MH: That note, which has generated some controversy, was my way, perhaps clumsily, of enjambing a number of themes. Benjamin somewhat anticipates Foucault in seeing the author as a locus of historical and cultural forces. Remember that, for Benjamin, the ideal critical work consisted solely of citations, that the critic would exist primarily as an arranger of those quotes, and that that arrangement would show forth, like a Poundian vortex, the luminous moment of history in which it was constructed. Faced with capture, possibly torture and murder by the Gestapo, and fearing that he, sickly and without much physical strength, would hinder his companions as they sought again to cross into Spain, his suicide has, in some sense, an illuminating logic to it beyond despair or desperation. Benjamin elected the Diaspora as his arena of activity, despite Scholem's urging him to emigrate to what was then Palestine. As late as 1939, he was claiming that "there are still things to be done in Europe," this even as he was aware of the possible fate that awaited Jews in Europe. So even near the end, the Diaspora for Benjamin was not a place of alienation but a place from which to re-engage the old texts. In my recently published essay, 'Diasporic Poetics,' which borrows some material from the memoir, I refer to Emmanuel Levinas' remark that Jewishness is not a metaphor but a "category of understanding." He goes on to suggest what this idea might mean for a poet: "Is it certain a true poet occupies a place? Is the poet not that which, in the eminent sense of the term, loses its [sic] place, ceases occupation, precisely, and is thus the very opening of space…" and "displays the bottomlessness or the excellence, the heaven that in it [sic] is possible…." For me, this is almost a siren call to be in the Diaspora—I'm sure it was the call Benjamin, that most poetic of thinkers, kept hearing. In this regard, *Living Root* is my attempt to enlarge my own category of understanding, to find in my life, my family history, my work as a poet and writer, and my surroundings, the heaven that is possible.

THE CLOUD: Exodus 35:1–40:38

Exodus, powerful and empowering in its narrative sweep, nevertheless ends on a couple of odd notes. The first concerns the construction of the tabernacle, that portable, proto-temple of a wandering people. Not only do the details of fabrication and construction seem beyond the capabilities of a nomadic band of workmen, but they clash tonally and intentionally as well with earlier instructions to Moses concerning the rough, natural stone to be used as an altar in *Exodus* 20:25. There is controversy over whether or not such a complicated structure could actually have been built or whether Moses and the Israelites communed with God in a simple tent. The elaborate description of the tabernacle may have been inscribed into *Exodus* by a later priestly cast, and is a product of the latest stratum of the Pentateuch, the Priestly Code. The details of the tabernacle's ornate magnificence were, presumably, designed to justify the Levite's class position as dictated by the Second Temple complex with its restrictions on movements and off-limits spaces. As well, the details may have been overlaid on that earlier wilderness story, partly to undermine ideas of a more democratic, less authoritarian and even voluntary priesthood which may have existed when the Exodus story was written. The original tabernacle, if it did indeed exist, must have been a rather simple thing, protecting the ark of the covenant from the elements as the tribes crossed wildernesses and inhospitable deserts. After *Exodus* it receives barely a mention, and as the theocracy develops and hardens into a kind of statehood, soon temples and great codifications are required to sustain and control the religion.

But let us go back to the biblical story. Consider that the desert wandering is temporarily stopped, and that the vision which interrupts the travels is the making of this edifice, begun on the day after the day of atonement. Page upon page of text for its construction, four short passages for the spirituality as symbolized by the cloud that then will follow above and inhabit it. What strange cloud passages they are, and yet they signify in a way that the ravishing details of the tabernacle do not.

Contemplating those last passages, one can envision the spirit cloud laid over the tabernacle. I don't say it hides the work of the laborers or ever could, but it certainly obscures it the way a scrim or slightly frosted window blurs what you are trying to see through it. It is the very uncertain, amorphous quality of the cloud that has meaning to me. The cloud is omnipresent. It is out, it is in, it is over and under. Waters reflect it, and when the sun is at a certain angle, the airy edifice hangs in the sky pink and green and with a luminous silky look. Or it is angry red and jagged. Depending on one's approach, it is fire, it is rain, it is mere fog, indulgent of the seeker. I'm sure that on some days, it is more substantial than the solid objects it obscures. It could block out cities, blanket the mountains and make the landscape look positively flattened. In a sense, the cloud humbles the simplest of knowledge: does a man aswirl in its vapors have his head raised or lowered, is he on his knees or upright and does he wear a hat or is the reddish scalp bared to the heavens.

I can't say I have walked under such a cloud nor can I describe in any sense my proximity to it. But as I stroll through city streets, thinking and following the paths of my thinking, I imagine its indefiniteness may have a purpose, to make a mockery of edifices, to humble the Law, the Concept and the Idea. This humbling reaches back to Moses's experience. It was he who had the vision, and he who marshaled the resources and oversaw the tabernacle's construction, and yet he could not enter the tabernacle when the cloud was present.

The original tabernacle is gone into history; the present-day versions are so much fine marquetry and gold leaf. So, in a sense, the cloud, in its presence and ephemerality, whether raised by the tramping feet of wanderers and seekers or by something divine, has outlasted the tabernacle. The kabbalists speak of the separation which exists even in the most intimate and unifying of experiences with God, and perhaps this separation is signaled for them by the cloud which always shows forth the divine presence but allows only intimations and indirect knowledge of it. Like the idea of the tabernacle itself, we don't know whether we are encountering myth or reality. But there is no need to resolve this issue; only the literalist requires the certainty of the edifice. The cloud is, in the last words of *Exodus,* the one constant for Jews "throughout all their journeys."

ON THE POETICS
OF THE JEWISH GODHEAD

Norman Finkelstein and Michael Heller in conversation
7 / 7 / 15

Dear Michael,

"Imagining the Jewish God": First thought is that Jews are forbidden to imagine Him, as per the Second Commandment. But to cut through endless commentary, I think that basically means that graven images or visual representation is forbidden. Representation in language is something else again. Second thought: given our years of shared reading, writing, and thinking on the subject, especially in regard to the centrality of commentary in the tradition, I think we are bound to turn to thinkers like Gershom Scholem, since it is in the kabbalistic literature (and Scholem has been our guide here) that the boldest verbal representations of God are to be found. So perhaps we can begin with a passage that I'm sure you've encountered, from Scholem's 'Reflections on Jewish Theology' (in *On Jews and Judaism in Crisis*). It is a passage, I confess, that has haunted me for many years, and has shaped my thinking and belief. Scholem is discussing the concept of Creation, and how for the kabbalists, the concept of *tzimtzum* becomes necessary: "By positing a negative factor in Himself, God liberates Creation"—and in this way, Creation perpetually renews itself.

But what really resonates (and mystifies) me is what follows. God's withdrawal into himself produces a Void in and through which Creation takes place. Scholem observes:

> This, to be sure, is the point at which the horrifying experience of God's absence in our world collides irreconcilably and catastrophically with the doctrine of a Creation which renews itself. The radiation of which the mystics speak and which is to attest to the Revelation of God in Creation—that radiation is no longer perceivable by despair. The emptying of the world to a meaningless void not illuminated by any ray of meaning or direction is the experience of him whom I would call the pious atheist. The void is the abyss, the chasm or the crack which

opens up in all that exists. This is the experience of modern man, surpassingly well depicted in all its desolation by Kafka, for whom nothing has remained of God but the void—in Kafka's sense, to be sure, the void of God.

There have been times, I have to admit, that I have identified strongly with this vision of the "pious atheist," and I know it has informed a good deal of my poetry. And I think this is preeminently a modern, or even a modernist, vision—distinguished from a postmodern vision, in which the void is somehow flattened out into a meaningless surface, or maybe filled up with the endless detritus of language. What does that then do to our sense of Creation, to which, I think, it has been the traditional role of the poet to attend? And this in turn can lead us to another of our dominant interests, that of Objectivist poetry. The locus classicus would be Oppen's 'Psalm,' in which it is revealed that the natural world, "this in which the wild deer / Startle, and stare out," consists at the same time of "The small nouns / Crying faith":

    Veritas sequitur

    In the small beauty of the forest
    The wild deer bedding down—
    That they are there!

             Their eyes
    Effortless, the soft lips
    Nuzzle and the alien small teeth
    Tear at the grass

             The roots of it
    Dangle from their mouths
    Scattering earth in the strange woods.
    They who are there.

             Their paths
    Nibbled thru the fields, the leaves that shade them
    Hang in the distances
    Of sun

The small nouns
Crying faith
In this in which the wild deer
Startle, and stare out.

And this, I think is as far as I should go before hearing your reply.
Perhaps I've already said far too much…

07.31.2015

Dear Norman,

I'm using your text to me, the one citing Scholem's passage, as my take-off point. First, let me register the problem as I see it at its most basic, the idea of "god" as the named (yet *designated* the Unnamable), the forbiddenness that brackets the designation, the prohibition of the graven image. Scholem, in *On the Mystical Shape of the Godhead*, discusses the clash between those, who through contemplation of God's sublimity do not conceive "the idea that man carries the divine form" and those who speak of God creating "man in His own image." Scholem describes the clash between these views as "vehement," and giving rise ultimately—and we have to think of that rise as one of enormous tension—to the resort to mystical representations of God, the most well-known perhaps, the varieties of forms discussed in Kabbalah.

Kochan, in *Beyond the Graven Image*, develops an argument between the image and the *making* of images that echoes the tensions above, the latter "making" being the assimilation of the divine to man (*imitatio dei*). (This would be an activity in contrast to that of worship of already created images or idols). As poets, this is full of suggestion for me.

A couple of phrases in the Scholem extract caught my attention: "the horrifying experience of God's absence," in its collision, "irreconcilably and catastrophically" with a Creation renewing itself. The atmospherics of these words and their alignment with Kafka suggest something static and perhaps problematic.

As A. N. Wilson describes it in a recent *TLS* review of *The Book of the People: How to Read the Bible*, the Romans in 63 BCE, after entering the Holy of Holies in the Temple in Jerusalem, were puzzled that, according to Josephus, "in the sanctuary stood nothing whatever." Yards of literature and commentary have been written about that Roman astonishment, not only as it relates to the nature of Judaism and its God, its difference from the god-filled pantheons that surrounded it, but also, as Kochan so pointedly puts it in his section on 'Holiness of the Land', the "*Problematik* of the land of Israel" as opposed to the people of Israel. If I understand Kochan's discussion properly, sanctity is problematized for the thinkers on Judaism and holiness because both space and matter, *i.e.*, "holy" places, temples and the land itself, are in danger of being transformed into idols. In this sense, the empty chamber of the Holy of Holies which so shocked the Romans is also a commentary on the transience of the sacred.

This astonishment and puzzlement also strikes as a lead-in to other questions of imagining God. My own sense is that, as one whose traceries are through language, that God, the idea of God (this nowhere/everywhere of his being) as conceived by Scholem's "pious atheist" is that this God consists of *that which is markable*. That the appearance of the sacred is revealed by marks, by our marking and writing. Unlike the Romans, we do not make an image to worship—we do not worship anything—but instead make sacred by making marks.

You refer to Oppen's 'Psalm' earlier. His "small nouns crying faith" in the "this in which" is a phrase that reminds me of another poem of his, 'World, World—' containing the line "the mystery is that there is something to stand on," a line that leads to the mystery (and a kind of "faith" in itself) of the surface on which he writes 'Psalm,' the surface on which any of us write, which is not blank but the "something we stand on," the background space of possibility. The mark on the background is the beginning of inscription and also of the possibility of the sacred because the sacred must be visible in order to be sensed or seen, which is why, in my view, the supernatural is not necessarily a component of the sacred. Quite the opposite: I would define the sacred as that which has been made intelligible and in that process has made the world intelligible. The "mystery" (not the supernatural) of the sacred—the arena beyond its literalness, the possibility that this arena is invisible, is to be read via the offices of language.

8/3/15

Dear Michael,

Without digging further (yet!) into Scholem or Kochan (the latter having shaped my thought on the subject years ago, when you first introduced me to his work, to the point that it has become part of my unconscious, and I was amazed to discover yesterday how thoroughly I had marked up the copy which he himself sent me, at your urging…)—let me respond to some of your remarks, and see where that leads.

"…the problem as I see it at its most basic, the idea of 'god' as the named (yet *designated* the Unnamable), the forbiddenness that brackets the designation, the prohibition of the graven image." Surely we are immediately faced with the basic paradox: *named* (or *designated*) the Unnameable, though the pious refer to Him not as the Unnameable (shades of Beckett—or Lovecraft!) but as *haShem*—the Name! The name of the Unnameable is the Name. As you say, we whose traceries are through language—we who weave the web, the openwork of words—understand "that this God consists of *that which is markable*." Yes, but also *that which is unmarkable as well*. How could it be otherwise? So that in one respect, our writing occurs (*cf.* Zukofsky) in the space between the named and the unnamed, a liminal space, or a space between the sacred and the profane. (Liminality, for the anthropologists, is that condition of uncertainty in the middle of the ritual, when one is no longer one thing but not yet another.) As for me, the alleged "pious atheist," it strikes me that such writing must be simultaneously sacral and transgressive. As I write in *Track*:

But to profane
this sacred history

But to sacrifice
this deserted writing

To call and call
knowing he will answer

To answer
not knowing if he calls.

Which leads me to your entirely justified concern about my original quote from Scholem, "'the horrifying experience of God's absence', in its collision, 'irreconcilably and catastrophically' with a Creation renewing itself." Yes, atmospherics—the atmospherics of cosmic or existential dread. I confess to be attracted to this stance, and its version of mystery, but I can certainly understand the objections. No doubt that some of Kafka's critics, and some of Kafka himself, reifies that sense. As I say, very modernist, so that a writer like Oppen, without becoming "postmodern," may oppose such static dread through his bracing sense of open possibility. And in religious terms, wouldn't that be analogous to Creation renewing itself? So a writing practice like Oppen's (and here I think your poetry inherits this stance) does indeed become a sacred practice because of its intelligibility. That the world is always open to investigation, an investigation being continuously written by the poet. Again, I take the liberty of quoting myself from *Track*:

      ##
And yet the poem
must sustain all things

All of the orders
as have been prescribed

As have been ordered.

      #
Therefore and
therefore

Not that it can be explained
not that it can be inscribed

But still.

      #
Nor is language magic
as in some cabal
waving their wands

Not magic but mystery
into which one may go.

      #
Into which one may go
when one's name is called

Called by the Name
the nameless Name

Called into the nameless.

    #

Not mystification
but a simple mystery

The self and the world
are made manifest in language

Called out of the nameless.

If I'm not mistaken, I wrote that section while we were staying with you
and Jane in Colorado. Makes sense to me.

08.04.15

Dear Norman,

Your note of 8/3/15 continues our round of provocations, useful ones.

My first quick response was to ask myself, should the poet concede
too readily to the idea of "that which is unmarkable?" Unmarked, yes,
but "unmarkable" seems to give over too much to the kinds of mysticisms
that have led to dogma, intolerance and, in the poetic field, a vocabulary
of abstractions and even weary fatalism (I could probably name a few
more). I presume that the poet's job, *à la* Bialik's word, is "revealment."
In this, the poet resembles the kabbalist in assenting to the idea that in
creation Torah preceded God. Scholem has an interesting passage in his
essay on Benjamin and his Angel that resonates with this idea; writing
of Benjamin, he talks about "his ties to the mystical tradition and to a
mystical experience which nevertheless was a far cry from the experience
of God, proclaimed by so many oversimplifying minds as the only
experience deserving to be called mystical. *Benjamin knew that mystical
experience is many-layered, and it was precisely this many-layeredness that
played so great a role in his thinking and in his productivity*" [my italics].
This succinctly defines the activity of our "pious atheism."

Following this back to the putative subject of Imagining God, I at
least want to put the emphasis on the gerund, that the act of imagining

creates the sacred—as opposed to the idol worship of bowing down before what has been designated "sacred." I think this is what I read from your excerpt from *Track*.

In my poem 'Mappah,' in my recent book, *Dianoia*, which in a sense is about the fate of the cloth protecting the Torah in particular, its being burnt along with the scroll in the Shoah, I wrote:

> Let this be put another way: the cloth that wrapped the Torah in darkness shielded the light from the dark.

> Let this be put another way: let this be put differently, the wish to call out.

The "dark" at the end of the first line above is the historical dark of that period, the light emanating from the Torah, from the ground of creation—in this case, language, was to be protected. The "wish to call out," is the wish to sacralize to make poetry of that horror.

In a way, we are brought back to Kochan's imagery, as I mentioned above, in his chapter 'Symbolism in Action' where he writes: "But if, in the process of the unmediated cleaving to God, the symbol disappears in the agent's performance of the actions dictated by God it reappears. This is consonant with man as the 'icon of God' and the only way in which God can legitimately be represented. In the *imitatio dei* man becomes his own symbol" Can this be a picture of the poet sitting at his/her desk? Is this picture the one that imagines God for us? *That*, to use your word, is already transgressive.

Which leads me to another contemplation *re.* "transgressive," that like the "sacred," it is for me less the name for something than for being some kind of enacting.

·

8/9/15

Dear Michael,

It seems that we are both moving to a position which insists upon the necessity of "transgression" insofar as it insists upon "markability" when it comes to representing or imagining (making an image of) the Jewish God. This would be congruent with your references to Bialik's task of "revealment" and to Scholem's understanding of Benjamin's God-less (?) mysticism, a position which certainly appeals to me personally and probably could be found throughout my work. In any case, one is still led to ask of Bialik, "What is revealed?" And of Scholem, "With what did Benjamin mystically commune, if not with God?" The answer in both cases, if there is an answer, may not prove especially kosher.

Imagining may create the sacred, as you propose. But in going back to Kochan's chapter ('Symbolism in Action'), I also find this: "…although a symbol may perform a large number of functions, primary among them is its supposed capacity to bring together two entities, one seen and one unseen." Kochan, if I understand him correctly, sees this as a potential problem, since the symbol, whether visual or verbal, tends toward idolatry. He thinks that in some instances, Jewish verbal symbolism (the making of Jewish poems?) becomes permissible "if symbolism, as is normally the case, inheres in the relationship of the profane with the holy or actually structures the holy." Closer to the passage that you quote, he argues that "The symbol that is both material and immaterial attains its apogee in both respects when it is wholly annulled and at the same time brought to perfection. [This sounds like Benjamin's version of dialectic, by the way.] This state is synonymous with the human imitation of the divine—to be more specific, it is synonymous with man's performance of the commandments."

This is both heavy lifting and very slippery thinking. Are we performing the commandments when we are producing sublimely self-annulling symbols in our poems? I wonder. One important reason that Jewish writing, including modern Jewish poetry, has tended to be oriented to commentary, is because commentary does not appear be a matter of "imagining" or inventing the new: it appears devoted to rehearsing and explaining, opening, the tradition, however that is construed. Yet this has always been something of a strategy, if not a self-conscious ruse (cf. the supposed authorship of the *Zohar*). Scholem's great essays 'Tradition and New Creation in the Ritual of the Kabbalists' and 'Revelation and Tradition as Religious Categories in Judaism' provide ample proof that engagement with tradition through commentary or rehearsed ritual may actually prove to be a means of invention and innovation. Anxiety over idolatry, sacrilege, transgression proves to be an immense spur to creativity. Then again, so does (to draw on another Scholem essay), 'Redemption Through Sin.'

But to what extent does all this truly apply to modern Jewish poets, who understand themselves to be secular, embrace the profane, and yet yearn for a sense of the sacred or the numinous? Is this yearning merely nostalgia—keeping in mind that nostalgia is, at least for Benjamin, a powerfully enabling psychic force? It would appear that we simply cannot dispense with traditional religious categories, because in the past, if not the present, they named the existential, psychic, and indeed, social experiences which remain the most crucial subjects of a modern poetry which seeks to make important cultural contributions. I think one of the texts which make this case most strongly is your essay "Remains of the Diaspora," certainly required reading for anyone concerned with imagining the Jewish God.

Another thought occurs to me, and here I will end for now. Isn't imagining a Jewish God another way of imagining the Jew? Doesn't raising the first question inevitably raise the second? And aren't the questions all the more relevant today, both in the diaspora and in Israel, when there is so much uncertainty and conflict around Jewish identity? For me, the claim that secular Jewish culture has real, substantial, and historical validity hinges on what Jewish literature—Jewish poetry—may say to such questions.

8/12/15

Dear Norman,

We should put Kochan and Bialik in a room to debate our question. Bialik responding to Kochan's "one seen and unseen," would probably respond as he does in 'Revealment and Concealment,' that "language with all its associations does not introduce us into the inner area, the essence of things, but that, on the contrary, language itself stands as a barrier between them. On the other side of the barrier of language, behind its curtain, stripped of its husk of speech, the spirit of man wanders ceaselessly." He remarks that there is "only a perpetual search, an eternal 'what?' frozen on man's lips." In truth there is no place even for this "what?" A few sentences later, Bialik refers to the barrier of language as covering the void, to "prevent the void's darkness from welling up and overflowing its bounds."

For me, Kochan's "unseen" and Bialik's "void" are the manifestations of the unknowable divine, and language is hiding them from sight. But Bialik, operating as poet, seeks a dynamic in which the poet is "forced to flee all that is fixed and inert in language, all that is opposed to their [the poets'] goal of the vital and mobile in language… [they, the poets] by this process there takes place, in the material of language, exchanges of posts and locations: one mark, a change in the point of one iota, and the old world shines with a new light…. The profane turns sacred and the sacred profane."

We would agree, if we follow the above, that the category of the "sacred" is a created category, that nothing, *ipso facto*—I would go so far as to say, *ipso facto*, nothing that already exists is "sacred" from the point of view of the poet, in the sense that to call "sacred" that which has already been created or labeled sacred would be redundancy. I'm not trying to debunk the category as much as I'm trying to emphasize that from my point of view as "poet," the marking/making is the creating of the sacred. In our task of imagining God, it is the moment of making sacred in which He is revealed. The noun and pronoun here are only handles. The locus of "God" or "He" (or any other nominative at which one can point, or better, use to point) is somewhere moving along the process of the marking.

You may recall in my 'Remains of the Diaspora'—which you mention so kindly—the two categories of "rabbini" and "ribboni," the former living within the Law, the latter seeing or transforming "Law," as Robert Alter writes, into "Lore." My emphasis on "the markable" and "markability" is to place the act of transforming, the marking, the act of creating, at the very center of making sacred. (And I don't want to exclude the reader from this act as the one who recognizes (or experiences and is affected by) that which has been newly marked as an instance of encountering the sacred). Bialik calls this approach "the way of the world: Words rise to greatness, and, falling, turn profane. What is essential is that language contains no word so slight that the hour of its birth was not one of powerful and awesome self-revealment, a lofty victory of the spirit." "Transgression," then, is the refusal to keep within the stock of already existing things, even (especially?) those called sacred, to override, to replace or re-order, what we seek to do by the act of composing (inscribing).

If all is language (Adorno insisted that even idols and images be read as writing), perceived through language as both the Kabbalists and Bialik maintain, then isn't every new construct of language also commentary? I'm thinking that Benjamin's "now-time" poetics is very much of this order of understanding. Am I making an unwarranted leap here or is this the "heavy lifting and very slippery thinking" you are warning about?

But our thinkers above would probably see composing as commentary, an act of marking. And therefore conceiving the blank page, the untouched stone or canvas not as truly blank but as the suppressed representation or repository of all previous markings. (And wouldn't this conceiving actually be an aspect of Tradition, the jump-off point of what has previously been made intelligible?) To repeat: the dynamic force here is the hunger, to use Bialik's term for "the void," to reveal it, but which is then concealed again by the words we mark it with, the words that have now concealed the revealment. And so one must go on.

The matter of the "modern Jewish poet's" nostalgia, which you bring up, seems a question that can only be addressed by a discerning criticism that can evaluate various modes of nostalgia. Oppen's yearnings, for example, cannot be lumped in with X, Y or Z's, any more than we would lump Baudelaire's spirituality with Claudel's. And Benjamin's nostalgia— think of his ride on the Angel seeing the ruins as it flies toward Progress— is less about a golden age than for a cleansing violence embedded in an image that can set the world right. As to the religious categories you invoke as necessary, aren't they also entangled in the process of the profane becoming sacred and the sacred becoming profane, so that each term, at every instance, each term is scrutinized/scrutinizable?

As to your last paragraph, yes, imagining a Jewish God would be another way of imagining the Jew, bound up with his/her Jewishness (what is strikingly strange is that the amplitude and freedom of that imagining may lie with the outside secular Jew more than with the Jew bound by religion), and the implications for what identity now means in such places as Israel or the Diaspora makes the imagining of great importance, culturally, politically and socially. What remains as part of the construal of an answer to that question is transmissibility (not in the poetry world sense but rather as a question of "legitimacy"—is there a legitimacy to the transgressive—the wingéd horse of our discussion?) But that may yet be another topic entirely.

The hunger for the profundity of a word leads us to marking (WCW "tuning?")

The way of looking at language as we have discussed above, and as you can intuit, is contrary to the experimental mode based on the idea that we are enclosed in language, and that poetry is the endless generation of language, such that it always refuses closure.

8/19/15

Dear Michael,

To begin, a few words about Bialik's essay, to which I return after many years (and it's always revealing—so to speak!—to see what I chose to highlight when I first read it). This time around, I'm deeply impressed by his suspicions regarding language, how it serves mainly to conceal, even in the hands of "the masters of prose," the philosophers, the builders of systems, and so on. Even at the end of the piece, when he looks directly at the poets (in the passage from which you quote), they must first "*flee* [my italics] all that is fixed and inert in language...." Yes, certainly, such is basic law for our tribe, but even when the poets assert their power, "words *writhe* [my italics again] in their hands; they are extinguished and lit again ... put off a soul and put on a soul." Such, I imagine, relates to the constant risk involved in writing poetry, especially a poetry imagining a Jewish God, or even a poetry in any way invested in some notion of the sacred. Bialik, it seems to me, cuts us no slack (and good for him): the uncertainty, the risk, the extremity of the void, is just a hair's breadth away from overwhelming. And furthermore, in case one was even thinking about it: "No reply to the question of essence is ever possible in the process of speech." Which includes, I suppose, poems.

And yes, Bialik's "void" and Kochan's "unseen" are indeed "the manifestations of the unknowable divine." In this respect, we seem to be spiraling back to my original letter and quote from Scholem about Kafka and the void. But I'm also getting a sense of an all-or-nothing dialectic operating just beneath our discourse. Let me try to bring it to light. In imagining the Jewish God, we move, you and I, given our studies and predilections, to a conception of divinity in terms of absence, *Ein Soph*, if you want to use the kabbalistic term. But given our Objectivist orientation as well, there is also a sense (cf. Oppen's 'Psalm' once again) of a fullness of Creation, a presence that approaches the sacred which language *can* reveal, rather than conceal or veil. And how is one to consider this (divine) plenitude. In your last letter, you note "that the category of the 'sacred' is a created category, that nothing, *ipso facto*—I would go so far as to say, *ipso facto*, nothing that already exists is 'sacred' from the point of view of the poet, in the sense that to call 'sacred' that which has already been created or labeled sacred would be redundancy. I'm not trying to debunk the category as much as I'm trying to emphasize that from my point of view as 'poet', the marking/making is the creating of the sacred." I certainly can't argue with this, but I would have to claim that the converse is true (or operative) as well: *everything* that already exists is sacred, again, when the poet marks the created thing as such. Oppen's "That they are there!"

So: plenitude or the void; a totally sacred creation or a totally profane one; language revealing divinity or concealing it. The paradoxical situation in which we find ourselves recapitulates that which Steven Wasserstrom chronicles in *Religion After Religion*, his study of Scholem, Corbin and Eliade at Eranos. Wasserstrom notes that Scholem preferred his religion "the more paradoxical the better" (those are Scholem's own words). Wasserstrom also writes of Scholem that "The crisis of tradition is still tradition, both remaining within its spirit and yet leaving its current forms behind. If this relationship to tradition was paradoxical, Scholem did not shy away from this conclusion." I'm content to "rest" within that condition—and more importantly, to write from it. As for God, Jewish or otherwise, Wasserstrom quotes Scholem's colleague Eliade: "the true dialectic of the sacred: by the mere fact of *showing* itself, the sacred *hides itself*." And again, this may not serve as any sort of ground of belief, but it may well be a condition, a dimension, of a poetics.

8/20/15

Dear Norman,

The "sense of an all-or-nothing dialectic operating just beneath our discourse" stems, I think, from two aspects of our discussion on which we most likely agree, aspects implicit in Bialik's "*flee* all that is fixed and inert in language." The first aspect, which I believe permeates so much Judaic thought, concerns the fear of the petrification of the sacred, which, as I hinted earlier, leads to a dogmatic law-driven theology, repressive and unable, except by pressure and/or enforcement (sometimes violent), to deal with the variability of the human condition or with historical change. The saving tools that enable fleeing in this regard, are Talmud, midrash, commentary, poetry. The Kabbalah is perhaps the supreme monumental endeavor of such flights.

The second aspect relates to how the sacred is realized: for the poet (one of Bialik's "masters of allegory") it is through the poet's engagement with the dynamic of language as it is combined and recombined in new creations, its fleeing act from the "fixed and inert." But there is also a restlessness which consigns this new instance of creation, this new node of the sacred ultimately to the category of what has been "fixed and inert." As I put it at the end of my essay 'The Uncertainty of the Poet,' "The next poem is always the aim of the prior poem, and this is how poetry develops, not by offering truth upon truth, but by reminding us of how truth is always passing into a lie." A number of people have asked me what I meant by "truth passing into a lie," and I've answered with Bialik's thought in mind—that, on the spiritual level, the sacred must constantly be made anew. (I.e., to go back to one of your worries about the contemporary Jewish poet in the Diaspora, he/she should not be concerned about writing "self-annulling poems," since, where the sacred is concerned, from Bialik's point of view, there are no other kind.) This idea of renewal does not contradict your words, your "converse" above that "*everything* that already exists is sacred, again, when the poet marks the created thing as such." It is in the *act* of imagining, in making the mark, that divinity is possibly manifest, in a way, recovered from its invisibility. Wilson, in his *TLS* review, cites Étienne Gilson's remark that "God is not a being, he is being." The emphasis here, then, is away from idolizing an object and toward a notion of the inherency of the divine, possibly realizable through the act of a reader or poet. Such a process is suggested in Judaic thought, even in the earliest conceptualizations leading to Kabbalah.

The thought-trains leading to and from this conception are multiple, possibly originating in commentaries on Ezekiel's descriptions of the throne of God, one of the most "anthropomorphizing" passages, as Scholem describes it, in holy scripture and leading toward Kabbalistic notions of word, naming and the sacred. I am by no means a scholar of this material, and what I take from it, as a "pious atheist," is its suggestibility that the divine is manifest in utterance (our "marking" of it) and then recedes into silence and invisibility as the moment of utterance passes. That is the condition in which divinity offers its simultaneous image/invisibility to the poet (and I might add to the reader who experiences the sacred through an encounter with a poem, a text).

One of the lines in my poem 'Mappah,' reads: "The teacher remarked that to regard the earth as the shrine-room floor is enlightenment." This is a Buddhist version perhaps of your "everything that already exists is sacred." And the Kabbalistic literature is replete with echoes of this attitude, even to its insistence on the "sparks" of the good lying hidden in the realm of Satan or Gehinnom. The particular genius of the Kabbalistic view and of the potentialities within the sphere of contemporary poetry lie in their abilities to resolve the dualisms of sacred/profane, good and evil. "Their common denominator," as Scholem puts it of such points of view "seems to be the assumption that, fundamentally, all of the divine potencies wish to operate in the existential realms of Creation."

An aside: in some of the Buddhist traditions, particularly in the Tibetan Vajrayana tradition in which I have studied, the cosmos in all its manifestations is sometimes referred to in the literature as "the Great Wrathful One," the source of the potencies (as in the Kabbalistic vision), "the trees, the greenery, and so forth," that make up worlds and are "wrathful" in the sense that they are incitements to creative action, irritants that punctuate the habitual and conventional overlays of our mind. The sutras and the endless commentaries and refinements on them constitute a movement toward spiritual realization similar to midrashic studies. Both traditions seem, before all else, to have a desire to keep both sides of our dualisms alive, hence always in interaction and hence resolvable into something which for want of a better word we call a path.

The *Tsaddik*, as Scholem cites from an early description in *On the Mystical Shape of the Godhead*, is tasked with setting "all the inner things in their place within, and all the outer things in their place without, and nothing leaves the boundary set for it." It would be an impossible leap to equate the poet with the *Tsaddik*, but certainly it is the possible righteousness in the relationship (practice?) of the poet to his or her language that sets "all the outer things in their place." Bialik puts it this way: "The profane turns sacred, and the sacred profane. Long established words are constantly being pulled out of their settings, as it were, and exchanging places with one another. Meanwhile, between concealments [our poetry?] the void looms. And that is the secret of the great influence of the language of poetry."

Perhaps for the Jewish poet, an image of God would be synonymous with that looming void our very words enable. In this we create the one divinity that seems boundless.

GROSSMAN: BENJAMIN: SCHOLEM: BEYOND THE "POETICS" OF POETICS

Before opening my discussion on these three influential figures in 20th century thought, I want to note that in the indices of the three collections of Allen Grossman's essays that I own, there is no reference to Gershom Scholem and only one parenthetical aside (to his *Theses on History*) concerning Walter Benjamin, two writers who have dominated my thought for many years. This fact makes something of a fantasy of my project here, its dreamscape, a sound chamber made by a bunch of Jewish carpenters where different voices and hammer blows seem to produce near echoes of each other. I might add that references to Scholem and Benjamin are mostly *en passant*, in perhaps the best, most lucid essay on Grossman that I know, 'Allen Grossman's Theophoric Poetics,' by Norman Finkelstein in his 2001 book on Jewish-American poetry, *Not One of Them in Place*, though references to them are liberally sprinkled throughout the rest of the book. This talk borrows from Finkelstein's essay and I hope builds upon it.

Builds on it in what way? Finkelstein's essay, like its subject Allen Grossman, is vast and wide-ranging; however, its deep concern with Grossman's complex sense of Jewishness is what I will focus on here. In describing Grossman's complicated response to his ethnic background, Finkelstein cites the poet's writing on Allen Ginsberg's *Kaddish*, which testifies to the "Jewish-American poet's mixture of nationalism and ethnicity" as a "highly unstable mixture." For Grossman, Ginsberg's *Kaddish* is "the most momentous record in English of the problem of the passing of the older sociology and meaning of the Jewish family-centered culture in America." Finkelstein, in his reading of Grossman, speculates on that passing and what is to replace it, remarking that the "problem that ethnicity poses is quite clear." He then quotes one of Grossman's most problematic and controversial thoughts: "Ethnicity, and Judaism is an ethnicity, is also *merely* [my italics] another violent phantasm, out of scale with human life, which drives us against one another in conflicts so dangerous as to be unimaginable as a desirable state of affairs." Grossman's "merely" and "violent phantasm" are maelstroms of oceanic depths and controversy, but the bottom line, as can be seen from earlier passages in his book *The Sighted Singer*, is that "ethnicity" is a dangerous trap and yet, for Grossman, a way out of the trap. If Jewish ethnicity embodies the divisive aggression within the concept of the "chosen people," it also at the same time contains a lineage of thinkers and poets whose historical experience as Jews inflects, for Grossman, the deepest meaning of what a poet is and, with respect to poetics, what his acts as a poet are seeking to accomplish What Grossman wants is "to take into my hands as a man the particular powers which the poet administers and to use those powers for the ends of poetry; that is to say, to make others both beautiful and also (what is from the point of view of the poem the same thing) free in a specific way." The meaning I take from this passage is that, among the near-infinite variety of available poetic practices, the administration of "particular powers" constitutes a poet's poetics. He/she makes choices.

Grossman describes what he considers proper or divine poetics as a function of his Jewishness, a term, which for him, is not one of "Jewish ethnicity" in the usual racial sense. "Jewish ethnicity," as he tells us above, that "violent phantasm, out of scale with human life," is a weaponized ethnicity which he opposes to the determining aspect of his Jewishness (no doubt equally a kind of 'ethnicity'), one based in a broad concept of lineage involving not only poets but culture and therefore history, in particular the cumulative experience of exile, homelessness and the *Shoah*. In *The Long Schoolroom* he describes what determines Jewishness: "the Jewish people, like all other peoples, *requires a place to be* (a teaching place, a place of Myrrh, a place where God sees), and the Jew's place is the word."

The word, the text as "homeland" (as George Steiner has said), paradoxically situates the Jew within a homelessness from which he or she cannot be banished. Grossman compares the entrapment of "the Jew's word," which he describes as "hard," in contrast to the "split word" of the gentile nations "who know the little word of the muse (the word half-raised up, divided—signifier and signified), or (again) who know the little word (as fiction), *and* the big word of the god or God." A certain kind of secularity is denied, denied especially to the Jewish poet, and to all other poets who swear a kind of fealty to language. For the Jew's word, strictly speaking, is "an undivided One (holy, sacred, *Kadosh*), and is unlike all other words in that it does not signify by difference but rather serves the Master who is difference—which is to say, existence itself." For Grossman, unlike the Western (or gentile) usage of language, which sometimes labels itself divine, the language of the Jew is always directed to the undivided One (or God, the Master who is difference, and *for this reason, the category of the sacred and the poetic repel one another.*

I turn here to contemplating Walter Benjamin's possible influence on and resonance with Grossman's work. How much to make of this? In his 'Theological-Political Fragment,' written in 1938 when the Jewish catastrophe to come was already self-evident, Benjamin both echoes and critiques Grossman's thinking. In suggesting a vector for Jewish thought in its very first sentence, he writes: "Only the Messiah himself consummates all history." Here, Benjamin reifies the distinction between representative language and the language of the sacred, yet, almost in the same breath, reinforces the impossible belatedness of a sacred world and insists that "the quest of free humanity runs counter to the Messianic direction....", that "[j]ust as a force can, through acting, increase another that is acting in the opposite direction, so the order of the profane assists, through being profane, the coming of the Messianic Kingdom." As with Grossman, Benjamin believes that the "Jew is the sufferer," because the restitution of the sacred (spiritual *Restitutio in integrum*) leads to immortality, something dematerialized and beyond the precincts of earthly existence. "For nature," Benjamin writes, "is Messianic by reason of its eternal and total passing away."

Such a realization prefigures in a number of ways the even more problematic realm of Grossman's later poetry in such books as *How to Do Things with Tears* and in his final book, *Descartes' Loneliness*, books in which Grossman's sense of the "death of parochial culture," leveled perhaps by the roiling of all cultures by the profane, become the occasion for a new poetics, one perhaps always implicit in Grossman's thought. If ethnicity was a binding (it's sacred promise), Grossman's recent work seems to seek a complex unbinding, one that is simultaneously "Jewish" and, in Grossman's word, also "transcendent."

The title poem of Grossman's last book of poetry, published in 2007, 'Descartes' Loneliness,' presents us with a case study of his late transformative thought. Its first stanza lays out, in the spirit of Descartes, the implicit paradox of perception by which one is led to believe in a comforting common world, led in a sense not only by the mutually perceived existence of the world and others, but as well by a language we share and tend to agree with in its signifying power. The first lines of the poem, "Toward evening, the natural light becomes/intelligent and answers, with demur:/ *Be assured! You are not alone....*" The diction here is interesting, "demur" being both mannerly and hesitant, an atmosphere in which "light" becomes "intelligent" and "answer"-ing suggests a Baudelairean correspondence, or, close to it, a resonance with some of Benjamin's thought as expressed in his essay 'On the Mimetic Faculty' and on the non-sensuous similarity" of world and language. This assurance, however, is immediately, even shockingly, rebuffed by the following lines: "But in fact, toward evening, I am not/convinced there is any other except myself/to whom existence *necessarily* pertains." In this opening stanza, I believe, lies the key to a singular *poesis* that is yet generally communicative to any reader.

It should be noted that Grossman's seeming lone reference to Benjamin is placed in the opening paragraph of his late essay on Celan, Whitman and Kant, ironically titled 'Poetry and Enlightenment,' in his book *True-Love: Essays on Poetry and Valuing* published in 2009, two years after *Descartes' Loneliness*, his last book of poems. (Ironically, because it is yet another call to drawing attention to the requiring singularity of a poetics that Grossman is insisting upon.) Grossman sees Enlightenment in its Kantian form ("I'm with Kant," he proclaims) as "the human being's emergence from his self-incurred minority," where "minority" is defined as "the inability to make use of one's own understanding without direction from others." Taken at face value, Kant's words themselves are an indictment of the group think "ethnicity" requires of its tribe.

Amidst a beginning discussion on 20th century literary and historical barbarism, Grossman's use of Benjamin consists solely of a parenthetical aside referring to Benjamin's "theses on history." It lies in the essay between two of modern poetry's most controlling thoughts, or "epigraphs" as Grossman chooses to call them: Adorno's "*No poetry after Auschwitz*" and the "second epigraph", invoking Celan: "*Only poetry after Auschwitz.*" There is no way to pinpoint any specific aspect of the *Theses* that influenced Grossman, but a good guess might be Benjamin's 'Thesis II' with its "idea that happiness is indissolubly bound up with the idea of redemption. The same applies to the idea of the past, which is the concern of history. The past carries with it a secret index by which it is referred to redemption." For Grossman, this "past," the past of his Jewishness which he seeks to distinguish from a crude "ethnicity" is related to lineage, an idea only viable if one's lineage is one of homelessness, of "Word" (which I would call a tuning of language, dealing with its baggage as well as its "erasures") instead of a lineage of place, the home of the immovable Arks of other religions, which must be fortified and protected by their heroic figures against the Other. This other "home" and its defense creates the violence of barbarism that precludes redemption, unless its existence is thought through historically.

Benjamin seems to be involved in a project with many similarities to Grossman's project, well described in *Fire Alarm* by Michael Löwy, one of the most important scholars of Benjamin's work, who insists that Benjamin sought an "elective affinity between Jewish Messianism and libertarian utopia … an authentic *fusion*—that is, to the dawning of a new way of thinking which could not simply be reduced to its components." Like Benjamin, Grossman sees the difficulty of achieving such a fusion, and herein lies the bitter logic of the schoolroom of Grossman's poetics, that it is always a contestation between the self and the Other, endlessly present—and yet for that very reason, also endlessly fruitful.

The stance of Grossman's poem resembles both Benjamin's "shock defense," its messianic unrest, and Scholem's oblique command to Benjamin that "you must sue for your own necessity." Scholem saw in the Kabbalists "a rather small group of people [who] were able to create symbols that expressed their personal situation as a world situation," which he contrasted to the modern individual who, according to Scholem, lives "in a private world of his own," coining subjective symbols that do not "obligate." Yet Scholem, in his work on Sabbati Zevi, meditating on the "strange holiness" of the Sabbatians, which mirrors the exclusive entanglements of the mystical Kabbalists, claims that the more ardent believers found themselves "becoming increasingly restless…. And soon the cry was heard: Let us surrender ourselves as he did! Let us descend together to the abyss before it shuts again. Let us cram the maw of impurity with the power of holiness…" producing a "great nihilistic conflagration."

Grossman identifies a similar transposition, though in a less existential tone, in the arena of American and English poetry. In 1981, in *The Sighted Singer*, he decries the modern image-maker in similar terms: "It is important to observe," he writes, "that the idea of poetry carries with it the prestige of functions which it can no longer execute." He alludes "to the use of poetry *for conserving the human image*—because I think *that* function constitutes the singular importance of poetry now and also specifies the particular dangers within the practice of poetry to which we are heir." Grossman continues in this passage to describe what older poetry contained: the "laws of Solon," "the Delphic oracle," "the laws of Moses and the agonies of Job" as poetic structures, the function "of making persons present to one another in that special sense in which they are *acknowledgeable* and therefore capable of love and mutual interest in one another's safety." This critique leads toward Grossman's considerations of technique and form. He asserts that Whitman's innovative lines and images are guided not by an aesthetic principle but by the language of the American Constitution and that Milton's blank verse "revolution" in *Paradise Lost* speaks to the idea that "rhyme is a form of bondage." The old poetics, the "intimate features" of earlier poetry were less about innovation for innovation's sake; in their most important sense, they were "fundamentally political."

Modern events, the two world wars, the threat of nuclear annihilation, inflected in works such as Eliot's *The Waste Land* and Pound's *Cantos*, signal for Grossman, poetic loss, "great erasures," threats of human oblivion and forgetfulness, "the disappearance of persons," which, in effect, have destroyed the old functions of poetry. Poetry cannot properly enact its ancient purpose, "the act of civilization." Poetics has become "poetics" (in scare quotes), the faded simulacrum of poetry's attempt to achieve its original binding effect of love and desire for "another's safety."

In the pages I'm referring to, Grossman talks about his Jewishness and "the word," but the *topos* lies under the penumbra of the Holocaust. This is a complicated matter. "The Jew," claims Scholem, "thinks linguistically," but, as George Prochnik in his semi-autobiographical study of Scholem, *Stranger in a Strange Land*, reminds us, "Scholem's decision to write his thesis on the linguistic roots of the Kabbalah was undertaken partly as a Zionist action. Every text hid a primal scene of inspiration and transcription, the recovery of which might electrify present-day Jewish consciousness." Scholem hoped that vision "would culminate in the utopian restoration of humanity as such." The split-word is to be healed, to become the "hard" word of self, undivided from world-saving holiness and the sacred. Yet, as we know, basing this idea in a physical, already inhabited homeland, even one conceived as sanctuary and utopian in nature, produced untold difficulties.

Benjamin, less resistant than Scholem to messages emanating from his own interiority, recognizes the "split-word" in sociopolitical terms as resident within himself. Löwy reminds us that Benjamin liked to describe himself as "a Janus figure, one of whose faces was turned toward Moscow and the other toward Jerusalem." Benjamin described his own position to Scholem in an early letter of 1926: the "sudden paradoxical change of one form of [religious or political] observance into the other (regardless of direction)." This wavering between sides and its refusal of commitment, as I have described elsewhere, strikes as the key to the powerful originality of Benjamin's thought.

So, too, Grossman's tightrope of a construction between ethnicity and his universalist position as expressed in his poetics runs parallel in the realm of language to Benjamin's balancing act. It is in this light of intellectual freedom and distancing objectivity that Grossman insists on the necessity for aloneness as the pre-condition for his poetry.

We can project this state of affairs onto the literary and poetical sphere as the conflicting tensions between materialist and spiritualist tendencies in literature and poetry. But perhaps another way of looking at Grossman's thoughts is to see these tensions as unifying, and in their way predicating a style. I'm thinking of something like the perspective suggested by the painter Arikha, one of Beckett's major influences, that "style is a way of protecting truth" or Oppen's lines in 'Five Poems About Poetry' about not mistaking "the bauble" for a "style."

In his essay on Celan and Kant, Grossman writes "Let me say as a poet, and for the moment as a thinker, that *the idea of the New is at this moment under pressure*." He despairs over the "inadequacies of our communicative structures." There is history here, for earlier, in *The Sighted Singer*, Grossman describes his astonishment at "the poverty of the utterance of those persons who call themselves poets" with "a full sense of the privilege of the art that they practice." He sees a poverty lying within the division induced by the parochial and the universal, as with Yeats, for instance, who he imagines as trying simultaneously to be an Irish poet and a European one, which led to "a division of self which was never (and particularly at the height of his greatness) healed."

This "unhealedness" manifests in both Benjamin and Scholem. For Scholem it signifies the distance between the ideal, holy—call it what you will—sanctity of the scriptural poem and the isolated figure of the Kabbalist, who seems homeless (perhaps "unofficial" is a better word) in his homeland, where his only recourse is to his mystical commentary, to Talmud and Midrash.

Grossman's "Jewishness" in this regard must be seen as a pathway not to an ethnic identity but to a subject position that not only stands for an ethical signpost against the experiences that overtook Jews catastrophically in the twentieth century, but also has been part of a dark undercurrent of culture for a couple of thousand years, part and parcel of the culture Grossman claims as his lineage. (David Nirenberg, in a chapter of his book, *Aesthetic Theology and Its Enemies*, entitled 'Every Poet is a Jew,' a line taken from Marina Tsvetayeva—herself not Jewish— quotes Kierkegaard's questioning of the idea of the "chosen people," writing "that they [the Jews] were not the happiest; rather that they were the sacrifice … they were the chosen people in the same sense that poets, etc. are, *i.e.,* they are the unhappiest."

At the center of Grossman's meditations is Celan's poem (I give you the English here) 'Speak You Also' where Celan writes "Speak—/ But keep Yes and No unsplit." Scholem's emphasis on "commentary" not only signifies an artifice, the separation of text from thinker of the text but also shows commentary (*e.g.* midrashic activity) as the compensatory mechanism of contact and understanding, as, indeed, the bindery across the inadequacy of communicative structures.

Allen Grossman concludes his book *Descartes' Loneliness* with a short prose apologia in which he writes of Descartes as "not just one name in the history of philosophy, but a name which stands for all persons insofar as we—you and I, *each of us alone*—discover the world for the first time and, therefore, must think (*each one of us must do so alone*, there is no other way) as if no one had ever thought about the world before. It is this person who writes *poetry* and for whom it is written." If the concept of an enunciated poetics is a universalizing concept, that is, if it demands or suggests a way of looking at or of writing poetry, then it would seem, at every point, to rub up against the thrust implicit in Grossman's "*each of us alone*," a statement which at one level of reading, a minor level I might add, becomes an injunction against any kind of group or clique or school that insists on formulaic or prohibitive sets of manners under which the making of poetry is to be ruled. It is this formulaic "poetics" against which Grossman enjoins, not so much because he sees it as puerile factionalism as because it fails to undertake the mission of a poetics as sacred activity, as a drawing towards scriptural authority and divinity. This scare quote "poetics" fails for Grossman because it does not attempt to transcend what divides forms of poetry in order to arrive at the deepest source of difference, which is world and God or, to put this in a phrase used by Finkelstein in *Not One of Them in Place* to describe Grossman's position, it fails to operate within "a culture of holiness."

Grossman's poem, 'Descartes' Loneliness,' is fully aware of this situation. "Because I am mostly a thinking thing" he first writes. And then, later in the poem, finds himself forced "to conclude that/I am not alone in the world. There is/some other who is the cause of that idea." As Celan would say to Grossman, your poem is refusing to keep Yes and No apart. And yet, the maintenance and collapse of distance in an unknowable opacity, is something only language seems to accomplish. It gives Grossman, finally, a realizable image of the poet's situation:

I have been unable to discover the ground of that
conviction—unless it be imagined a lonely
workman on a dizzy scaffold unfolds
a sign at evening and puts his mark on it.

Reading these words, I too can only imagine a conclusion, a desire really,
to place a mark next to his.

NOW-TIME POETICS:
UNDER THE SIGN OF BENJAMIN

In the 1960s, I had two extraordinary bits of luck. The second of these, occurring in 1967, was meeting George Oppen, an encounter that lasted until his death which, as I have described elsewhere, halted in its tracks, my abandonment of writing poetry. The first bit of luck, which was much subtler, still evolving, and even now growing more complicated, took place during my "expatriate hegira" in the seaside town of Nerja in Spain in 1965. At the time, I was trying to decide if I would be a writer at all, when the Irish novelist Aidan Higgins, who also lived in the town, gave me a copy of Walter Benjamin's *Illuminations*, just published in the United Kingdom. I read it, thrilled and absorbed as much by Benjamin's life as by his writings.

My title intentionally echoes Susan Sontag's path-breaking essay on Walter Benjamin, 'Under the Sign of Saturn.' In the essay, Sontag reminds us that Saturn is the planet of wobbles, of an eccentric orbit that brings it now nearer, now further from the sun. That irregular motion characterizes the life and thought of Benjamin, and indeed, such an imperfect ellipse of encirclement around the subject of Benjamin is what I now make in this writing, an activity I have been pursuing since I first encountered his work and fell under its influence.

Benjamin's exemplary poetics begins, I believe, in this errancy which, as many commentators on him have noted, is an essential aspect of his work. If errancy can be a ground, then this is Benjamin's. Theodore Adorno, writing to Hannah Arendt, notes "how far it [Benjamin's thought] distances itself from every traditional conception of philosophy." And Michael Löwy identifies the active element of Benjamin's thought as an "erratic block in the margins of the main schools of contemporary philosophy." These views of Benjamin parallel the modern poet's situation in which one is no longer able to tell the tale of the tribe but rather must instead relate the tale of the tribe's uncertainty, the story of our adjustments and compensations to our own transformed sociopolitical and cultural worlds, worlds, like Benjamin's, always in motion. To borrow from Pound, the contemporary poet has lost his "Aquinas map," Pound's term for the socio-religious and political ordering of culture to which a poet like Dante, for example, could continually refer. Today's poet finds instead that he or she has entered into a field of disorientations and linguistic traps created by media, culture—including the arts themselves—as well as by the debasement of thought and language in the public realm. No contemporary thinker has more powerfully thrown off the "Aquinas maps" of his and of our culture than Benjamin, a life's gesture that cost him dearly.

Benjamin's dynamic thinking resembles that of Keats's "man of negative capability" who exists "without seeking after fact or reason." But unlike the conventional view of Keats's figure, Benjamin yearned deeply for certain "facts and reasons" of ethics, of politics and philosophy—in this we could say he was something of a moral or ethical actor, searching always for the redemptive gesture that could free mankind from oppression. His quest, we know, is marked by a capital "R" Romanticism. His earliest influences were the high German Romantic writers like Schelling and, especially, Novalis, and he wrote probingly about Hölderlin, Goethe, Hofmannsthal and Rilke. Before contemplating Marx, he had made these poets part of his intellectual makeup and confessed that they co-existed with all his other influences. Their impact on his thought makes a shimmering textual fabric of his masterpieces such as his studies of Baudelaire 'Central Park' (1938–39), 'On Some Motifs in Baudelaire' (1939), 'The Arcades Project' (begun in the 1930s and unfinished at his death) and his 'On the Concept of History' (1940), These rich influences account for one's flailing inability to fully grasp Benjamin's writings, to fully master or even summarize them by discourse—above all, they help explain the difficulty thinkers have with attempting to make Benjamin's works into instrumental documents. Only by reducing or ignoring parts of his thought, can you make a program out of Benjamin.

Benjamin's writings, as Irving Wohlfarth, puts it, are "both in and against their time". The concept of "now-time," one of the central pivot points for Benjamin's *poesis* of materialist history-making, is, as Wohlfarth sees it, always untimely. And yet that untimeliness, Wolfarth insists, is always set "within the measure of the possible," a phrase constantly repeated in Benjamin's writings. Benjamin juxtaposes the actuality of the "now" (its oppressive and inhumane character) within "the measure of the possible," the range of available redemptive, political and social acts that might counter oppression. He positions this "now" against "the revolutionary hacks," as he calls them, who "stand entirely to the left of the possible." He describes Baudelaire as desiring "to interrupt the course of the world… to be a Joshua (stopping the sun)." Yet the poet's chastened revolutionary poetics, eschews prophecy; there is in it, Benjamin writes, "no thought of reform." This complex inherently conservatory stance is, in Benjamin's thinking, among the most important elements of Baudelaire's poetics.

Benjamin's sense of the poet, of his "now-time" poetics (Baudelaire, as he notes, finding "the new in the ever self-same, and the ever self-same in the new") can, in my opinion, be situated beside Emmanuel Levinas's question/description of the poet. Levinas writes: "Is it certain a true poet occupies a place? Is the poet not that which, in the eminent sense of the term, loses its place, ceases occupation, precisely, and is thus the very opening of space, neither the transparency nor the emptiness which (no more than night, nor the volume of beings) yet displays the bottomlessness or the excellence, the heaven that in it is possible...."

Levinas's phrase, "loses its place," describing a relationship to tradition (the "place" that one must be lost from) rather than a sundering or abolishment of the present from the past, echoes the Benjaminian untimeliness as it structures "now-time" within the field of the possible.

"Now time" poetics cannot offer itself up as a salvational program; rather, its *correspondances*, as Benjamin said of Baudelaire, are a "spectacle," its images depicting or showing forth a "petrified unrest." Like the "shimmer" I spoke of in Benjamin's texts, Baudelaire's images are perfectly clear, yet deny us any head-shaking approval, any sense that "we've got it." Encountering their power and their appeal, we experience a pause, a stoppage, what Benjamin, in 'On the Concept of History' will call "messianic arrest" or "shock." We are uncertain what is to follow. The motions of culture and thought have been captured dynamically, yet, to borrow a phrase from Ernest Bloch, they are still "unfated." Perhaps, as some commentators have noted, Benjamin may have drawn inspiration from the ancient Jewish prohibition on prophesying the future.

As Benjamin asserts, Baudelaire's images demand—more than pleasure or novelty—that they be thought about. The poet's loss of or willingness to give up "place" is thus seen as enabling, creating the condition or possibility of an openness that works against the securing of a position. If the dogmatism of a strongly held idea creates violence, in the way that works of art and thought, according to Benjamin, are always barbarities, then poetics must involve receptivity, openness to contingency and resistance to closure rather than justification of theories about art and art-making.

It was Benjamin's example (Adorno describes him as "standing apart from all tendencies"), his endless shuttlings, his hope and despair, that drew me to him. The question he raised for me, the question he answered in both his life and thought was: how does one make a kind of home in homelessness. And here I am not referring to his physical wanderings all over Europe, but to his chosen intellectual and psychic journeys, and, as I think of it, his ever dynamic refusals.

Among the myriad ways of responding to the pressures of Benjamin's thought, I will name only a few, almost methodological perspectives. Naturally, when I first encountered the story of Benjamin's life, I was drawn to the romance of it, to the drama of his outsider-ness, to the many pitfalls it led him into, on up to the fatal decisions he made in not emigrating to Palestine in the 1930s or in abruptly ending his life (as we believe he did) rather than waiting out the Spanish authorities at Port Bou. But as I contemplated Benjamin over the years, I began to sense two very important issues for me: one involves the ethics of his life, his peculiar realism-idealism which went hand in hand with what seems an almost willed impracticality. The other, the intellectual and emotional "poetics," especially as filtered through Baudelaire, its capacious embrace of methods and techniques, its strategies (if they can be called that) which interwoven with his ethics, ultimately transforms the romance of his life into an exemplum, into a use-value for the poet. This transformation is what I mean by its methodology, a word I use with tremendous caution with respect to both Benjamin and Baudelaire.

I want to begin first with his notion of "messianic arrest," which involves a double-sided conception of "shock." In 'Thesis XVII' of his 'On the Concept of History,' Benjamin writes that "thinking involves not only the movement of thoughts, but their arrest as well. Where thinking suddenly comes to a stop in a constellation saturated with tensions, it gives the constellation a shock, by which thinking is crystallized into a monad." In the crystalline structure [of the monad], the historical materialist, Benjamin tells us, "recognizes the sign of Messianic arrest…, or, to put it another way, a revolutionary chance in the fight for the oppressed past." To be taking "a revolutionary chance" gives us, *en fine*, a Benjaminian poetics, one translatable to a poetics of poetry.

If I read Benjamin correctly—as a poet doing the reading—the moment of "messianic arrest" is something intelligible in the nexus of events that constitute what he calls "now-time" (or *jetztzeit*), something readable to the historian or the poet. As well, the expressions of this moment (and elaborations from it) as history or literature are themselves arrests, moments where the progress of time is interrupted in order that the messianic moment, the possibility of understanding or even deliverance from suffering is presented.

Benjamin's constant intellectual outsiderness is a major element of this messianic moment. His lack of a home within a systematic or coherent set of ideas, is both consciousness and potential for action. In his writings on Baudelaire and Poe, it is precisely such homelessness, both physical and psychic, that describes and constitutes the conditions of much modern poetry. Further, Benjamin often expresses this "homelessness" in terms of shock. He sees it as a poetic principle in 'Central Park', referring to Baudelaire's 'Tableaux parisiens' which exposes the urban landscape as "no longer a homeland" but "a spectacle, a foreign place." For him, Baudelaire's act of poetic "defamiliarization" is not a conscious strategy as it is with the surrealists or with more contemporary experimental modes of composition, but a reaction to nineteenth century Paris and what Benjamin called its "era of High Capitalism." Everything is made strange by an intense and close attention to detail at an almost granular level, from grand historical documents to the filigree of the arcades' rooftops, from newspaper opinion to courtroom witnessing. These details constellate and resonate with the dissonances between "actual" and "official" or conventional reality.

Benjamin's analysis of urban life, his tracking of Poe or Baudelaire through the cityscape, exemplify the poetics. Baudelaire's discomfort at being jostled by the crowd is partly the horror of being carried along by senselessness, by a mass wave of conventional thinking on everything from politics to religion and by the movement of sluggish mentalities diverted by commodity culture and its fake promise of an easy consumer erotics of urban life. Baudelaire's dandyism, engarbing him like a life-jacket, buoys him up while he is being carried along. His linguistics are protective: seeing into triviality and banality: they shield him from a deadening absorption in mindlessness and stupidity. The jostle, in effect, produces the shock of awareness.

Benjamin sees Baudelaire's "petrified unrest" as simultaneously an effect and a generative act, one capable of producing the intervention that poetry seeks. "Every second," he writes, "finds consciousness ready to intercept its shock"). For Benjamin, the poet's resistance to the zeitgeist is, in effect, the foundation of poetic production. His poetics, his way of apprehending and dealing with the world of shocks and messianic arrests, involves many aspects and strategies, but they strike me as being encapsulated in one of his phrases for literature: "the hieroglyphs of redeemed life." Within the arena of these hieroglyphs lie subsumed more narrow or focused sets of terms deployed by Benjamin such as "messianic arrest" and "monad" by which the historian (the "historical materialist" in Benjamin's words) perceives in the "flash of an instant" the critical connection between a fragmentary element and the crisis of the present. In order to form the hieroglyph (the "monad" or image) of the moment, as Benjamin calls it, the past must, figuratively, be stopped. "Every second," he writes, "finds consciousness ready to intercept its shock." The poet's resistance to the zeitgeist is, in effect, the foundation of poetic production. The strength to refuse is very nearly equated with the power to produce.

Websters defines the monad as "an elementary, unextended individual spiritual substance from which material properties are derived," a data point or concretion which, to borrow from the history of our literary poetics, bears resemblances to our Poundian-deriveded concepts such as image, vortex or gist and pith. I think Benjamin meant his hieroglyphs as something more complicated than these literary concepts (as I'm sure many poets do), containing not only the products of observation or of the visual imagination, but historically and culturally determined monadic "spiritual substance that gives them ethical or truth-value status." For Benjamin, this ethical aspect derives from past knowledge. "The crowds of today shaped by dictators," he tells us, are the "cores of resistance" rekindled by memory, by the "monad" carrying the past into the present as the vehicle of deliverance, making it bear on the present.

Monads, then, are creations of "messianic time," moments where language and thought come together as both prophecy and dread. They are the result of shocks to the system, and where they are deployed as poetry, as in the case of Baudelaire, they have a revolutionary character, rescuing individuals and even whole epochs from the darknesses of chronological time. Benjamin's notion of the photograph as the "posthumous moment" and his discussions with Scholem on the Kabbalistic ideal of Devekuth or "adhesion" add additional reinforcements to this sense of his poetics. These conceptions, surrounded by various ideas about revelation, about light and seeing, and the need to articulate the social and historical dimensions of what is illuminated, are the tools by which he sees historical content transformed into something like truth.

Benjamin joins the "monad" to the idea of the name (as the name or naming is historically conjoined to the making of the poem). In his critical speculations on language use, Benjamin sees in the monad "a primordial form of perception in which words possess their own nobility as names." In his schematic 'Antitheses Concerning Word and Name,' a chart of topics he culled from his previous writings, he comments: "All human language is only reflection of the word in name. The name is no closer to the word than knowledge is to creation. The name is the translation of the mute into sound and the nameless into the name."

History inflects the name with power. Elsewhere in his writing Benjamin suggests that this form of perception by which word is transformed into name does not simply correlate words with the things of the world. It is not merely referential, but, as he says in his essay 'On the Mimetic Faculty' (1933), words participate in a kind of "non-sensuous similarity," creating an immediate and powerful relation between past and present, thus short-circuiting conceptual thought. At the time of this writing, Benjamin was concerned with the most primal aspects of language, especially the idea of naming, which, if we read him carefully, is actually an idea of "re-naming" a term I use to clarify the dynamics of poetic composition. I am thinking here of what textuality and commentary, at root, actually consist of. From the biblical perspective, the original pre-Adamic field of play can be seen as namelessness, as a silent and unlettered cosmos. But if it ever did exist, this undifferentiated namelessness is no more. It has been replaced in the contemporary consciousness by the totality of Adam's act, by Babel or, as the Kabbalists insist, by the world and all its forms as already, albeit secretly, a form of Torah, lurking as a written out and inscribed universe hidden behind apparent phenomena. Adam, then, as he names things, is our first textualist and, possibly, by these acts, the first Jew in the Bible. As Benjamin sees it, "God made things knowable in their names. Man, however, names them according to knowledge."

As I have written in my essay 'Diasporic Poetics', "for the poet, then, renaming is the essence of poetry, renaming in the sense that the poem is a name for a thing or state of affairs which did not previously exist." By the time I encountered Benjamin's writings, I had already been exposed to the Objectivist poets, poets who most deeply influenced me. In their work, at least as I saw it, they honored Zukofsky's "code," as expounded in 'An Objective.' They sought for what he characterized as both "sincerity" and "objectification," qualities that gave the poem its aesthetic and intellectual resolution as indissoluble content and form. Zukofsky had termed this resolution "rested totality," and I was struck by the idea's resemblance, albeit secularized, to the notion of messianic arrest in Benjamin. Reading the Objectivists, in particular Reznikoff and Oppen's poems or Zukosky's essays on poetry, brought constant reinforcement of my views on Benjamin's poetics. The last lines of Zukofsky's poem 'Mantis: An Interpretation,' with its intent to seek "the simultaneous,/ the diaphanous, historical/ in one head," presented, in my mind, a kind of parallel to Benjamin's notion of "arrest."

For Oppen, who along with Benjamin, was the major influence on my work, such naming, as he told L. S. Dembo, was a "test of sincerity, the moment … when you believe something to be true, and you construct a meaning from those moments of conviction." In this, poetry repeats the Adamic act; it bears the force of "non-sensuous similarity," of original conjunction.

I have posed these thoughts from the perspective of a diasporic poetics, not only of someone in the actual diaspora, but from the embrace of the diaspora as the condition of poetry. I've tried to intuit here, as I did in reading the Objectivists, a sense of the transmigratory aspect of words and names, of a re-naming which floats or drifts into wandering based on the polyvalence of words as though one could send a word towards a meaning it did not begin with and hence disperse it, placing it in diasporic motion.

In Benjamin's notion of "aura" one finds a sympathetic—hence transmigratory—magic of words, an inkling of the powers conferred on words. Benjamin writes: "the name no longer lives in [the human word] intact. It has stepped out of… its own immanent magic, in order to become expressly, as it were externally, magic."

Levinas's conception of the poet as properly not having a place dovetails with Benjamin's errancy of the word. Like Benjamin, he testifies to the dynamics of the word-experience phenomenon; he regards the poet as transmitter of a worked upon physiology into language, the re-namer. Implicit in this line of thought is that the poet is not perceived as an experimenter with language *per se*, for there is nothing more confident than the experimenter in the laboratory who can objectively manipulate materials (language in this case) in a fanciful manner. On the contrary, Levinas's poet (and Benjamin's as well) is anguished and exposed; he "loses place," "ceases occupation," that is, he does not perform but is performed upon by experience, by adversity, by love and history.

For Benjamin, there is an obligation associated with something having been given a name. Cryptically, he tells us that "the atonement for damaging the name lies in the word of judgment, which is also the root of abstraction." If the name represents an imposed authority prior to understanding (if it is damaged by arbitrary power, by the coinage of power), it must be questioned. Such a received name is dogma incarnate, not experience; it is, in Levinas's terms, "a place." The poet's obligation is to grow, to move out from under this place, this authority of a prior name, and to express that movement as a new understanding. In this sense, the poet's work can be seen as an undoing of authority or at least a testing of it.

* * *

Benjamin developed another principle or strategy as he tried to bring over the name or image (or the monad) into historical analysis, using collage and the making of the montage, "to detect," he writes, "the crystal of the total event in the analysis of the simple individual moment." The acts of disruption and recombination inherent in montage could be seen as a form of naming or renaming writ large, acts that by creating unique juxtapositions offered a new or formerly hidden narrative of events. Benjamin wanted to "rub history against the grain," to create juxtapositions of thought and citation that would sunder the purposeful chains of chronicle. He wanted to place the so-called historical narrative in question, especially the stories which mandate "official" sense and "official" views which sanctify the idea that history was moving toward some sort of progress. Everywhere one looks at or remembers a past, Benjamin insisted, chronicle is broken open into contradictions and ambiguities so that another logic is impelled, one that builds contrary to the flow of time. He remarks that for the chronicler (and he could have said poet as well) "every day is judgment day", that "nothing that has ever happened should be regarded as lost." Benjamin counsels a kind of interventionist poetics, one in which recognition—he defines it in 'Central Park' as the "flashing up [of the image] in *the now of its recognizability*" and contingency (the circumstances and environments of that recognition) weigh more heavily than invention or poetic fancy.

Benjamin was very much a critic of *l'art pour l'art*. In his writings on Baudelaire, he makes a severe attack on the concept. "This doctrine [of *l'art pour l'art*] and its corresponding practice," he maintains, "for the first time gives taste a dominant position in poetry ... In *l'art pour l'art* the poet for the first time faces language the way the buyer faces the commodity on the open market." Such poets, he maintains, "have nothing to formulate with such urgency that it could determine the coining of their words. Rather they have to choose their words... the poet's taste guides him in his choice of words. But the choice is made only among words which have not already been coined by the object itself—that is, which have not been included in the process of production." Benjamin is responding to the lost sacred bond between word and object. The "urgency" of the poet restores that bond, a bond he contrasts with the more modern tendency, in the poetics of *l'art pour l'art*, to accept the divorce of word and referent and treat language from the side of its manipulated surface effect. Such manipulations may be a path to art, but not necessarily to truth.

* * *

Benjamin's writings have a dialogical character, what I have termed a sense of oppositional counter-continuities. This idea of counter-continuities comes out of the many comments on Benjamin's and Scholem's exchanges on "counter-history" (most prominent is David Biale's book on the subject), a conception derived from Nietzsche. Nietzsche, in *The Use and Abuse of History* defined counter-history as "an attempt to gain a past *a posteriori* from which we might spring, as opposed to the past from which we do spring." History, in this sense is redemption and rescue, rescue from ourselves and from our penchant for myth-making and reification. "Messianic arrest" becomes the doorway through which this past can be viewed and utilized.

The articulation of needs is what modern culture works best at silencing. Benjamin in 'The Storyteller' (1936), mourning the loss of the storyteller, observes: "It is as if something inalienable to us, the securest among our possessions were taken from us: the ability to exchange experiences." As he realized, the difficulty of establishing both connections and limits to the notions of self and world lie buried in the nature of our terminology, in the antinomy of our categories such as "public" and "private." These terms are less actual entities than the vectors of gestures, institutionalized gambits, ways to aim an emotional arc. As categories, as mythologies, they begin to collapse once we trace their arcs from their beginnings to their endings (or vice-versa), once we arrest language and investigate it closely. Benjamin sought to plumb this social mythology in order to reach for something simpler: how individuals can give meaningful shape to their experiences, and how they will be able to enact their desires, to sense what obstructs or limits desire and what can then be undertaken.

His formulation suggested to me that if political action and literary works have a meeting ground, it lies in the work's or poem's capacity for a kind of local revelation. What culture has silenced, literature will articulate, not because words represent realities but because they offer us the sites of negotiation. The "data of the world" is incorporated by the poet into meaning-structures (Benjamin's monads and crystallizations) through the agency of the poem. The poem does not replicate the value-structure of the data but wrenches it from the utilitarian/socialized matrix in which it occurred. These are the poem's counter-continuities. On the other side of the disjunctive act, the wrenching of words from their contexts within the structures of power is not silence but new conjugation, new oppositional counter-continuities.

My studies of Benjamin led me toward a conception of poetry as a redeeming art. If "art is to rescue us," Oppen wrote, "as only the true might rescue us," then it must have this character, of exfoliating memory and history in a new way. Benjamin explores the dynamics of this exfoliation. "Man's inner concerns," he writes, "do not have their issueless private character by nature. They do so only when he is increasingly unable to assimilate the data of the world around him by way of experience." The key words of this passage, "inner concerns," "assimilate" and "experience" and in fact the main thrust of the passage, is sociopolitical and cultural. Benjamin is less concerned about a "self" attempting to express its interiority than about an individual attempting to articulate needs which cannot be isolated as either public or private.

Recently Xavier Kalck, in his essay "'Politics is history': Testing Oppen's 'Test of Truth'" asks a central question of poetics at this time: "what happens if the poem's truth is to be sought in the poem's relation or incorporation of that something we decide to call 'history'—at the same time as that poem as object becomes part of history? Have we not then come full circle, looking at history for a greater truth value in the poem, while that poem would be repeating the truth-value we assign history as such in the first place?" Kalck, in this passage, would seem to veer close to solipsism, but the words "relation or incorporation" and "decide" speak to a poet's act of intervention, its potential for challenging a historical narrative or discourse. One "inevitable" discourse, the positivist, progressive march of art into the future might well suffer rupture in such an act. So another way to put Kalck's question might be: what if Oppen's test of truth relied on the historical awareness of our political predicament, rather than on abstracted dialectics? Poetry, Kalck seems to tell us, needs a real enemy. It needs to be worked through and worked on by politics and history rather than being a response to the last mode of poetry that captured the poetry-commodity market.

Kalck's questions correlate with Benjamin's "now-time," suggesting a thinking that resists those discourses and programs of and on poetry that seek to universalize a particular practice or propose this practice as sufficient for the utopias we want to construct or the regimes we want to overthrow.

In 'On Some Motifs in Baudelaire,' Benjamin writes of the "covert laws" of Baudelaire's poetry as they show forth in 'Spleen de Paris,' that dream of "the miracle of a poetic prose, musical yet without rhythm and without rhyme, supple and resistant enough...." "Resistant enough" strikes me as the embodiment of that covert lawfulness Benjamin sought in a poetics that never loses touch with its situation in the world, one that is always more about articulating our hopes and fears and those of the culture around us than it is about the making of art. That resistance which he deeply admired was to be just enough of a force to keep open "the small gateway in time through which the Messiah might enter."

A CONVERSATION:
FIONA McMAHON AND MICHAEL HELLER
ON *THIS CONSTELLATION IS A NAME*

Introduction by Fiona Mcmahon

This conversation with Michael Heller follows upon the publication of
his most recent volume of poems, *This Constellation is a Name: Collected
Poems 1965–2010*, and the subsequent readings he was invited to give
in France and in Great Britain during the winter of 2012–13. By way
of entry, the weave between tradition and experiment is one pattern to
follow as the diasporic consciousness underlying his poetics unfolds. His
writing will just as soon delight in the vitality of the poet's eye in the
world as in the mutability of the Word at the hand of the poet. Though
suggesting modes of experiment along a transmigratory path, poetry for
Michael Heller holds fast to a ritual ruled in equal parts by skill and desire.
As he explains in his essay, 'Diasporic Poetics', poetry is experienced as
the endeavour "to gather two intimacies at once, that of the very things
words named, the trees, the rocks, the persons and images, etc. and that
of a renaming" (*Uncertain Poetries* 174).[1] Against the background of
discussions on experimental poetry, Heller's volume, *This Constellation is
a Name* brings to light a careful yet uncertain placing of intimacies. The
reader is distinctly drawn to consider the nodes of thought, of feeling and
of craft that comprise any one poem.

The gathering of poetry into a *constellation*, as the title suggests,
means reflecting with the poet on the formation of language as though
part of a network of experiments. For the contemporary poet, the circle
widens to acknowledge and to query the relationship of language to the
circumstance of history. If the poet never steps out of that circle, it's
because he remains, as he is described, a "supplicant before words" (*UP*
173), a modest player of sorts setting forth amongst the signs of language
that others have inscribed before him. If we sift through the substantial
body of work collected in this volume, we gain a sense of Michael Heller's

---

[1] In his essay 'Diasporic Poetics', MH defines "renaming", the second of these
two intimacies as the "construct of the poem which collocated all these names of
things and yet held them in some new order and relationship and so constituted
a new name."

itinerary in and among words, and importantly, his itinerary alongside other writers. In his poems there are encounters with Apollinaire, Celan, Rilke, Mallarmé, encounters with Paul Blackburn, Carl Rakosi, Robert Duncan, Walt Whitman, as well an enduring conversation with Walter Benjamin. The poet for Michael Heller, in the act of "re-naming" (*UP* 180) is something like the figure encountered in one such conversation-poem entitled 'On a Phrase of Miłosz's':

> He has found vertiginous life again, the words
> on the way to language dangling possibility,
>
> But also, like the sound of a riff on a riff,
> it cannot be resolved. History has mucked this up. (*TCIN* 387)[2]

Constellations emerge with Michael Heller as a bastion of possibility in spite of the impediments that history has thrown across the path of language. This latest volume, stretching over a period from 1965 to 2010, exposes the poet continuously in the act of revisiting words, thus forming new constructs, new arrangements. This comprises his task, if he is to ponder the loss of intelligibility and yet refuse solipsistic routes: "and if our words are off not by being / in another place but in a nowhere / of no help to ourselves or anyone, / if they are just stuff and the proof of stuff,"… (*TCIN* 385).[3]

In response to the finality of a "nowhere" for language, there is a move to retain the potency of modalities that may foster, as Kenneth Burke once said in reference to Charles Reznikoff, a "usefulness to living" (xvi)[4]. These entail concentration on sight—on what may be reclaimed from the visible world—and concentration on language through efforts to fathom transmissibility. As we consider the matter of poetic allegiances and divergences that develop over time, Michael Heller's relationship to the ideals and shapes of Objectivist poetry appears as one example of a lasting poetic companionship. What may not find its way into the present conversation, we can remember from the influential study *Convictions's Net of Branches: Essays on Objectivist Poets and Poetry* (1985) and Michael

---

[2] 'On a Phrase of Miłosz's' (*Eschaton* 2009) in *TCIN*, 387.

[3] 'Looking at Some Petroglyphs in a Dry Arroyo Near a Friend's House' (*Eschaton* 2009) in *TCIN*, 385.

[4] Kenneth Burke, 'The Matter of the Document', Introduction. *Testimony* (New York, NY: The Objectivist Press, 1934), xvi.

Heller's extensive thinking through of George Oppen's poetry in his collection of essays, *Speaking the Estranged: Essays on the Work of George Oppen* (2008; 2012). Our conversation will touch upon this mapping of poetic practice, as it relates to Michael Heller's involvement in European poetry and the contemporary American scene.

* * *

FM: Your poem entitled 'Poetic Geography' (*Eschaton* 2009) planted the seed for my first question. It pertains to the formation of what you've termed a "diasporic poetics" alongside the figures of geography generated in your writing. Reading the poems over the expanse of your volume *This Constellation is a Name*, we are carried along as though through the geography of your experience as a writer, many poems casting light on the different places where you've made your home or travelled through. At the same time, language appears contingent upon place as poems retrace the itinerary in and out of the myth encoded in an American landscape: "Lost. / To be lost / in that old American hope // of words / enfolded in the continent," (*TCIN* 424). Beyond these examples however, the mobility of your sympathies direct us beyond the limits of a place-specific poetics. I'm thinking for instance of your ties to European culture and European places as defined through your Jewish cultural heritage. The reaction against the transparency of the word, which defined much experiment in poetry since the latter half of the twentieth century (beginning perhaps with the Concretists) may also be tied to your heritage as a writer. What fascination do words, sometimes "enfolded in the continent" continue to hold over writers today? Is geography a helpful or an adequate image to replicate the experience of language?

MH: First let me partially exempt myself from the strictures of being labeled "Jewish American." As I write in my memoir *Living Root*, I'm a secular person, and any label such as "Jewish" or "American" has to do with history and location and with others identifying me as "Jewish;" in other words, the label, as labels must, feels reductive. As you remark above, I hope I'm working "beyond the limits of place-specific poetics." On the other hand, and this is also partly historical, diasporic, cultural, even Shoah-related, some of the most profound writing I have encountered on attempting to understand the situation of being beyond place-specifics, trying to grasp something fundamental about human beings, well, some of that writing has been, quite naturally, given their history and culture, written by Jews. When I say fundamental, I'm thinking of the comfort or discomfort in my mind of being locked in a place-specific context. Yves Bonnefoy wrote a remarkable little book on Rimbaud that I recently discovered in which he remarks that Rimbaud's whole career as poet can be seen as trying to undo the rite of his baptism, his entrapment in a powerfully marked category or identity. Such an urge to undo possesses me, especially with respect to poetic and cultural categories.

We know, however—and who better to remind us than certain French writers—that the trace, if I may sound like O. J. Simpson's lawyer, is there even as we attempt to erase.

To go back to your question of words: to my mind, any poetic "sublime," the American Sublime (and the American "nuclear sublime," the subject of Rob Wilson's book, which is why I dedicated 'Poetic Geography' to him) represents an effort to render words superfluous to a vista, to a "vision." The source of our so-called "American exceptionalism" lies there in its utter mutedness, in its anti-dialogical character. It is not to be argued or trifled with. As a thinking human being, not only as poet, I seek an erotics of words that forces them to be encountered again, to be dealt with. So really I have to say that no geography, no image of geography is sufficient to language, unless one buys into some sort of nationalism. That is why the narrator of the poem puts his hope in a vertiginous fall "homing/like a smart bomb/from signifier to signified/ and there, oddly,/identifying/with a lover/instead of oneself." But yes, as the poem goes on, this is something of a "Lost hope!"

FM: As Norman Finkelstein has suggested in his review of your volume, *This Constellation is a Name: Collected Poems 1965–2010*, the relationship between intellectual inquiry and lyricism has been a constant concern in your work[5]. It is described not as a seamless binding but as a necessary dynamics of resistance enacted by the poet through language. In the same respect, your writing brings us to contemplate, after Wallace Stevens, "the poem of the mind in the act of finding / What will suffice" (*Parts of a World*). Mindful of the past and yet seeking to write outside the "script", as Stevens' modern poet, the very act of writing becomes inseparable from an investigation of the world. Anticipating an approach diversely explored in the contemporary context, the investigative quality of poetry equates it to some extent with the logical rigors of philosophy.

---

[5] *Notre Dame Review* 35 (Winter/Spring 2013)

At the same however, as you have suggested in your 1995 essay, 'The Uncertainty of the Poet', "the poet is caught in the secret knowledge of language, that it speaks not certainties but explores uncertainty" (*UP* 25) In a manner that recalls your understanding of "diasporic motion" in poetry (*UP* 181), Henri Meschonnic has described language as "unquiet" and poetry as "the organization in language of what has always been said to escape language: life, the movement no word is supposed to be able to say" (*Rhyme and Life* 181). When I read this I think of the following lines from your poem 'The Oath', in a group entitled 'Partitions' (*In the Builded Place* 1989; *TCIN* 316):

Not the power of speech
Nor the note blown into wholeness.
We seemed never to converse in the now as now.

What poetry there is
Is always late. Strange merely
To have thought. What
[...]

Has negation become a method of redefining language so as to become, in the end, a form of affirmation? If so, do you see this stance as part of the elegiac quality of your writing – inherited from the Romantic tradition? Do you join in with Stevens who writes in 'Sailing after Lunch': "It ought to be everywhere. / But the romantic must never remain."

MH: Oppen's well known lines seem to bear here: "One can use words provided one treat them as enemies ... not enemies but ghosts that have run wild in the streets, etc." I wrote an entire chapter in my book on Oppen based on that pause between "enemies" and "not enemies," on the swerve in the poem from "enemies" to "ghosts," and so the question has been not one of negation but of a kind of tuning into and exposing as articulation the haunting of language. "One by one," writes Oppen or, as my friend Jonathan Morse entitled his book, 'Word by word.' Admittedly, this has left me on occasion somewhat indifferent to some of the programmatic aspects of experimental poetry, though "word by word" is, as far as I am concerned, the most experimental as well as experiential modality, because it encompasses so much by way of possibility and is at root a sense of not quite knowing where you are going, but wanting "to cohere" (if I may be Poundian for a moment).

FM: To return to the notion of "uncertainty" or what you refer to with disarming simplicity as "lostness" in the same essay: "Perhaps all that a word can do is remind us that, in order to experience lostness or uncertainty, one has to remember when, whether for an instant or an eternity, something was 'true'." (*UP* 24) In a different essay, 'Notes on Lyric Poetry, or at the Muse's Tomb', you describe the lyric as a "point of radical undoing" (*UP* 246). Once again a negative framework appears to paradoxically give rise to an opportunity for poetic production, for a form of renewal. Do you understand lyricism as an expression of "lostness"?

MH: I understand the human condition to be an expression of lostness. I don't want to be esoteric, but, for instance, in the Buddhist tradition in which I studied (and the various traditions are by no means the same), the expression was not that "the world is an illusion," but that "it was like an illusion," characterizing our disorientation from both a grounding and a groundlessness simultaneously. When Oppen writes that "the miracle is not that we exist but that we have something to stand on," I feel that he confirms the endless duality of our situation in which the lyrical—"lyricism" sounds too musical-theater for me—the breaking into the discursive constructs, opens up the possibility of seeing a path to freedom, momentarily at least. And you can sense, from what we've discussed here and from our shared knowledge of some of these subjects, that Benjamin's "now-time" was among the most seductive formulations of this range of ideas I was to come across. So, to answer your question, the lyrical "act" of the poet, can be the expression of "lostness." I say this with caution, because the words lyric, lyrical, etc., carry such horrible baggage. In my essay, 'Notes on Lyric Poetry, or at the Muse's Tomb,' I tried to delineate what I meant by the word, but whether or not I could overcome in the reader the idea that I was not talking about "poesy," I can't know.

FM: I would like us to touch upon your exploration of memory with respect to your long-standing conversation with Walter Benjamin. In his tracing of the evolution of the "epic mind" since the example of the early Greeks, Walter Benjamin makes a distinction between how memory is made manifest by the novelist and by the storyteller. In the first instance, he speaks of the "perpetuating remembrance of the novelist" and in the second instance, the "short-lived reminiscences of the storyteller".[6] As a poet whose writing turns repeatedly to the agency of memory, how

---

6

do you conceive of the "epic mind" in the present day? What future is there for the "epic mind" if we live in a period of "short-lived" memory and rapidly changing modes of communication? To quote from 'After Class', a poem that appeared in your 1989 volume, *In the Builded Place*: "I hear the dead leaves scrape my voice: history" (*TCIN* 225). Is memory sounded out at a cost? Is it necessarily an antagonistic process?

MH: This question has an odd resonance with my previous comment on lyricism—the poem invokes Shelley again, which must indict me as some hapless Romantic who has not caught on to the change of rules. The Mr. Wolfgang of the poem, a student of mine in the 1960s, an aging German lawyer who had lived in Berlin during the Shoah, was, without meaning to be, a confrontational figure, one who stopped up my speech without any awareness, and certainly no animus. Memory, "the dead leaves" that I wouldn't/couldn't query or mention, had its cost, which here was a kind of quietude. As Benjamin tells it, if we sit on the back of his angel of history, our view is a landscape of disasters, and whoever wishes to speak must overcome memory not by negating it but by being willing to speak through it. Poetry, as Aristotle insisted, could do this more accurately than "history." It's part of why I am in the game, so to speak.

FM: As a writer of prose, your ties to a chain of tradition, derived from your family and their Jewish cultural heritage come alive most vividly in your memoir *Living Root*. How does the task of poet align itself with that of the chronicler, the history-teller? In the poem, 'The Chronicle Poet', the process of telling is wracked with failure: "A noise seeking to reach / its fundament, trying, out of pure sound, to form itself / as honest language, and by that failure, painfully embarrassing" (*TCIN* 401). What difference is ascribed to prose? Does it succeed where poetry fails?

MH: A tough question, which entails all the answers I've been trying to give all along. I think such a question can no longer be asked in a binary way, since the interpenetration of poetry and prose, the boundary markers of each, no longer are distinct. I have put this question to myself and in print more in terms of discourse as opposed to "lyric," a word which I put in scare quotes lest someone think I'm talking about Joyce Kilmer's 'Trees' rather than a figured language that leads a writer or poet on to something unplanned and unannounced about it. I would add that any number of writers who are designated as "philosophers" fall between the stools of our categorizations. "Pure language," a language supposedly having nothing else but the writer's pure intent died with the second- and third-level imitators of Mallarmé or Stevens. At best, to borrow from William Carlos Williams, we "tune" words by ordering them through our craft, for me the greatest pleasure of writing.

FM: Considering still your conversation with Walter Benjamin, it seems to me that as a writer you demonstrate how memory works as both an obstacle and a path to language. For instance, the memory of Benjamin's thinking is furthered through a defining, affirmative tonality in your 1989 poem, 'Strophes from the Writings of Walter Benjamin' (*TCIN* 241). At the same time, the poem appears to recognize to some degree the alienation of memory from language:

> In shutting out experience,
> the eye perceives an experience
> of a complementary nature,
>
> less the product of facts
> firmly anchored in memory
>
> more a convergence in memory
> of accumulated facts,
>
> the replacement of older narrations
> by information of sensation.
>
> According to theory,
> fright's significance
> in the absence of
> of ready anxiety.

If poetry, as in this poem, reads as a search for a conduit of memory, could you briefly discuss the modality intimated in the phrase, "by information as sensation"? Does this relate with the Objectivist notion of "rested totality" or Carl Rakosi's "hard/ Inevitable quartz[7]".

---

[7] This is the raw data. / A mystery translates it / Into feeling and perception ; / Then imagination; / Finally the hard / Inevitable quartz / Figure of will/ and language. ('Shore Line'; *Amulet*)

MH: The poem is taken word for word from a passage in Benjamin's writings. It is related to Freud, to Bergson, to trauma. Its lines must be looked at in terms of his thinking on "shock," an occurrence, which like fascination, opens pathways to a redemptive view of history. When information is suddenly potent, when it passes out of the low-energy sphere of factuality and heightens consciousness, as poems or historical events can do, it becomes a source of cultural and political energy. And yes, if "rested totality" or the quality of "hard/inevitable quartz" were achieved by a verbal construct, it too would be a possible moment in human affairs.

FM: You have discussed on various occasions the extent to which another Objectivist, George Oppen has been a shaping influence from the very start of your career. You emphasize for instance how Oppen presents a model of kinship between poetry and philosophy that has been important to you. This entails the poet being "caught between a philosophical sense of his or her craft and a religious sense of the mysteriousness of the world." ('The Uncertainty of the Poet' 24) At the same time, in your deeply perceptive review of the last edition of Charles Reznikoff's poems by Black Sparrow Books ('Dantean Reznikoff'), you discuss the activity of the poet in the context of modernism and a world emptied of symbolic and spiritual meaning. As such, you identify poetry as performing the role of witness in a world where there are no longer any "designs" with which to shape meaning. You put it this way in the essay:

> Recording takes precedence over making; it can be likened to the act of the saint or bodhisattva, or to the Talmudist's insistence on living for others. One's own salvation or enlightenment is put off for the saving of other people. The artist puts off the self-display, the novelizing trick because what he or she has to say must be rendered with straightforwardness.

Is the philosophic mode the only worthy "design" as the poet tries to navigate a course? How does your understanding of Buddhism find a place in this encounter between philosophic and religious thought amongst contemporary poets?

MH: Well, without quite having come to this question, it seems I have scattered a few answers to it. First, let me say that Reznikoff is perhaps the ultimate poet-bodhisattva in both his writing and in his literary career as someone whose work is at once a power, a witness and a non-aggression. I don't know if that even begins to cover it, but it was what I wanted to imply when I first wrote about Reznikoff that he practiced "a modernity with a vengeance," the witness making us come to terms with what he has witnessed.

But let me not use the term "Buddhism" or its terminology too much. It leads to more misinterpretations and has much more baggage associated with it than "lyricism," and one finds that instead of what empowerment certain ideas have given one, that he or she is, instead, defending against all the misconceptions a word can entail. Suffice it to say that poetry exists, at least in one sense, to deconstruct philosophic ideas, and that the Buddhism I studied also seeks to deconstruct all sorts of ideas, including the idea of Buddhism itself.

FM: Writing in a world often labelled today as 'post-religion' or 'post-faith', do you feel such distinctions are relevant when describing objectivist writing? In their own time, though it may be difficult to generalize about such matters, did the Objectivists experience loss of faith as a crisis? Or was it quickly absorbed by a search for what you described as Oppen's search for an "adequate language" (*Conviction's Net of Branches* 86), the "truth-value of poetic speech" (*CNB* 81) or even by a readiness to humour? You mentioned an episode to me where you were invited with Reznikoff to read poems in a synagogue...

MH: Yes, it was for a *Yom Kippur* service at an Upper Westside Synagogue. There is a portion of the service devoted to the remembrance of the dead and to the suffering visited throughout history upon the Jewish people. Reznikoff read from *Holocaust*, and I read from my 'Białystok Stanzas.' But we both seemed to have been a little less thoughtful about the ritual space we were reading in. We arrived at the synagogue together and strolled down the aisle to our seats at the front of the congregation, neither of us stopping to put on kippas. There we sat, two bald heads gleaming back at the assembled congregants when shortly the sexton approached us and held out kippas for us. Reznikoff looked at me and shrugged, and I shrugged back, and, wordlessly, we put the kippas on our heads. We were not trying to be defiant in any way, but perhaps, unthinkingly, we came as poets rather than congregants. Yeats writes somewhere that the poet can come to the threshold of the chapel but must not cross it in his role as poet. Perhaps it was something like that which led us to act the way we did. By the way, I've written about the "Jewishness" of that shrug as a typical gesture made in the face of what is unknowable or unnameable. The Jewish God in his namelessness? And there is a line in one of the "old photographs" sections of 'Białystok Stanzas,' in which an elderly Jewish man is shrugging into the camera as he is being rounded up by the Nazis. Also, I might add, the "shrug" reminds me of certain verbal gestures that I've discussed, the "involuntary voice," like Aristophanes' hiccup in Plato's *Symposium*, that Mladen Dolar writes about which has the power to alter discourse. I liken the hiccup to Oppen's use of the dash in his much-cited lines in 'A Language of New York,' where he writes "Possible/To Use/Words as enemies./Not enemies—Ghosts which run wild…." For me, that dash-line from enemies to ghosts, the kind of effect which Dolar calls an unparaphrasable "high elusive meaning" is one of the pivotal moments in Oppen's poetry and poetics. That's the kind of thing Rezi's shrug meant to me—the silence of it spoke volumes.

FM: To return to the difficult question of mapping influences or allegiances… You spend and have spent a significant amount of time in Western Europe (Spain; France) and there are specific poems in *Wordflow* (1997) and *In the Builded Place* (1989) that convey that experience. Does the past weigh more heavily on you as a poet when in Europe? To put it differently, does the present elude the poet more deftly? I'm thinking of your poem 'Fifty-Three Rue Nôtre-Dame de Nazareth' (*TCIN* 266) where you write:

> While at best one writes
> The lightning's thunderclap:
> Not the event itself, but the event's
> Near after. Poet, this is the husk
>
> Already burnt, the belated desiring
> Of an image on command,
> O not one's own, never one's own.

The poem, 'Operation Cicero' also appears to thread this same theme, with its reference to World War II and to the deceit or the slipperiness of "idiom": "as the words / all go toward the sight / of secrets" (*TCIN* 68).

MH: I think I will invoke again Rakosi's "hard/Inevitable quartz." The poem that I seek to write takes up language in order to produce silence, that vast silence in which all our secrets are buried or, better, not yet articulated, until someone writes a poem that reveals them.

FM: Is the source of poetry for you (as you say of Charles Reznikoff) "less the bookshelf than the sidewalk" ('Dantean Reznikoff' 6)? Do you have a strong affinity for what may be termed deambulatory thinking?

MH: Are you an American poet, these two questions seem to ask? Of course, I'm an American, have American tastes and interests, but I am not a post-Whitmanesque American, feeling a special duty to define our culture against another, or—horrid thought—to claim an exceptionalism for my country, which is a great country and often, in the quest for freedom and dignity, an ennobling country. Living in New York City, I love urban spaces, I love the layered thickness of history, of culture, so when I am in Europe, I experience its even more apparent thicker thickness as a great pleasure and resource.

As for ambulation, being a flâneur and being a poet seem very much like the same thing. I think of Rezi's great circumabulations, of Mandelstam's linking of Dante's *Commedia* to the tread of his feet, and the Baudelaire-Benjamin nexus as examples that animate me and get me away from my desk.

II

from OPPEN'S THEMATICS:
[what are poets for?]

(A talk given at Kelly Writers House on the
100th anniversary of George Oppen's birthday.)

So I am reading George Oppen yet again. After much thinking and many hours writing hundreds of pages on his work, I am still trying to know what kind of poet he is, what is the nature of his poetry. The labels: modernist, objectivist, classicist, etc., tell me almost nothing.

It seems I'm not writing an essay but an assay. Most often, the essay form involves a whirl (or swirl) around a subject—it's a bit of display. An assay, on the other hand, is an analytic procedure to test the properties and/or composition of a particular material, a mineral rock, a bit of ore. The assay tells you a story of substance, what makes it up, what qualities are possessed within its materiality. (Recall that Kenneth Rexroth titled a volume of his critical writings *Assays*.)

But back to Oppen, that hard, perdurable poet, a worthy subject for assaying. Influenced by Heidegger. Perhaps more important, he seems to participate—in the Heideggerian sense—as a foundational poet (the term Heidegger used to describe Hölderlin). The foundational poet alters not only poetry's paths and modes of creation but alters or suggests a new way of looking at the basic themes of poetry, love, desire, language, history, memory, the sociopolitical and cultural worlds we inhabit. He is extra-literary.

Oppen, I feel follows Heidegger's thoughts on Hölderlin, that "it is a necessary part of the poet's nature that, before he can be truly a poet in such an age, the time's destitution must have made the whole being and vocation of the poet a poetic question for him." The parallels between Hölderlin and Oppen are numerous—the odd disjunctive look and feel of their late works, both written in the shadow of mental disease. Both worked in a "destitute time." And both careers involved important reversals—Hölderlin's investment and then rejection of German Idealism; Oppen's embrace of Marxism and the Party and later his taking up of poetry after twenty-five years of silence. This "non-return," as I have called it, follows the contours of such a questioning, first his abandonment of poetry rather than composing "socialist realist" verse, then his long silence, followed by a working through as poetic career of trying to understand and relate to the human destitution that surrounds him.

Oppen's most characteristic gesture, I would suggest, is posing the question of being a poet to himself across the entire spectrum of his work, a question that can only be asked (and possibly answered) as part of a consonance or simultaneity with the process of time itself, as in these lines from his poem 'Return':

> For the wood weathers. Drift wood.
> And the footprint in the forest grows older.
> This is not our time, not what we mean, it is time
> Passing, the curl at the cutwater.
> The enormous prow
> Outside in the weather.

"Destitution," and the response to destitution must invoke a sense of how untimely ("This is not our time") his poetry must be within his own era. He must also sense the very ungainlessness of his efforts, his "not what we mean," evoking the poet's dis-ease with his own vocation, with the ambivalences and inadequacies that are raised as he re-reads what he has written. To write may be to originate, to create, but to read is to sense, as Oppen puts it later in the poem, to acknowledge "the very/Ceremony of innocence that was drowned." So it is not only time (and history) which occurs and which is one of the seemingly implacable forces in the poem, "the enormous prow," that rives culture and society and the very task of the poet as tribal singer, it is also the act of re-reading.

It is with this notion of time passing, with the sense that culture and society are in ruins (in 'Return,' Oppen invokes everything from the Depression to a razed city to the depredations of the Romans), that I take up Oppen's thematics of love and desire, not thinking of romantic or sentimental effusions, but because love and desire are effectively the substances that allow the poet to be sustained in a destitute time. I begin by re-reading the poem 'Solution,' (45), one I have written about a number of times in the past, because the substance that I am looking for is, by Oppen's design, the poem's subject *as an absence*. This absence, though its meaning to me has changed over the years as I read the poem, is what makes it work. Here is the poem:

The puzzle assembled
At last in the box lid in the box lid showing a green
Hillside, a house,
A barn and man
And wife and children,
All of it polychrome,
Lucid, backed by the blue
Sky. The jigsaw of cracks
Crazes the landscape but there is no gap,
No actual edged hole
Nowhere the wooden texture of the table top
Glares out of scale in the picture,
Sordid as cellars, as bare foundations:
There is no piece missing. The puzzle is complete
Now in its red and green and brown.

The second line with its deeply psychological "at last" sounds like a metaphysical sigh of relief. A satisfying moment for the assembler. It's as though now syntax could go on all by itself, a little machine manufacturing the rest of the poem, enumerating its building blocks, the puzzle pieces, the "green hillside," "a house," "a barn," "a man/and wife." What else to have in a 'solution' but a 'wife' rather than a 'woman,' where "wife," perhaps designates an entrapping domestic role as it stands in apposition to the more generic, open-ended "man." "Wife" operates like a number of other words in the poem, such as that "at last" above, or the words "lucid," "crazes" and "sordid," each rippling with disorderly presence within the confines of the "solution" proposed by the word's title. Such words are not simply pictorial, descriptive or informational. They carry rhetorical auras that illuminate powerful tensions in the "solution" thus undercutting its putative stability. It is these words that undermine the ostensible subject of the poem and make the "at last" seem prematurely self-satisfied. In fact, the metaphysical relief of that first line break/sigh becomes powerfully ironic. It is both temporary and false.

For once "assembled," the 'Solution,' the completed puzzle is fakery, its "jigsaw of cracks/crazes the landscape." "Nowhere"—the thing being solved—can one sense the sordid cellars, the foundations of the puzzle's pictured world. (Such cellars might contain anything from old junk to the family's dead bodies, to the skeletons of dead Native-Americans who lived on the spot before the house or barn were built). The puzzle expresses, even as it suppresses, the cost, in terms of psychic health, world politics, markets, ethical well-being, of our "lucid," "polychrome" living arrangements ("lifestyles?" Oppen would have hated the word). In fact, the assembled puzzle could be Oppen's Dante-esque picture of the frozen, solidified lowest depths of Hell, its stasis, its moral and psychic entropy, its stifling absence of risk or imagination.

Is there more than one backstory to the poem? The poem strikes at first as a critique of American bourgeois middle-class existence. But now that we know more through the published letters and the *Daybook* about Oppen's complex relationship to the politics of the nineteen-thirties and later, doesn't the poem also suggest a critique of his own experience in being guided or seduced by a rationalistic, all-encompassing "solution," the cultural and political straight-jacket of American Communist Party Marxism?

Oppen himself posed such a critique, repeating it to me and many others in a number of letters, and in his notes:

The type of mind necessary to the artist—or simply the mind of interest—is touched always by experience, by particulars, cannot remain within dogma, no dogma but this which is not dogma but another and overwhelming force which we speak of or speak of nothing

Aren't Oppen's words, "no dogma, no dogma but this," a *cri de cœur*, disguised as advice? Even as they shed light on his late poetics and its insistence on perception and openness, don't these words constitute a stance against "solutions" themselves?

Fifteen years after he published the poem, Oppen in a letter to Frances Jaffer, the San Francisco poet and one of the founders and editors of *How/ ever*, a magazine that focused on feminist issues in poetry and poetics, said of the poem 'Solution,' that "it describes the refusal," as he puts it, "to think outside a field, a set of rules, of definitions.... Whereupon 'it' becomes a complete puzzle." If the solution (or the concept) is complete, if for sociopolitical or cultural reasons—or coercions—it cannot be falsified i.e., it is not allowed to be falsified, then it must be false or worse (I'm alluding here to Karl Popper's thinking that a theory should be considered scientific if, and only if, it is falsifiable).

Let me turn to the poem entitled 'The Forms of Love.' "Love," is a word, that in a crucial sense, we might imagine Oppen seeking to avoid.

The word lacks the thingness or suchness, the inhering physicality or precision of his small nouns like "tree" or "sun" "crying faith/in this in which" that made his poetry, as he claimed "realist." On the other hand, the word "love" presents itself as a focus of exploration, much as the unwritten word "humanity" does in 'Of Being Numerous,' raising the question of its graspability and hence the possibility of it being undefined and therefore not "believable." Believability is a primary aspect or quality of the linguistic experience that Oppen seems to have insisted on, the factor which makes the moment of sincerity seem like something true.

My first assay then might be to try to find out what the substance of love is in Oppen's work. Clearly, the reader must feel an inherent and uncontrollable quality of believability. Believability, because like Oppen's "small nouns," there must be a reader's faith in the experience of reading the poem. This is not about courtship or romance, but some quality that exists within multiple possibilities of experience. And yet surely it cannot fulfill a dogmatic requirement for love.

Oppen's 'The Forms of Love' seems to demonstrate such qualities. For instance, the word "Forms" in the title makes it difficult to define "love" as a convention or to mold it into a singular cast. Certain elements of the poem, "the groping downhill" of the lovers, the wanderment as to whether the lovers will encounter fog or the lake, all taking place in "the bright incredible light" reflect the poet's struggle with meaning. "Love" in Oppen, is one of those words that we must re-read because we cannot read it in the first place.

So the question of the substance of love, while it can't be resolved by any single material fact or quality, is shown as a quest, an inspired quest, a participatory action not only within the context of the two lovers but by a feeling of authentic (some would say near-divine) contextuality with the world, the source of the "bright incredible light" that seems to be a kind of sanction or protection. Yet the poem is saved from being a pure romantic effusion by the repeated "I remember," an insistence of its own on the poem as artifice and construction, as a thing in its own right.

* * *

We can titrate much of Oppen's work for its many echoes and transformations of Heidegger's thought. Oppen's poems can veer close to solipsism, and yet, as Oppen's notes and letters show, the cause and effect he focuses most attentively on are those of the mind making and unmaking worlds. Did Oppen read Heidegger's quote from Hölderlin that "man is a conversation?" For we sense that Oppen's reworkings are governed by the relational aspects of language, language not as constructing worlds but as such a Hölderlinian conversation.

I'm concerned with how the dynamics of these cross talks are amplified in the poetry, for instance in the complex poem 'Time of the Missile,' a poem that brings the idea of nuclear disaster into adjacency with the presence of the loved one. "My love, my love," Oppen exclaims, "we are endangered totally at last." Here, raised to a kind of international level of conflict, our boundaries and adjacencies, "the realm of nations," threaten "viviparous" space, the space that gives birth to new life. The poetry here becomes almost vision, seeking out a sheltering modality with respect to the "other"—to the largest of othernesses, the "Place of the mind/And eye," that can win back the life-producing space of creativity from the death-producing peril created by our own minds.

The backdrop to this poem and many others of Oppen's is that, as Heidegger writes, "poetry is the inaugural naming of being… poetry never takes language as a raw material ready to hand, rather it is poetry which first makes language possible" i.e "gives life-producing effects in a destitute time." So when Oppen insists in 'Leviathan,' that "we must talk now," i.e, we must be *in conversation*, "talk" is already embraced and enfolded into poetry. The title, with its hints of Hobbes and Jonah in the whale (viviparously?), stresses that our "talk" occurs amidst the precariousness of the human situation. "Fear/Is fear." Oppen writes, "But we abandon one another." Without the "talk," without poetry, we have no way to place ourselves outside of that fear, to open to love, my initial theme of this talk.

Like the "bright incredible light" of 'The Forms of Love,' Oppen's poems express the space and articulation of poetry as a kind of surrounding love, as in 'O Western Wind,' where the woman, (his wife Mary, we suppose) moves in "a world around her like a shadow," where "something is being made—/Prepared/Clear in front of her as open air?" The poem is made in the very place that love makes clear. The poet can "write again" where the face of the beloved , her "Beautiful and wide/blue eyes /Across all my vision" signals that for an instant the loved world and the poem's world are a simultaneity. This is the simultaneity replicated in 'The Forms of Love,' and like Oppen's idea of the poem as disclosure, this is also love as disclosure, not possession, but discovery, a theme he develops further in his poem 'Of This of All Things…,' which ends with these lines:

We have wanted
not comforts
but vision
Whatever terrors
have made us companion
to the earth, whatever terrors—

Oppen's feeling is that love is neither privacy nor shelter but this companionate search for "visions." Its subtext is a grounding in an ethics of tact, of apartness and solitude as fundamental human condition. "We will not breach the world/these small worlds least/of all," he writes in 'Penobscot,' a sentiment rewritten from yet another viewpoint in 'Ballad,' which concludes "What I like more than anything/Is to visit other islands." The ethical awareness of these lines pushes against hubris, cultural pride and universalized utopian ideas. For Oppen, the arena in which love or desire are worked out, then, involves a kind of alertness that transforms the usual ironic distance of poetry into an embracing spaciousness in which thing and fact can stand by themselves.

And while the beginnings of this outlook are contained in the poems I've mentioned above, the later poems are suffused with it. Take for instance 'A Morality Play: Preface' in *Seascape: Needle's Eye*, which begins with the astonishing picture of the loved woman lying naked on the bed, in the "feminine light//feminine ardor" that define love in terms of otherness and distance. There's more than the hint of non-possession, of separation in the "eyes turned inward." Here the poet is "pierced and touched," as Oppen defines love away from the usual romanticism of possession and control that aroused and jarred his sensibility in the poem 'Solution' above.

This later poem is a "morality play" for him, not only because it seems to argue against our usual conventional middle-class ideas about love, but also because in a very compassionate way, it defines itself against a kind of fear-love in the mass movements (especially among the young) described in the poem where togetherness is bonded not by visions but comforts. This poem draws on the Oppens contact with the young protestors in the nineteen-sixties, including their experiences of going to the Altamont Rolling Stones concert where, unbeknownst to the Oppens, a young black man was killed by a group of Hells Angels. Yet Oppen, in his remarks on the poem, notices the long hair of the young who "seem to be mourning." He writes about the young "Huddled among each other" giving an almost craven picture of emotion on a mass scale that mirrors the closed up spaces of 'Solution,' the poem I began with above. In a way, the entire San Francisco series is an investigation of the authentic and inauthentic bases of community.

Oppen's thematics of love is also offset and entangled in a thematics of poetic truth, as in 'The Little Pin: Fragment' where Oppen enjambs that idea of truth with his idea of love. The possibility of this entangling is then posed against the "dishonest music" of the present which makes it possible for the imagination to realize its surroundings, for "world/ sometimes be/world…" "O western wind to speak of this," he writes, as if the entire project of Western poetry were moving toward a conception of love that healed the dissonances between individuality and community.

In a letter concerning the translation of his poetry into French, that Oppen sent to the French critic and poet, Serge Fauchereau, he writes of his own work: "The line sense, the line breaks, and the syntax are intended to control the order of disclosure upon which the poem depends." "Disclosure" as applied to what I have called Oppen's thematics of love, seems always to involve a sense of revealment and furthering understanding.

Oppen, whom we honor today, is seen more and more as a kind of foundational poet, one who alters not only our thinking about poetry and how it is written but also how we look at the most basic themes of poetry such as love or history or culture or politics. He makes us ask again, Hölderlin's question: What are poets for? A question that Oppen continually asked himself.

The largeness of that question, the largenesss in which Oppen asked it of poetry and of his own work is what compels the study of his thematics. To read his work, to be moved and absorbed by it, is to be reminded how much we desire to be caught up, as he was, in the question of poetry, how much we desire to participate in the act of discovery—of disclosure—as the central act of a poet, disclosure not only of how a particular poem works but of how its unveiling enables us and gives us insight into our lives and our world. We ask these questions within the company of Oppen's work, we frame them through our readings of him because of the depth and significance his work has for us.

"GLAD YOU'VE INITIATED THIS CORRESPONDENCE…"

In a number of my essays and talks, I've described how I met George Oppen, and how intimately that meeting was connected with my becoming a poet, indeed, with maintaining the desire to write poetry. A long correspondence with Oppen ensued; it was unlike any other I have had with another writer. Clearly his side of it, in its beauty, variousness and syntactical originality, remains beyond any easy categorization, but looking back, even my own letters to him are hard to define specifically. Reading again the letters exchanged between us, I see that my attempts to formulate a response to the provocations of his words were really guideposts leading to a deeper comprehension not only of his work but also ladder-rungs or pathways into my own poetry.

Our correspondence started before 1968 shortly after I met George and Mary along with Charles Reznikoff and Carl and Leah Rakosi at the house of the poet Harvey Shapiro in Brooklyn Heights. In May of 1968 I wrote George, hoping he would not be offended by my telling him that I had been "alternately consoled and terrified" by *Of Being Numerous*, particularly by the poem 'Route' which "seemed to matter" and yet "that neither detachment nor compassion give me any peace of mind." I was thinking about section 8 of 'Route,' where, witnessing a car wreck by the roadside, George writes, "I don't mean he despairs/I mean if he does not/ He sees in the manner of poetry." These lines, rendered with Oppen's characteristic authority, exemplify the nature of the confrontations embodied in his poetry. He wanted, he told his readers, to write with clarity poems that "could not not be understood." Such "clear pictures in verse," (another phrase that described his intent) have the effect of forcing the reader to make sense of his own responses, to probe deeply into one's self in order to resolve a meaning. What is ambiguous, what is unclear or yet to be worked out in his lines lies not so much with the writer as with the one who reads and responds. For someone who wants to make poetry, such passages—and there are many in Oppen—suggest an urge toward psychic depths in which any would-be program of poetry-writing must first take account of contingency, of the life that impinges upon us, whether it involves meeting other poets, car wrecks or the wrecks of the self and the world. Possibly this openness to the contingent was the first "lesson" I took from his work.

From those early exchanges, our correspondence evolved quickly. By 1971, I was telling him:

> I write to you not in search of a father figure, but because I am weary of talking to and reading all those—including my friends—burnt-out cases. I do not write here even questions, only looking into what may be mutual; forgive me for sounding like I am addressing an article of faith rather than a human being. I mean to pose no burden... (November 20, 1971)

George wasn't a "father figure," though I felt the greatest affection for him, as well as total admiration. He was something much more profound, a kind of bulwark or shoring for others in both his work and life. I called him an "article of faith" because I wanted to convey how they were quite different from father figures, the latter seeming to demand a psychological deference, a constant thematics of hope and fear in relation to the parent, something I never felt with George. The article of faith, however, represents something fixed, impassive, immovable, something you return to when you think you have strayed or are in peril, as was the case with George when he lay wounded in the foxhole and recited Reznikoff's poetry to himself to keep himself sane and alive. George was in so many respects my "article of faith," the whole construct of his thought and work like a poem or text that one must constantly relate to or come back to for all sorts of reasons from seeking hope to finding a way out of despair.

Certainly a lot of fathers appear in George's work, though not many father-figures. There is that cryptic excerpt from Kierkegaard in *Of Being Numerous* that ends "but he who will work shall give birth to his own father," as though engendering led to self-engendering, to renewal, as though the labor of poetry, if it were honest and clean and precise enough, could stand for the entire Tradition with a capital T.

More often, the word "father" is freighted with ambivalence. 'Of Hours,' one of his most powerful poems, concerns the terror and disappointment that lies under the shadow of the father. It situates a problematic fatherhood in Pound, a misbegotten lineage of modernism and politics, in which Oppen's experience of the war and his knowledge of the fate of Europe's Jews suffuse his mind. "As a Father did you know that" the poet asks Pound. He asks this into Pound's anti-Semitism and his admiration for

Mussolini and fascist thought, into a darkness that, despite his affection for the poet, has made this aspect of Pound utterly intolerable to him. The memory of Oppen burying his dog-tag, with its "H" for Hebrew, in the war rubble of Alsace cannot be erased from the constellation of memories surrounding Pound, his old mentor and champion. It is the poem's pivot. "*I must get out of here/Father* he thinks *father*," Oppen exclaims, as though he were the ever-endangered son of a despotic monarch. No wonder 'The Lighthouses,' dedicated to Louis Zukofsky, who holds a position (mentor, encourager) similar to Pound's, plays out its poetics across the ambiguous and ambivalent territory of male parentage: "*saying yes* in loyalty to all fathers or joy of escape from all my fathers."

If my own experience of George makes me see him as that "article of faith" rather than as another escaped son of a literary father, it is at least partly due to his own poetics. It is not about feedback from a beloved poet, but about finding in his words the formula of one's own longing. George himself seems to understand the nature of this self-work—it too has its painful and powerful emotions, as I sense them in the end of his letter to Harvey Shapiro which occurs on the same page of *The Selected Letters of George Oppen* as one of his early letters to me:

> What one wants, to know what one wants, to move toward it—What is it? Fear or loss of oneself as one knows himself, is familiar with himself? ? 'Fusion of subject and object' where all is acted upon? I don't know I suppose fear's a great part of our lives I don't know
>
> George

Fear would not necessarily be the motive for anyone's poetry, but the experience of it could be salutary—it gave an ethics to the writing. George's dislike of *a prioris*, of mechanized schemes of composition, of blithely letting some formula work its will, lay in part because it seemed to eliminate risk from the process. Possibly it is too simple to say necessity ruled over 'art' or logorrhea, but I believe this was what George communicated to me.

Certainly, as expressed in his work and letters, this essentially conservatory stance (though stance already seems too fixed for the openness and even wiliness of George's maneuvering through a poem) was ever-present: "New arts! Dithyrambic, audience-as-artists!/But I will listen to a man, I will listen to a man, and when I/speak, I will speak...." It lay at the core of our correspondence, which is why our letters did not focus on how to be a poet. That is we rarely discussed issues of technique or publishing. The question we both addressed was some version of why should one be a poet at all.

George is, of course, one of the great self-questioners of contemporary poetry. In his return letter of early December, 1971, it was he, my "article of faith" and by then supremely important to me, who wrote back: "not sure what is getting accomplished—in poor shape to pontificate." This thread of doubt is a constant of the letters and of the work, a tremendously important thread. There was *always*—how to say this—in an authoritative sense, George's own uncertainty. It was his ground, the wonder, as he put it, that "there is something to stand on." Embedded in his letters, this ground that is almost no ground provides a foundational model or prototype not only for my relating to George but to his poetry, perhaps to all serious writing I ever encounter.

Let me explain. I had received this letter from George while in a very complicated state of mind, halfway between deciding to continue writing poetry and abandoning it (I would never have given up on reading it). My central question to him was: "is it a poetry that one writes?" And he answered me as follows:

> this is, of course the question one MUST not attempt to answer or think of answering, this is what is wrong with all the 'courses' is it not? The question: 'is it a poetry that one writes?' is the question not to answer
>
> Is it a poetry that one writes? Don't answer
>
> Is it a poetry that one <u>writes</u>? alright: one's typewriter and one's desk could answer this.
>
> and this can sustain discussion: the act of writing

Oppen's work—the exemplary figure of integrity and endless questioning he represented—was in itself the open-ended answer to what I had asked, one which I explore in the many essays I've written about him, most concentratedly in my *Speaking the Estranged: Essays on the Work of George Oppen.*

In the late fall of 1971, I had picked up a book by the critic Erich Heller (no relation), *The Disinherited Mind,* and it left a powerful, confirmatory impression on my mind, especially concerning the thoughts that were flowing between me and George in our letters. In December I wrote to him:

I think you touch the whole of it [the emotional impulse in the making of the poem], that staying in anguish and not in shame, which is the burden—for to move into shame is to pass the judgment that you have not accounted for what you could, and so falsified the thing. For the artist now, I suspect, as Erich Heller puts it: "Uncertainty alone is ineluctably real." Hence the simultaneity of the pulse and the dread of the pulse in rebeginning.

George wrote back:

Your namesake's sentence also very fine These things, these things that can sometimes be said ! the direct feel of living replacing the abstract 'soul.' And finds, thereby, the soul. The love of the world. (Could one imagine, as the first moment in the history of the sacred, not personification of the known, but the imagination of the first moment at which object become [sic] object: among sensations, object—)

"The love of the world." The "first moment in the history of the sacred:" what George communicated to me in these words, among the articles of his faith, were pressures, not to try to write like him, but to seek the depth of realizations in language that he sought. They were words so earned by Oppen in his life and work that they seemed immune to criticism. One approached them worshipfully, even warily, because to pursue them was constantly challenging to the way you thought about life or the work you did.

* * *

I don't want to give the impression that all we wrote each other were ponderous thoughts on the fate of poetry, though these words were no doubt the most formative texts of my life as a poet. There was much irony and much self-deprecatory humor on George's part. In an undated and unpublished letter to me, he speaks of

the academic environs, the iron maidens in which or with which you break bread: yes, I realize the problem   How to escape, how to escape, for 'out there'

among the greasers and the new which is becoming less new
Bohemia
things is rough too   Not rough, but weary

He goes on to repeat some lines of Zukofsky:

My home is where I hang my hat
My head is my home,

Zuk's joke. Spoiled now by the rarity of hats. But the only answer is?

'S' in the hat, keed."

I think George meant 'A', the letter closest to 'S' on the keyboard, the title of Zukofsky's epic poem.

George could make wonderfully incisive comments on his working conditions, as in one letter he wrote, scribbling in the margins to me: "forgive the script. working in a very temporary small shack in dense fog from an island in Penobscot bay" (unpublished letter to MH, early 1970s).

His attentiveness to place and his sense of where the culture was going, which fed into his poetry, also marked his letters. He invited me to visit in San Francisco:

it's a pretty place… tho—well, it's tearing itself apart for one reason or other like the rest of the country. Puritanism replaced by a strange viciousness without pleasure—a freedom of sexuality which is an attack on sexuality, etc. etc—Maybe strangest here on this very pretty bay and the mountains across the bay—
It's a pleasanter place than most cities, I meant to say, and still and still: all these people desperately eager to board the sinking ship—well, it's reasonable they want to be 'in the swim'—how else but from a sinking ship
Me? I'm the ancient mariner Tied round the albatross's neck. That half-witted bird.

There are many more passages in his letters than I could cite here.

* * *

Going over the correspondence allows many memories to surface, but it also prompts an impulse to explore Oppen as an exemplum, *the* article of faith in the ongoing arena of contemporary American poetry that I have looked up to over all these years.

We might imagine these last seventy or eighty years of poetry writing in America as being a time-space continuum filling an area between one of Zukofsky's *summa* signs in 'A,' that mathematical symbol he uses to define poetry with its famous "lower limit speech," "upper limit music." Let us imagine the summa sign at this moment in time bracketing what I would call the *task* of poetry (Zukofsky himself referred to the poem as a "job" of having a "job of work" to do). The honor code of 'An Objective' written in 1931, defined the task of poetry for its period; it sits next to the lower limit of the summa sign. And something like Oppen's more recent thoughts about poetry, his comments in the *Daybook* for instance, a product of the 1950s and '60s, may mark its upper limit.

Take for example how Oppen, writing late in his life, qualifies Zukofsky's thought in 'An Objective' of "thinking with things as they exist." In his *Daybook*, George notes that "what concerns the artist is that the thing exists—and he starts with a ruined language *day by day and then by man, destroyed* achieves language." By "ruined language" Oppen means the linguistic environment in which we are now immersed in the public sphere, in politics, culture, media, the arts, but also in the private sphere, in an everyday life sapped of "truth-value" by the depredations of technology and corrupted word-usage. In between the two, the Objectivist honor code was operating for George, not as prescription but rather like a shield, a code that, if it were kept in mind, would enable its adherents to write poetry and yet keep safe from the pitfalls of "style" and mannerism. George's decision to abandon poetry rather than write "socialist realist" verse is a case in point.

This code, this stance, embodied in him, has gone through numerous tests and tribulations, not only of aesthetic thinking in literary circles but in culture and politics as well. One way of looking at his thought is how it encompasses the fate of the Objectivist impulse as it moves through enormous times (and time's enormities). George's "ruined language" I believe describes the arena of modernist and contemporary poetry, an arena the Objectivist poets were especially sensitive to, and it is this sensitivity most of all that distinguishes them from their mainstream or 'establishment' contemporaries in modern American poetry and, more subtly, from the avant-garde or experimental wing of that group.

For me (and it is why I return again and again to him), it is the problem of language, of its corruptions that brings him to the rescue from the entangled dilemmas of form. For it is Oppen who places all of Zukofsky's hopes for form, for "thinking with things as they exist" under the signs of fear and uncertainty. He is the mountain climber up the rocky arduous pathway of Objectivist honor—it's not just thinking, it's not just seeking out a method for him—his is the work of constant testing and re-testing of every word, of every motive for its use, recasting and recasting again, along with an almost obsessive recursiveness in which passages and phrases from already written poems and letters and re-readings get tried out once more. For Oppen, that "ruined language" of mankind is a gauntlet, a test of every imaginable trait that a poet can embody. I think of Duncan's "I make poetry like other men make war" as sympathetic statement.

It is the passage of time, the sense that culture and society are in "ruins " that animate the poems. Oppen gave up poetry to help workers: he lived through the Depression, found his home in razed cities, studied the depredations of politics from the Romans to the present, returned to poetry. His thematics are tested and co-exist within a Dantean landscape of the frozen, solidified lowest depths of a contemporary hell, its stasis, its moral and psychic entropy, its stifling absence of risk or imagination.

* * *

[early to mid-September 1977]

Dear Michael,

—couldn't deal with New York—Dazed by the wreckage
—afraid to look back at my Of Being Numerous. Couldn't have written it now—we've become alien (alien to streets in Brooklyn where we knew, I think, almost everyone in every apartment Alien then, no doubt, in that we had lines of retreat open to us that we never admitted—and now perhaps their revenge. And where are we? As the walls fall

….

I'm sorry we missed you.

George had struck me as, in a particular sense, our quintessential urban poet, not so much because an urban landscape was often one of the major scenic elements of his poems. In fact, much of the poetry beautifully renders the seascapes of Maine and California, the open spaces of light and air, the cosmology of the white space of the piece of paper before him. What is 'urban' about the poetry is its registration of every nuance and shock of the sociocultural, political and artistic milieu in which we live. Its gods or demons throng the space of composition as though the poet's desk were being carried through a city mob that jostled and cajoled, threatened or seduced him on all sides. Oppen not only lived through the Depression, World War II, knowledge of the Shoah, Vietnam, Altamont and Woodstock and the actualities of political assassination, he had also been a participant, a worker, a Party member, a soldier, a writer. "Dazed," in the incipience of his later illness, replaced his "lured by the dazzle." His flight from New York was a signal to me.

I saw him last in New York City when he and Mary traveled to the city to be tape-recorded reading his poetry—a bizarre coming full circle for me, since the recording session was held at Harvey Shapiro's house where I first met George. Only this time he was without strength, mentally as well as physically. The taping was interrupted every few minutes so that he could lie down and recover himself. It appeared that he had lost the power to meet the very contingencies and impingements upon him that were the source of his work. I saw what lay in that strange claim in the letter above of having become "alien."

Like the "bright incredible light" in his poem 'The Forms of Love.' Oppen's work expresses the space and articulation of poetry as a kind of surrounding love, that for an instant the loved world and the poem's world could be a simultaneity. The arena in which love or desire are worked out, then, involves a kind of alertness that transforms the usual ironic distance of poetry into an embracing spaciousness in which thing and fact can stand by themselves.

All my encounters with George insisted on a subtext or grounding in an ethics of tact, of apartness and solitude. Letters, with their simultaneous feel for companionship and distance, seemed the perfect medium for conveying that grounding. "What will one ask" he wrote me in an undated letter, and answered himself in his powerful and inimitable way: "The benevolence of the real."

DANTEAN REZNIKOFF

The Poems of Charles Reznikoff 1918–1975. Edited by Seamus Cooney.
A Black Sparrow Book. Boston: David R. Godine, 2005.

Here, in profile, is Reznikoff complete:

> *March 1, 1930*
>
> *Marie,*
> *I am on the way to your house, and have stopped at the post-office*
> *at 169ᵗʰ St, to write you a note. There is nothing new, and I am just*
> *going to copy*
>
>> *The fog lifted; the tops of the buildings stood out against the*
>> *blue sky,*
>> *And in the street a thousand automobiles speeding toward*
>> *New York were shining*

And then, a bit further down in his letter:

> *Here is the restaurant window that I have been threatening you with:*
>
>> *The store had been a restaurant, but had been empty for months.*
>> *In the window there was still a dusty sign "All kinds of Soft*
>> *Drinks for Sale";*
>> *Bottles of "near" beer and soda had been grouped in a pattern*
>> *about the rubber plant.*
>> *This had been taken away, and all that was left was a leaf,*
>> *tightly curled*
>> *In two shades of brown, the darker brown spreading from the*
>> *middle like a stain.*

The 'poem' continues, describing the burst or missing bottles seen behind
the glass, and then we get to the vision culled like a gleaner from the
scene:

"And whatever design might have been it was no more.
A bit of dark was also on the oil-cloth, covered by a grey
fungus of delicate hairs.

I am sorry," the poet writes, *"that I haven't a beautiful bit of verse to send*
at present.

Charles"

Everything is quite clear, from the impulse to share a perception, that
"shining" of momentary beauty to the darker adventure of discovery in
the restaurant window, that slight feeling of the eye's wandering here, then
there, until it forces something like a conclusion in language ("whatever
design… was no more"). Mission accomplished, but then that half-apology,
half-the-way-it-is truth to the woman he loves, this is how the world is, at
least today. Most days, if one surveys Reznikoff's entire corpus.

For Reznikoff is a secular-Jewish Dante writing after the fires of
the Inferno, the punishing fires fueled by a judgmental god, have been
banked. Like Pound, he is without a religious "Aquinas map," certainly
without the divine authority that hovers over *Leviticus* or the rabbinic
sages. There are few mentions of Dante in Reznikoff's work. And I don't
mean to suggest that Dante is a model or even a serious source book for
the poet. Rather, the central attitude and approach of Dante's *The Divine
Comedy* are also Reznikoff's. In his letters to Marie Syrkin, his wife, there
are two mentions of Dante, one of which strikes me as significant, his
citing from the *Inferno* of "the river of blood, canto XII." The important
lines for him were probably these: "The river of blood, wherein are
boiling those/who live by violence, and on others' fears" (lines 47/48 in
Laurence Binyon's translation). For Reznikoff's seemingly self-imposed
task has been to give voice to those who have suffered the violence, who
have lived in fear. His scope is epical, but necessarily of a different order.
Some time before the French *annalistes*, he made a habit of seeing history
from the ground up, from the point of view of its victims rather than its
makers. Even his reworking of Biblical material is often bottom to top:

As when a great tree, bright with blossoms and heavy with fruit,
is cut down and its seeds are carried far
by the winds of the sky and the waves of the streams and seas....

Out of the strong, sweetness;
and out of the dead body of the lion of Judah,

the prophecies and the psalms;
out of the slaves of Egypt,
out of the wandering tribesmen of the deserts
and the peasants of Palestine,
out of the slaves of Babylon and Rome...
out of the greatly wronged...

Contra Pound, he follows to where the idea has its consequences in ordinary lives, but also, if I may slip for a moment into jargon, follows to where, "the action is" when one has political leaders who exhibit an undramatic if highly dangerous banality.

Our new hell is cold, secular, and, in the linguistic sense, uninflected. For large-scale heroes and villains, the aristocrats and mad kings of Shakespeare's plays or the neurotic nobility of the Jacobins, the use of highly figured language seems apt. But now a Barthesian "writing degree zero" of almost anonymous victims and oppressors obtains. The steamroller of history or the mass death of civilians in war, in holocausts, genocides and plagues, seem to require a different register.

To play with metaphor or to whomp up a style or aesthetic is to indicate a belief in the effectiveness either of the "new" or in the effectiveness of literature itself. Literature *is* "effective," but at times, its only power comes from the act of leaving its language alone, even to itself, thus allowing it to work as the instrument of witnessing. The "work" of literature, then, in the present is to return or, better, to strive forward toward a certain clarity, to transmute figural power into something like rhetoric, to take up the rhythms of the body and mind as argument before delight. Osip Mandelstam, in his 'Conversation about Dante,' hints at a formula that could be applied to Reznikoff's poetics, to his constant city walking:

> Both the *Inferno* and, in particular, the *Purgatorio*, glorify the human gait, the measure and the rhythm of walking, the footstep and its form. The step, linked with breathing and saturated with thought, Dante understood as the beginning of prosody.

In Dante, Mandelstam says,

> a composition is formed not as a result of accumulated particulars, but due to the fact that one detail after another is torn away from the object, leaves it, darts out, or is chipped away from the system

to go out into a new functional space or dimension, but each time at a strictly regulated moment and under circumstances which are sufficiently ripe and unique.

Here is Reznikoff chipping away:

A row of tenements, windows boarded up;
an empty factory, windows broken;
a hillside of dead leaves, dead weeds,
old newspapers and rusted cans.
Now come a group
in old clothes and broken shoes
who say politely,
The way, sir? If you don't mind
tell us
the way, please.

Reznikoff's eye, his Virgil, moves left to right as he walks through the streets of New York, a kind of touch and go of images, now this, then that, none lingered over for very long—the cadence of the activity forming the layout of his pages. And then, in the poem above, that sudden encounter and question, "tell us the way, please." When Dante asks a tormented X banished to one of the *malebolgias*, why are you here?, the character answers back, and gives as reason the sin he has committed in life. But here in Reznikoff's dead weed lot, it is the Xs who ask the question, who rather than have an answer, can find no reason in their lives for the fate that has befallen them.

Modern suffering has almost no "design" of punishments and rewards, and the only holiness (if that is the word) to be achieved comes via the attentive witness. Recording takes precedence over making; it can be likened to the act of the saint or bodhisattva, or to the Talmudist's insistence on living for others. One's own salvation or enlightenment is put off for the saving of other people. The artist puts off the self-display, the novelizing trick because what he or she has to say must be rendered with straightforwardness.

Reznikoff's verse continually registers contemporary life, and its forces which seem, in equal measure, to be power and indifference, and, for the victims of these forces, confusion and pain. "Whatever design might have been was no more" he exclaims in his poem-letter of the deserted shop window that he has written to Marie above.

As with Dante, among the most powerful sources of knowledge for Reznikoff is contemplation of the dead. *Holocaust* and *Testimony* are Reznikoff's major threnodies, major *Infernos*, but one can look back to the very beginnings in such early works as *Rhythms* and *Rhythms II* and discern the pattern of the poet's thought. In *Rhythms*, nine of its nineteen numbers speak specifically of the "dead." Loss, chaos, an unresponding world, *i.e.* a world acting as though it were dead to the poet, typify many of the remaining ten numbers. Only numbers, 15, 16 and 17, those relating to an idealized female figure (Marie Syrkin, Reznikoff's wife as a Beatrice figure?) break with the tone.

Rhythms II is the sequence that clearly establishes much of Reznikoff's mode. Here, the technique moves from the literary to the near-documentary, from making to recording. But, one should not be naïve about "recording." What does seem to be happening is that the source of poetry for Reznikoff is less the bookshelf than the sidewalk, that the movement into the street is a revelation, a movement from the temples of literature and religious belief. Norman Finkelstein in his essay, 'Reznikoff's Tradition and Modernity,' notes that Reznikoff, a secular, *i.e.*, "fallen" Jew, finds his "faith" not in religion but in "history." And it is poetry, Finkelstein continues, that "rescues history from mere facticity."

Reznikoff defined himself as a "writer of verse," and it must be the meaning of "turn" in the word "verse" that brings the work closer to an implicit narrative than simply "accumulated particulars." With every eye movement and every coordinated step, Reznikoff makes a weave; his intelligence and moral bearing wrap the lines into meaning, neither that of the snapshots of Imagism nor that of Zukofskian word play. If, as Oppen and others have suggested, Reznikoff's poems have often gone unnoticed and unremarked because in their completeness there is no need to explicate them or to turn them over to the ministrations of the academy, it is still the duty of the critic to say how they work and what constitutes the sense of completeness they exhibit. Robert Alter, in *The Necessary Angel*, his study of Benjamin and Scholem, discusses the Judaic notion of the world's intelligibility, an idea that led both writers toward their sometime conflicting theorizing about language. One passage from Alter in particular, however, strikes me as directly applicable to the writings of Reznikoff:

> The world in which we find ourselves has an ultimate, though also ultimately inscrutable, semantic power: something is always 'in the process of appearing' *from the ground of being* that imposes

itself on us with the sheer force of its validity, even if it finally has no safely construable significance.

I can think of no other poet who is as true to those appearances as Reznikoff. To borrow a phrase from Zukofsky's *Bottom*, one that Zukofsky applied to Shakespeare, the sense of completeness that we experience in reading Reznikoff involves a thoroughly "inexpressible trust of expression."

And so we are watching this walker, this poet who more and more resembles a Jewish Dante. He moves through the city, through its suburbs, and his rhythms, as Mandelstam insisted of Dante, are those of his steps, of his eye's transit through worlds and peoples. Sight governs because, as he writes to his friend Albert Lewin, "our eyes are simply more attentive than our ears."

And like Dante, Reznikoff is witness to both the damned and to the saved. It has become a critical cliché to call Reznikoff a "serial" poet, but, of course, this term adds little to our understanding of his work. Rather, it places him in the company and in the tradition of poets he had no use for, and to know that he started and stopped poems, that he separated them by numbers or spaces is enough, but to call him a "serial" poet turns his work from poetry into academic labeltry. Clearly, he is the continuous eye, and the numbered breaks in his poems signal the raisings of his foot from the ground, the blinks of his eye-lid, and the need to refer back to the sky above him or the ground over which he traverses. Here is section IV from 'Epitaphs:'

The water is freezing in straight lines across the ripples;
the ice is so thin the brown leaves
are seen moving along underneath;
the wheels of the automobiles hiss
on the wet pavement;
the bridge has become only a few lines in pencil
on the grey sky—
even lines made by rule and compass.
The street curves in and out, up and down
in great waves of asphalt;
at night the granite tomb is noisy with starlings
like the creaking of many axles;
only the tired walker knows how much there is to climb;
how the sidewalk curves into the cold wind.

Everywhere he feels the urge to mark off where a phenomenon ends so as to be able to render it. Reznikoff, in a 1932 letter to Lewin, divides his work up into poetry and prose, poetry is: "the vertical… the moment, the as/is: if possible from the top of the sky to the bottom of the earth. For that my instrument is the poem—and of course I rarely succeed. But I try to write some verse every day, to keep whatever skill I have—for which I don't give a damn—and, above all, the seeing eye, 'the haiku spirit.'"

One finds this "haiku spirit" everywhere in Reznikoff as a complex brevity, lying somewhere between the eye's register and the semi-breathlessness of the walker who has something to tell us (Mandelstam, in his Dante essay, remarks that Dante thought the "teacher is younger than the pupil" for he has to run faster. Here is number 7 from Reznikoff's early collection, *Poems*:

> The house-wreckers have left the door and a staircase,
> now leading to the empty room of night.

No crowded metro, no petals on a wet, black bough, but rather out of a surround of lath and plaster, an ingathering of breath and then a rendering in accord with the deep loneliness of the observer who sees where the inhabitants once were and ramifies the vacancy to an almost cosmic level. As Mandelstam says of Dante, Reznikoff is a creator of impulses rather than forms. Perhaps one could tease out an ambivalence in Reznikoff, borne out of the biblical Jewish injunction against the graven image, for isn't Reznikoff's lightness of touch the result of the need to testify and to record, and yet to not bow down or serve via the image?

Which is why, in keeping with the idea of the impulse, even of impulsiveness, Reznikoff's fascination is rarely trance-like or obsessive. Rather, it is part of his tact to allow the reader to see what he sees but yet give space to that reader for judging and even making sense of what has been rendered. For "explanation" then, I would identify Reznikoff as a poet imbricated in the physiology of walking, in the feeling, which we find quite common, of being drawn to hesitate, to look at something charged with interest, and then being almost driven off by either a sense of capture, of completion—that "haiku effect"—or by the psychic pressures of what has been seen. Among his contemporaries, he is the lightest of poets and also, in certain ways, the deepest. Perhaps the most Jewish and most Dantesque aspect of his writing is his utter trust in his readers to see what is really there, to see something that is not his or their self-invention.

FIGHT FOR AN ILLUSION:
H.D.'S *HELEN IN EGYPT*, POUND'S *CANTOS* AND THE MASQUES OF MYTH AND HISTORY

Modernity is not so much a condition as a strategy, one of the ways out, as a Sartre might quip, for geniuses or at least intelligent minds in difficult cases. Both *Helen in Egypt* (in fact almost all of H.D.'s so-called post-Imagist work) and Pound's *Cantos* contain war-machine gestures, simultaneously defensive and aggressive, as they try to break the holds of restraining traditions, both aesthetic and cultural, and manifest new poetic dynamics.

So let me begin with my word "masque," recalling its use in the charged atmospherics of the aristocratic court, as both an act of projection and, with the artificiality of its distancing effects, an act of camouflage. A number of definitions swirl around the term, from its Wikipedia description as a "deferential allegory flattering to the patron," to, as *The New Princeton Encyclopedia of Poetry and Poetics* explains it, a dramatic attempt at "bringing divinity and royalty together," consisting of "representations more emblematic than mimetic," the "soul" of which according to Ben Jonson is its "themes and words." The authors and critics of "epic" works like *The Cantos* and *Helen in Egypt* may see them as enacting a mimesis, but given their theatrical dramatic structure and hallucinatory power, it strikes me that to see them as masques, as "emblematic" rather than "mimetic," makes them more comprehensible. We/they are perhaps the flattered reader/patrons of these works.

The two poems, as the *Princeton Encyclopedia* claims of the masque, "explore in a quasi-mystical way the sources and conditions of power." In both works, elements of myth and history become allegorical figures: they no longer 'represent' themselves but, wearing the masks of their enlisted duties, enter into dances and arabesques with the poets who deploy them,. If in Pound, the emphasis is on history and in H.D. on myth, in both cases the overt content of the appropriation is subverted to the desire, not of history-making, but of prophecy and visions of the "good" society.

So first to Pound whose *Cantos*, which have already generated mountains of critical attention, serve, for my purposes, as an exceptionally convenient foil to H.D.'s poem. In the *Cantos*, it is the progression of great men who emblematize artistic, social and economic power, whose representation is in the service of moral and political instruction. The way to a terrestrial paradise is through the examples of Malatesta, Mussolini, etc. Pound's loss of "his Aquinas map" leads to the plundering of culture and to the citational modalities of *The Cantos*. Yet, despite its immense hoard of sources and poetic techniques, the poem remains resolutely monological, as though Pound's "repeat in history" were the only repeat. Kenner describes this as Pound's "await [ing] with a vigilance of his own the exact events that will enter his purpose without modification." And Richard Sieburth writes of the poet in 'In Pound We Trust: The Economy of Poetry/The Poetry of Economics,' "language serves not to create meaning but to carry or convey or 'get across' antecedent facts or meanings or values." Pound subscribes, says Sieburth, "to the totalitarian plenum which institutes an absolute continuum among the signs of the natural, political and economic world, thus guaranteeing both the order and representation of order." The figures of Pound's pantheon are not people—we are not encouraged to wonder about their psychology, their hopes and fears, their doubts—rather, they are the characters of the masques, symbolizing, emblematizing, creating the dance of the plenum, "guaranteeing" the divinity and power by which Pound wishes the world were ordered.

And yet, in the same breath as I write this, I'm aware, as with many critics, how much the *Cantos* sometimes seems a poem divided against itself, especially in the preternaturally beautiful and often deeply moving *Pisan Cantos* in which Pound's remembrances of friends and lovers (H.D, for example, his "lynx" and "Dryad"), his focus on natural objects, "*la vespa,*" the cats, the landscapes, the cut of the language by which these are rendered, all either temper or resist our knowledge of the often brutal political systems Pound had embraced, and, despite the presumed air of confession and repentance in the poetry, continued to embrace. In Pound, this complicated (and to many, compromised) vision is in the form of a catenary, an unbroken series of links from the past to the present that not only shows, as Benjamin saw in modernity, an implacable, judgmental "immemorial gaze," but exposes—in fact indirectly claims for the poem—an "antiquity."

As Paul Morrison writes in his *Poetics of Fascism*, "Pound's commitment to a poetics of proper names (following Aristotle) [is] in opposition to an ethos of metaphorical displacement." "Proper names"—and here I allude to my own poetics—are quite different from a poetics of naming. The former, especially under Pound's regime of the "direct treatment of the thing," become already fixed historical entities, filling the poem, as Morrison insists with "so much inert subject matter." Inert because with Pound the proper name forms part of an argument rather than an interrogation. Names constitute the array of antiquity: museum captions turned into maxims.

A superficial typology perhaps might classify *Helen in Egypt* with Pound's *Cantos*. H.D. herself may have toyed with the idea or at least thought the ambition of the *Cantos* must be matched by her own effort. But her *Helen in Egypt*, by contrast, while in many respects also a work of cultural theft and appropriation, shows forth its uncertainty, not only between its versions of the Helen story but in the malleability of its project of *mythos* itself. And while its surface, triadic stanza upon stanza, seems formally regulated in contrast to *The Cantos*, it conjures myth and myth-as-history as dynamic illusion.

Helen in Egypt was written in part, perhaps subliminally, as a response to Pound's work, since its genesis occurs in the time frame in which H.D. devotes serious attention to the *Cantos*. The result is sometimes not favorable. In her prose diary-meditation *Compassionate Friendship*, begun in 1955, she describes picking up a small collection of the *Cantos* and finding herself

> lazy and I have not the power to concentrate and my own rhythms run in my head. There is beauty in every paragraph or stanza or page, somewhere, a dynamic, indissoluble beauty. The world and time are blasted, dynamited, shattered.... But long ago, I stepped out of the track of this particular whirlwind, this psychic landslide.

Nevertheless, both works do have some material in common, mythic gods and heroes, the poets and mythmakers who celebrated them and a deep feel for the language and cultures of the originals. But while Pound's poem is "presentational," *i.e.*, makes an argument that allows virtually no speculation, H.D.'s poem seems to make almost no argument, placing us instead in an endless mirrored hall of possibilities. The masque here is less processional, less conclusive, and far more dance-like, with interrelations between its figures complicated by issues of proximity, psychic attitude and pose. Any scene of instruction is temporary, replaced by another equally temporary. If patriarchal Pound wants to order men and their affairs, H.D. wants a looser freedom from men and their business of war and revenge and their domination of woman.

H.D.'s difficulties were many. In the war- and post-war years leading up to *Helen in Egypt*, they included living through the Blitz and the ongoing conflict, her fragile state of physical and mental health, personal disappointments such as those with Lord Dowding allegorized in *Majic Ring* and *The Sword Went Out to Sea*, and finally there were her concerns about the direction of career and work. At the same time, these years were richly productive, first came *Trilogy*, and then a great rush of prose and fiction, *The Gift*, *Tribute to Freud* and other works poured forth. Yet, as H.D. confessed to Norman Holmes Pearson, who had for several years been prompting her to write more poetry, the beginning sections of *Helen in Egypt* were the first poems she had written in five years.

The entire work, over 300 pages in length, was produced between 1952 and 1955; she received her publisher's copy the day before she died, on September 27, 1961. It consists of three major divisions, each broken into a number of "books," 'Pallinode,' 'Leuké' and 'Eidolon,' each containing a number of sections comprising cadenced tercets that are irregular in line length and beats. Above each section is a prose caption in italics. These were written and incorporated as part of the text as a result of H.D.'s experience in recording the poem for reproduction on disk. H.D. had used prose passages in both her 'Hymen' sequence of 1921 and in her translation of Euripides's *Ion* in 1936. But in 'Hymen' they are used to choreograph the poem, while in *Ion*, they are "explanatory," offering a poetics and a meditation on Greek drama. In *Helen in Egypt*, the captions and the poetry echo and intermix like two mountaineers speaking across a deep gorge to each other. Phrases bounce off the texts and rebound, only to become lodged in both, the source or origin unclear, so that the whole enterprise of the "epic" is suffused with an uncertainty that is foreign not only to the usual epic narration but especially to the Poundian assurance of voice and name.

Helen in Egypt is also a coded, hence emblematic autobiography, the stage for a confrontation (is it a battle?) between masculine will to power and a will not quite easily definable as feminine or feminist, because, if it has a project of ordering the world, that comes via a hope for peace and the powers of the imagination to offer up alternative realities. The "illusion" it resists is that woman causes war, that this war over beauty and sex, is both noble *and* evil, inevitable and, as with the Trojan war, ruinous. Instead H.D. proffers another "illusion," meant to be understood as illusion, even as its source materials, Stesichorus's poem (and then Euripides) substitute their illusions for the Homeric one. Stesichorus's example, blinded by his indulgence of the Homeric version, then restored to sightedness by moving Helen to Egypt although her eidolon remains on the walls of Troy, is the ur-motivation for H.D.'s vision: the war was "fought for an illusion."

H.D's re-imagining, seen in the potential of its largest context, is directed at the overthrow or breaking up of, if I may borrow from Blake, the "mind-forged manacles" of the basic roots and tenets of western civilization. In *Palimpsest* (1926), what H.D. is fighting against is made clear on page 1 of 'Hipparchia: War Rome', when the narrator Hipparchia, conjuring a poet, one of her "eternal Greeks," comments "I think differently but what does it matter? *That* poem, Marius, is religion." Writing heresy to that religion is H.D.'s intention. Her poem then is also something of an attack on the methods by which we process the products of the imagination and on the extent to which consciousness is mythic. For the poet's consciousness to hew too closely to myth is to make it iron-bound in its traces and basically unalterable, doomed to formulate and reformulate an eternal recurrence or in Pound's words to enact "the repeat in history.". In this transformative view, *Helen in Egypt* stands alongside Simone Weil's 'Poem of Force,' but H.D.'s poem also liberates—opens up might be more accurate, or interrogates the whole arenas of thought concerning what culture and society might be.

How does the poem work? The most obvious, at the macro level, is some admixture of apposition and opposition. Two versions of a story, one out of Homer, a baseline cultural datum, the other, making for a kind of interference in the transmission modes of that datum, are juxtaposed within the same work. There's more than a shimmer of instability, a rich, complex shimmer, because we never lose sight of either version—they begin, after a few sections of the poem, to interpenetrate each other. Yet *this is a poem*, the work shouts; nothing is exactly true. Even the autobiography underlining the motifs is subject to a poetics of role-playing, revisions and psychoanalytic scrutiny.

On a more micro-level, each section rather than furthering the narrative, as in a traditional epic, proposes a conflict. The captions, with lines and phrases repeated in the poetry below it, create echoes; they are not meant to clarify or explain. Thus, for example, in 'Pallinode,' the caption of section 8 of Book 3 begins: *But still Helen wants "some simple answer." She feels that Achilles can give it to her....* And the first tercet of the poem reads:

"Were you rapt in prayer?"
"no, Achilles, I wanted some simple answer
to your question";

"my question?"
"which was the dream";
"I asked you which was the veil;

the sea roads lie between
you and the answer";
"you called me Helena":

At least three questions and a confusion of who is speaking mark the poetic passage. Is the Helena, the Helen of the Trojan walls, as the caption suggestions? When Achilles seems to apologize for the impulsive leap to that false conclusion, it seems he also leaps out of character and admits: "I was afraid." The Helen who is in Egypt seems to transform him, which, as the caption indicates, transforms "all-history, bringing into question 'Fate, Death, Reintegration, Resurrection?'" Again, those key terms are followed by a question mark, as though emphasizing their instability.

Let me give another example: H.D. writes in the caption of section 8 of book 5 of 'Pallinode:' "*Helen compares Clytaemnestra and Iphigenia to 'one swan and one signet' who "must forget war and its consequences—but no, there is this yet, unresolved—without war, there would have been no Achilles, no 'Star in the night.'"* The poetry related to these lines reads as follows:

Have you ever seen a swan,
when you threaten its nest—
two swans, but she was alone,

who was never alone;
the wings of an angry swan
can compass the earth,

can drive the demons
back to Tartarus,
can measure heaven in their span;

one swan and one cygnet
were stronger than all the host,
assembled upon the slopes...

Clytaemnestra is made male by H.D., perhaps because she takes matters into her own hand, slaying Agamemnon, after he has tricked away Iphigenia with a fake marriage offer so that she can be sacrificed and enable the Greek fleet to sail to the Trojan war. Yet this is a double-sided revenge; it initiates war and establishes the figure of Achilles, the warrior, who in the polyvalence of the poem, is both cruelty personified and love object, one that Helen must create and recreate, illusion transformed into illusion:

I must wait, I must wonder again
at the fate that has brought me here;

surely she must forget,
she must forget the past,
and I must forget Achilles...

_____

...but never the ember
born of his strange attack,
never his anger,

never the fire,
never the brazier,
never the Star in the night.

* * *

There are many passages of the poem that work this kind of magic. What sorts of endings do we have here? Pound saw his world collapse around him. His "antiquity" had been still-born in nightmare, in the corpses of Europe, in the dead bodies of Mussolini and his mistress hanging by their heels in Milan, in the ever-constant stream of visitors to St. Elizabeth, some to try to understand, some to pay homage, some to reinforce a dark vision out of ruins. One of them, John Kasper, as virulent a proto-Nazi and anti-Semite as one could imagine, must have driven the old poet to both hope and distraction with his plots and dreams. James Laughlin reports that Pound had a food-taster, like a dotty old Roman aristocrat, fearing an enemy's poison.

"Antiquity" never happened for H. D, or at least it was a work in progress, not the fixity it had been for Pound. "Fear nothing of the future or the past," she writes in the draft of the first section of the poem, which she sent to Norman Holmes Pearson in 1952. *Helen in Egypt* is situated directly on the seam of past and future time. As Horace Gregory notes in his Introduction, the poem "infused with the action and memory of an ancient past ... exists within the mutations of the present tense." Pound was sure of his history, secure in it, in its rightness. H.D. acknowledged the tensions that inhabited her very being, the clash of visions within herself. Her project, with its minuet of myths, its midstream combining and recombining of partners, each exposed by the plasticity of their torn-away masks, seems, in its very uncertainty and ambiguity, to lay a simultaneous claim to the ground of both romanticism's freedom and modernism's strategic perception of the loss of the archaic. This was a conflict she embraced within her own materials, fighting for the present and yet envisioning it to be eternal. "Is it true, I wonder," she wrote, "that the only way to escape war is to be in it?"

THE *WAR* OF POETRY: DUNCAN'S HERESIES

In relation to each [Zukofsky and Olson] I was to be heretical—for in the face of Zukofsky's stripping to the essentials, I was working toward a proliferation of meanings; and in the face of Olson's drive toward the primordial roots, I was working from interpretations of the text.
—*A Selected Prose*, 138.

This declaration by Robert Duncan is only one of the ways that the poet sought to express the nature of his heresy, one that takes numerous shapes and is staged in the light of the condition we find ourselves in, as he puts it in his Preface to *Bending the Bow* (1968), amidst the "last days of our history," in our need "to defend a form that our very defense corrupts. We cannot rid ourselves of the form to which we now belong."

The collective "we" of Duncan's statement implicates the poet in the very condition he would ameliorate, or at least would see in the making of poetry, the one act that might offer some redemption to the "war of all against all" in which the last days of history has found us. The heretical aspects of Duncan's thought, as laid out in the epigraph to this essay, represent only a later statement of a deeper heresy whose origin lies in the poet's engagement with poetry itself. For Duncan, such thinking can be sensed in his earlier 'The Sweetness and Greatness of Dante's Divine Comedy' of 1964 that begins with a discussion of Dante's four-fold interpretation in which the doctrine of the literal, where "the literal sense should always come first as the one in the meaning whereof the others are included, and without which it were impossible and irrational to attend to the others." Pursuing Dante's thought, Duncan asserts: "The doctrine of the literal, the immediate and embodied sense, as the foundation of all others, is striking to the modern poet." The literal, however, "is the hardest ground for us to know, for we are *of* it—not outside, not observing, but inside, experiencing. It is, finally, I believe, the only ground to know."

For Duncan, the literal is a check on language (or Language with a capital L, as he sometimes writes). For "Not only in Theology but in Poetry too, something goes awry if in our adoration of the Logos we lose sense of, or would cut loose from, the living body and passion of Man in the actual universe." He warns that "words can float away in a light of their own, taking the light *for* their own, as if the universe of actual things, that we might rightly call Creation, were, as the gnostics believe, a material antagonistic to meaning."

So for him the primal heresy, stemming from his reading of Dante, is that poetry *qua* poetry is not a freedom. Musing on the role of myth, as deployed by the philosophers and historians of ancient Greece, he speaks of "Canto-recanto, the very genius, the creative will of the poem, alters what it would conserve.... The mythological poet ... struggles to keep the original, and to relegate all invention to the adversary of the poem: he struggles against the invention that moves him."

This struggle is the "war" that Duncan chooses ("I make poetry as other men make war"), in which he is a protagonist most often wrestling with himself, to liberate form—not to choose one form over another other—but to bring form to possibility, to express form as the creative artist's fulfillment of "the law that he creates," to see poetry's "every freedom," as leading toward human liberation, but, in the most complex sense, also to see poetry as the liberation of the poem from the poet. He wants a re-enactment of what he sees as Dante's movement from the realm of the *Inferno* to *Purgatorio*, the releasing of poetry from the dead, bringing it into the realm of his masters who, like Virgil, were for the most part pre-Christian, hence unaligned with either the Christian vision of redemption or with the doctrinal structures of the Christian theology. This thematics is hinted at in all of Duncan's major poetry, but especially prominent in the *Tribunals* as they weave together the personal, political and cultural worlds and in a sense transform the "literal" into a language, a poetry and poetics that would resist the tendency of poetry to "go awry" in its love of language.

Duncan's *Tribunals: Passages 31–35*, originally published as a separate book in 1970, and the prose surrounding it, form a central focus of the struggle of his war *with* and *for* form, the site of risk, undoing, and resolution. As World War Two haunted H.D. and haunts his *H.D. Book*, it is well to remember that these *Passages* are, in the most obvious sense, actual war poems, written during and deeply shaded by Vietnam and the battle skirmishes, the demonstrations and reactionary violences in the homeland, the United States, and by the collisions between its citizens and its government. *Tribunals*, then, can be seen as a conceit, a series of poems launched before a prosecutorial poet and reader, an arc of poetic activity leading to a verdict; *Passages 35*, the last in the series, denominates this specifically with its subtitle 'Before the Judgement'.

The arc has its beginning in *Passages 31, The Concert* in which the poet has already moved from the complex pastiches of *Roots and Branches*, with their alchemical and gnostic references toward a goal he sets forth in 'Structures of Rime XXIII,' to make "Only passages of a poetry, no more…. only passages of what is happening." Happenings that are ruled by Mnemosyne, "Memory," as he says in *Passages 2*, as presider over a new and deeper alteration of the poet's consciousness, a "weaver's shuttle" crossing and re-crossing image, idea and music replete with their attachments and consolations, the stuff which

> vanishes upon the air
> line after line thrown down

yet which can no longer quiet the poet's uncertainty, for what is recognized here is the moral problem of poetic artifice, here Homer's *poesis*, his very making coming under critique:

> Yet it is all, we know, a melee
>   a medley of mistaken themes
> grown dreadful and surmounting dread,
>   so that Achilles may have his wrath
>   and throw down
>   the heroic Hector who raised
>   that reflection of the heroic
>   in his shield

This critique is, in its way, a critique of Duncan's own practice. It is "heretical" in the sense of its being a self-heresy, one which deeply inflects the first of the *Tribunals*, 'The Concert,' which I consider to be one of the greatest of Duncan's poems, to be put alongside 'My Mother Would Be a Falconress,' and the Pindar poem, coming much early in his oeuvre, but with which the entire Tribunals series has much resonance. A rich catenation links the Pindar poem with the later Tribunals; one such link is established toward the conclusion of the poem where Duncan makes reference to the "old stories." He mentions "Mont St. Victoire," as an almost sacred object, with which Cézanne was obsessed, making it the subject of many of his paintings. Another link can be discerned in Cézanne's appearance in *The H. D. Book* where "his vision of Mont-St. Victoire" along with Salvatore Dalí "not only draw but are drawn by what they draw. From body and world toward another body and world, man derives meaning in a third element, the *created*—the rite, the dance, the narrative, the painting, the poem…." In the next paragraph Duncan writes: "The power of the poet is to translate experience from daily time where the world and ourselves pass away as we go into the future, from the journalistic record into a *melodic coherence in which words—sounds, meanings, images voices—do not pass away or exist by themselves but are kept by rhyme to exist everywhere in the consciousness of the poem. The art of the poem … is a cathexis: to keep present and immediate a variety of times and places, persons and events…. the experience we thought lost returns to us.*" [my italics].

'The Concert' can be read as a "melodic coherence" of the thoughts embodied in these citations, the poet instantiating his own existence as "severd *distinct* thing" but rhymed to the cosmos by the music and words of poetry. This distinctness, the enabling rhyme of language and hence poetry, its "resonances of meaning exceeding what we/understand," is what enables the poet "to release full my man's share of the star's/majesty thwarted." This word "thwarted" returns us to the Dante of Duncan's earlier meditation on the literal and the cautions by Dante to the poet, warning that the poet's view is not the theologian's. As a recent critic wrote of Cézanne's relationship with his subjects, all the art is in the distancing; "disparity," he writes, "as totality."

The thematics of 'The Concert' are perspectival, partially transforming sections of the *Tribunals* into documents of witness and prosecution—possibly there is a Zukofskian-to-Reznikoffian connection that I am not aware of—that mimes the Dantean progression from the dead language of the *Inferno* to its release in the *Purgatorio*. As with Prospero's speech at the end of *The Tempest*, the poem is an admonition and a measure—but is also a restoration, to use Olson's words that Duncan cites, "a restoration of man as force." It is in that restoration that the prosecutorial power of the poet lies.

Many volumes of sympathetic critique would be needed to unpack the range of references and the functions of their juxtapositions in *Tribunals*. One way, however, of looking at the references is to note a strange harmony in the discordant and interruptive character of their nature. The opening of 'Passage 32' contains lines from John Adams's diary contrasting monarchical and American politics, ending with his plea to "let the mind loose," and is immediately followed by a passage on the sound of the name, the Spanish name/sound of "Jesus, *Jesús (HAY-SOOS)*." "Say no more," writes Duncan, "than [that] the sound of the rime leads back from the American cry '*Let the American mind loose!*' to the Jesús." Loose/Jesús invoked to "take on the trouble as if time had a center/

and spread out its story from Bethlehem." This passage is immediately followed by references to the Vietnam war and the desolations of the Conquistadores, who we recall were bringing Christ to the New World. Duncan finds himself

Child of a century more skeptic than
            unbelieving adrift
between two contrary educations
that of the Revolution, which disowns
            everything
and that of Reaction
which pretends to bring back the ensemble
            of Christian beliefs

Heresy is here knowledge of the record of history made music through the offices of poetry; it's disjunctiveness is a cautionary warning which Duncan has already laid out in the *The Sweetness and Greatness*, in which he describes the "pseudo-romantic mirage" of the Siren in the slothful circle of Purgatorio, the seductions of the poet by fantasy rather than truth. As he writes "In this figure of the Siren we see what poetry is in the absence of the moral or theological virtues, in the denial of the good of the intellect." In Dante's and, by transmission, in Duncan's thoughts, the poet may lay claim to judgement by beginning in the literal, but, as he exclaims in Olson-like bold caps, "LET THE LINE SURPASS YOUR USES!"

'Passage 35: Before the Judgement' centers around the identification with Dante's thoughts where "the forces of Speech give way to the Language beyond Speech." The force of poesis, the mystical dramas surrounding Duncan's poetry, "the Master of Rime," is expressed in "the Overwhelming," who "sends her own priestess of the Boundless to the councils of our boundaries," on and on in the great weaves of participation that spring from the literal, including the great doubt, the "grasp faltering" of the poet's understanding, all these are the enablers of judgement. Duncan's rhetoric has now become one of accusation in which he decries the "Dream in which America sleeps, the New World floundering," in which he names names, their public faces, "Rubin, Hayakawa, Alioto, Reagan, Nixon," whom he names "The Hydra[s]" of corruption and deceit. And yet, as in the drama enacted by Virgil and Dante, poetry's movement is from Inferno to Purgatorio, with Paradise's "secret of a Life beyond our lives" ahead up the path. As he writes in the last lines, the poem offers a vision of possibility and redemption "against the works of unworthy men, unfeeling judgments and cruel deeds."

What seems to have made this journey possible lies, I believe, in the realizations of 'Passages 31 The Concert' in which the poet is suddenly at his most vulnerable, that induction into "objectness" where

> now he sings or it is
> the light singing, the voice
> shaking in the throes of the coming melody,
>> resonances of meaning exceeding what we understand…

* * *

I end with a kind of postscript: on the evening of April 16th, 1979, I introduced a poetry reading by Robert Duncan and Carl Rakosi at the 92nd Street YMWHA in Manhattan. I can't find the text of that long-ago evening, but I do remember a number of points I made. I recall most clearly that I referred to that old comparison of Isaiah Berlin's that there were two types of thinkers, hedgehogs and foxes; the hedgehogs rooted around and sunk their teeth into something and hung on to the subject or compact group of issues while the fox ran all over the landscape collecting information from and referencing all types of sources in making their arguments. For me on that night, Rakosi was clearly the hedgehog, wedded to the Objectivist principles of clear-seeing and following Hugh Kenner, as I have written of that group committed to "no myths." Duncan, of course, was the fox, roaming voraciously across the open field of other poets and poetries, spiritual traditions, myths, the occult, history, you name it. And my observations about Duncan were completely reinforced when, after the reading, a small group of poets and interested writers and readers gathered at Robert Wilson's apartment above the old Phoenix Bookstore on Jones Street in the West Village. Wilson was the owner of the bookshop, which, along with Ted Wilentz's 8th Street Bookstore and the Gotham, were almost the only places in New York where one could find an abundance of poetry not published by the mainstream publishers. Duncan was the guest of honor. Carl, already in his late 70s, had retired for the evening and did not attend. About 11 pm, Duncan started talking, and with very few interruptions, roamed like Berlin's fox across a landscape of discourses on anything and everything, continued a monologue into early morning; the sunrise light was beginning to show at the windows before he finally stopped. Throughout, however, at the center of the great Ferris wheel of Duncan's readings, lores and imaginings was his own attempt to confront the limitations of the human condition, to judge man's fate as man, to occupy that heretical space between the literal, as exemplified in Zukofsky's stripping to essentials and Olson's plunge into primordial roots. Duncan's heresy was that he too while being a fox was indeed a hedgehog, grasping tightly to whatever in poetry seemed to be an instance of human liberation.

NOTES ON THE SCRIBAL POET[1]

The scribe was one of a learned class in ancient Israel, charged with teaching, copying manuscripts, studying Scripture, even performing a juridical function at times. The word for scribe in the New Testament "*soferim*" suggests a transgressive figure, referring to "book men" who differed with the teachings of Jesus. In a combinatory phrase found throughout the New Testament, the scribe is linked pejoratively with the Pharisees. Finkelstein's beautiful new book (beautifully designed by Dos Madres) invokes all these senses of the term. In Finkelstein's work, the scribal poet is both scholar and outlier, and his work is the product of both his deep knowledge of the subject and an ambiguous, sometimes distant relationship to the text he offers up.

This scribal poetics lies at the center of Finkelstein's poetry. It can be found in *Restless Messenger* (1992) and the recently published *Passing Over* (containing poems written about the time of *Restless Messenger*), works that echo with the language of biblical parables and Jewish lore and yet demur from any embrace of the theological imperative. In his three-volume procedurally-oriented *Track*, narrative continuity and the lyric voice are disrupted by an exogamous set of mathematical constraints that give a Kabbalistic air to the poem. That simultaneous participation and distance from the overt "subject" of his poetry, reveal the arc of Finkelstein's poetics and its "history of renunciation," as he puts it in the title poem of *Scribe*. The poem, and ultimately the entire book, resolves and completes a movement of displacement that I think is the goal of Finkelstein's career as a poet. In this poem, the scribe observes himself:

> There is no sign upon you
> but there are signs upon the doorposts
> amulets of silver shaped like a hand
> with letters upon the palm and fingers.

The title poem, then, can be taken as a manifesto, though, given that that "you" is in the second voice, it produces the kind of complication that makes Finkelstein such a rewarding and yet difficult to pin down poet.

---

[1] *Scribe* by Norman Finkelstein. Dos Madres Press, Inc. 2009. 115 pp. $15.00.

The scribe, as Finkelstein envisions him here, is not exactly a maker nor a figure expressive of a particular interiority. Rather his constant motion involves both emptying and recording, an attempt at placing himself in an ever-ready position to receive the messages of the world while in some way accounting for and even compensating for the dross of private experience. As he writes in 'For Count Zero':

All this is quotation
Even if it is not all quotation

The aim is to transpose the energy of *logos* from self to the world, to arrive finally at the title poem's last line of making "a scribe into a scribe."

Scribe is divided into three sections, 'Drones and Chants,' in which the poems I've just discussed appear, 'Collages' and 'An Assembly.' As these titles suggest, Finkelstein intends to keep the impersonal, almost contingent quality of his poetry in the foreground. A certain mechanism is at work, both in the propulsive force of the drone that sweeps up the individual's voice beyond its own concerns and in the discourse-breaking mechanisms of collage and assembling. The scribe stands outside. He becomes a recording or constructivist instrument led on to writing by forces and new-found juxtapositions that in a sense take him out of himself in an almost mystical aura of self-abnegation.

The poetics of the work argue for an utter receptivity, the scribe attendant on phenomena, and so deeply absorbed in his task that revelation comes about as a kind of inverse contraction of reality. It can be likened to something resembling an emptying out or purgation. In the 'Collages' section, Finkelstein writes:

Take everything
From life but
Give nothing
To biography
…
You enact
The deed of presence
You pass
Into manifestation
…
Scholium:
"Poems create poets"

This passage highlights the logic of a scribal poetics. The concatenation runs something like this: secede nothing to time or to any sense of any individual moment in a life as being over ("to biography"). Awareness ("The deed of presence") then manifests as poetry. The final "scholium" or explanatory note, a quote from the work of Allen Grossman, is that the poet is made by the poetic act and not the reverse, a kind of caution against the hubris of creative power.

One of Finkelstein's touchstones is Jack Spicer, about whose work he has written brilliantly, and in his poetics, there is a distinctly Spicerian quality. But it seems to me that in Finkelstein there is also a reversal and even a critical investigation of Spicerian "dictation," whether in the sometimes lyrical and amatory passages of his work or in the need to give a more complex account of the contours of the self/non-self, that counterpunching radio so to speak, at the root of much of Spicer's poetry.

The modification of Spicerian "dictation" is clearly signaled in the last section of *Scribe*, 'An Assembly.' Finkelstein in his note to this section remarks on his indebtedness to Christopher Alexander's ground-breaking visionary book on architectural space and community, *A Pattern Language*. The epigraph to the section is taken from Alexander's book. It reads: "let the site tell you its secrets," a phrase which could well apply to Finkelstein's poetics. Here scribal energy is no longer a simple act of copying out, but a meditation on the physical objects of the world as they are transformed by human use until they yield up new articulations. Take the quiet gorgeousness and warmth of this passage from 'Marriage Bed';

> The poem as an idea of rest entwined
> around two bodies resting entwined
> around all their time together
> Always one wants to rest
> in the other, one wants a space
> that is the other resting at anchor
> One said there isn't an anchor
> in the drift of the world, "dissolution
> and struggles," and indeed one wakes
> in the midst of a dream, not in light
> but in enduring darkness

Nothing in human relations is secure, and the marriage bed is no guarantee of shelter. In the last few lines of this passage, we hear the echo of another of Finkelstein's influences, William Bronk's, "there is no anchor in the drift of the world." Bronk's metaphysical poetry continually provides a cautionary tale against any purely human interpretation of the world as a truth-value, a note that is struck here. The marriage bed as a site of love is invaded by the "darkness" of impermanence and the "dissolution and struggles" of any human interaction:

> One said the bed was a great distance
> between them, and we took it, rightly,
> for a bad sign

But the scribal act, informed by that Bronkian impermanence and in spite of seeming impersonality and freedom from a purely self-expressive intention or "biography", is capable of capturing a particular moment and thus perhaps making it timeless. Or if not timeless, then at least prophetic and consoling:

> But the dawn comes
> and love may return, out of intimacy
> love may return, seeing a place
> again for itself in the poem

In a recent note on his own methodology, 'A Few Thoughts About My Recent Work,' Finkelstein writes of his belief that "the poet's vocation is always constituted by and through the interrogation of his vocation." *Scribe* reminds us that such interrogations are a rich source of poetry itself, that the question leads to a return, one that is answered by the moving and intelligent poetry found in its pages.

III

CODA

LETTER FOR *ARCHAE*

I've been out here in Colorado for a couple of weeks. We'd spent June and half of July in England, Ireland and France, mostly on literary business or visiting relatives, and I had with me a letter from a friend, one in which he asked me to respond to recent developments in cosmology *i.e.* the seeming confirmation of the Big Bang theory or "instant of creation," and so I was thinking about many of the questions concerning the cosmos, or should I say, our relation to the cosmos, with theism and non-theism, which it raised. The letter brought up some old questions for me, not so much those concerned with the creation (or should it be *the* Creation); rather, as someone with a minimally scientific background who went over to literary activity, a kind of two cultures person, if you will, it raised up before me, the way our minds are inflected by our experience of scientific information and by the cosmos itself. I've lectured on the interaction of science and poetry, an ancient, honorable and continuing cross-fertilization. What the letter drove me to reflect on was one of the themes that has been a subtext in my poetry and other writings, our subjective-objective boundaries, the nature of the creative act. I would say, at the outset, that, for me, for my practice as a writer, poetry does not establish "facts" (the validity of the Big Bang, creation, etc.) but is a spiritual (I wish there were a better word) response to the facts or data of the mind.

I thought about it on some rather specific occasions, on our last night in Ireland, for instance, when an Anglo-Irish friend of ours asked us to see if we could find his family burial plot near the ancient Celtic round tower at Glendalough. It was a very clear night as Jane and I wandered among the headstones and crumbling ruins of the cemetery, one which had been in use for at least fifteen centuries. The tower, over a hundred feet high, was a flinty black monolith against the star-filled sky until one came up close and stood under its soaring cylindrical height whereupon it began to resemble something more like a bridge or tunnel to the heavens. You can perhaps imagine the flickerings of my mind: gravestones, mortality, the tangible feel of inconsequence and nothingness against the splayed out bands and clusters of stars. I felt sad for myself, for others, but also a deep, staining tinge of momentary abridgement, a psychic bounding between me and what was above, which in some way mitigated the aloneness I was experiencing. I wanted to say something, but I also didn't want to utter a word.

I am reminded now, as I think of this, of the worst of my undergraduate days at Rensselaer; I was a very unhappy student there (a story for another time) whose sole moments of tranquility and lucidity came on those Thursday nights when the observatory was open. There, as I first looked in the reticule of the telescope with its textured compactions of stars, as I concentrated myself into my looking, there was the initial, open shock of the thing, awe upon awe of uncurtained depths. Later, as I began in my mind to surround this occurrence, I would feel, or wish to feel, as though I were no longer on the earth, no longer stuck in the rundown grubbiness of Troy, NY, trying to blot out my problems with women or school by getting drunk every night. As well, the mathematics of astronomy or cosmology (though I was never any good at them) were also inspiring, relieving in their abstractness but also in their formal beauty.

Part of our travels this summer took us to Cornwall and its spectacular coastline where at night the stars drape down near the seaside cliffs and make the little clusters of village and farm lights seem almost an extension of the skies. I recall too that at a party in London, I talked at length with a Cambridge cosmologist, who is also a poet, about the "broad wrinkles" of interstellar space, something he is directly involved in. It led us to the subject and nature of perception, that is, what did it mean to suddenly have thrust on one the idea that the universe was actually twice the size originally thought. Suppose, he suggested, we had never known the lower figure (not that we can say we *know* these things at all); immense magnitudes, he felt, like Cantor's various categories of infinites, were all beyond a human taking in. It struck him, intimately involved in the scientific work, that his experience of the new knowledge, its emotional impact, was both more and less than might be the knowledge that his bank account had doubled. He told me, perhaps this is *apropos* as well, that, in Hawaii, on the upper slopes of Mount Mauna Kea, at nearly 14,000 feet, there are a cluster of observatories. The air at that altitude in that location is extremely clear and considered one of the best places in the world for visual astronomical observation. Cambridge is part of the scientific community on the mountaintop, and when new students or trainees arrive they are asked to go out at night on the slopes and observe the stars with the naked eye. Almost invariably, they report back that the sky was too cloudy for good viewing. Of course, what they thought were clouds was actually the star packed densities of the Milky Way, which in the excellent visibility of those heights looks like mist or cumulus.

Why am I telling you this? Certainly, here, in Colorado (we are at 9,000 feet) where I have been coming for the last thirty years, the clear starry skies have meant a great deal to me. You know how it is in the city, the moon is visible and an occasional planet and, if one is lucky, one might see a star of the first or second magnitude such as Arcturus or Vega. Here, only last night, as on other summer nights on the slopes of the Sangre de Cristos, I walked out on the deck of our cabin to watch the beginnings of the *Perseids*, the mother of all meteor showers in the Northern Hemisphere with arcings across the sky almost every minute. It is quite a show; along with the stars, with Saturn bright in the East and even a few high slow-moving satellites, the meteors blazed their delicate phosphorescent trails. Sometimes one caught them full; at other times, they flitted across the corner of one's vision. You looked at one, you missed another.

As you can see, I've been writing here about relativities, about, if I can crib from the theologian Martin Buber, the *me—it*, or the *me-Thou* possibilities of our connections with magnitudes which we cannot quite encompass. These have the structure of what we both might call "theisms;" that is, there is a form, an equation or a ritual, by which we are able to work our way back and forth across the dash-lines of two terms. We always think of magnitudes as what connects us, one term to another, like man to star. Magnitudes, the odd stepping-stones of those strings of numbers, like that round tower in Ireland, provide us with a mode of transport. As with the Greeks, who feared infinity—and cosmology brushes the dread of the infinite at every turn—far more important for us is the *fact* of a number rather than what that specific number is. Wittgenstein pondered this problem as he went about considering the notion of a foundation to mathematics. Almost anywhere one looks, science is adjusting and readjusting itself, to maintain the great Classical triad of ratios: microcosm :: human being :: cosmos. New calculations of interstellar distances are accompanied by new findings of sub- sub- sub-atomicities. Formulations establishing a psychological and emotional as well as a spiritual-religious sense of well-being.

Now science, one might conjecture, with its claims to "objectivity," has sought a non-theism of the objects it investigates, thinking, until recently, that there was some sense of the "impersonal" or transcendent to knowledge; it did this by denying or not reflecting on the problem of language, by not recognizing how its concepts were in fact the secret binderies of relations. It ignored the metaphoric-psychological aspects of scientific language and research. Yet, in the sense I'm talking about, the constructs of science, even something as remote as the Big Bang, are relational and are tinged with our desires for certainty, for surety. I distinguish here, the difference between the facts of science (its magnitudes, its formulae, etc.) and the *activity* of science, which like all creative human activity, takes place with both theistic and non-theistic components.

Non-theism, and of course you will recognize this idea from your knowledge of Buddhist thought, means, dynamically, (in the act of thinking the thing) to abolish, in some sense, such dualities. Let us leave aside, for the moment, that, as traditionally understood, "non-theism" is less a concept than an experience, a rather fleeting one, or, even more frangible to conceptualization, is the mere shadow-trace of an experience. Non-theism, then, seems to require that loss of reference point by which we establish the identity or meaning of something primarily in relation to ourselves. That is why the experience of "non-theism" is often referred to as being disorienting or panic inducing. Marlowe in *Tamburlaine* plays a riff on such disorientation:

> Our souls, whose faculties can comprehend
> The wondrous architecture of the world,
> And measure every wandering planet's course,
> Still climbing after knowledge infinite,
> And always moving as the restless spheres,
> Wills us to wear ourselves, and never rest

If the products of science are not free of theistic clingings, is anything? And then, what about your series of questions to me? Since my own personal history involved moving from the scientific field into one of language and poetry, let me speculate just a bit in these areas, on *poesis*, the act of and the resultant, the poem. Part of what I am thinking about here is inseparable from the nature and function of language, language's "divine" status in almost every culture. Such thoughts are very much on my mind, as I have committed myself to giving a lecture on 'The Uncertainty of the Poet' in which I will try to present a sense of the flavor of the non-theistic as conveyed through the idea or feel of uncertainty, manifesting as a disorientation or panic, the unstable ground that leads to writing.

In developing my argument, I maintain that the poem, the "strong" poem, *pace* Harold Bloom, can be called The House of Uncertainty. By this I mean that our experience of a powerful poem is that disorientation, of disrupting our conventionalized or habitual ways of looking at the world. Its alteration of our consciousness, its shock value, is in the act whereby we, as readers, are cast out of our conventional states of mind, from certainty into uncertainty. It can have, on the local level, the full force of a new scientific fact. In fact, Thomas Kuhn's notion of the "paradigm case" in his *The Structure of Scientific Revolutions* offers a scientific parallel to the literary model. My essay 'Poetry Without Credentials' published a few years ago in *The Ohio Review* covers this idea a little more fully, but it also connects not only the poem but the act of poem-making with the notion of gift or giftedness and uncertainty, as two aspects of the hint of non-theism in poetic creation.

Among the many influences on my own thinking about *poesis*, about the making of poems, one of the most powerful has been Walter Benjamin's ideas, specifically his thoughts on the "nonsensuous similarity" of language *i.e.* language, not as representing something, but as enacting, by fusing, as Benjamin put it, the semiotic and the mimetic. And, furthermore, in his concept of Naming: "Naming is that by which nothing beyond it is communicated, and *in* which language itself communicates itself absolutely." The poem as Name (or word or Word), the maker of the poem as striving toward the articulation of a Name, that most ancient of formulations, something which, according to Benjamin exists without residue, opens, in my mind, the way to an experience or idea of the "non-theistic" as part of (possibly the main attraction of) the creative process.

Poems appear to want to possess an experience, to surround it with image and word, as though a verbal net were being flung over an object. And yet we know that what poems contain is that verbal machinery and something mysterious and intangible that we call desire or heart-soreness, the knowledge that nothing is possessed. Of course, at this point post-structuralist thought often goes wrong, assuming the possessiveness but not rendering the dispossession that gives life and beauty to form. I have not sufficient room here to go into the subtle mechanics of this maneuver, but a hint of what I am reaching for appears in my essay 'From The Notes' which introduced my poems in the anthology *Beneath A Single Moon*. There, I speak of the possibility of "unconditioned" or "non-theistic" writing, writing "which, for the poet and reader, the giving over to the words, is the practice of vulnerability, where in every act of perception, one is reduced to a word. This is not a word that stands for oneself, nor does it represent oneself. The word (the poem) *is* oneself. And this word is not one that can be enjoyed or taken for comfort. Whatever else is contained in it, the pain of one's death is also there." That vertigo that I felt when I first looked through the telescope at Rensselaer years ago, long before I had any notion of committing a single thought to paper I would now say *gave me the cosmos as a word*. Before I wrapped it up in my needs and hopes. Such giving I take as the central possibility of art.

"IN WHAT SENSE…"

|

[In late 2016, the Editors of *Paideuma*, a journal of commentary focused on modern and post-modern poetry asked for responses to the question: **In what sense does the work to which you are committed share in the renovation of society?** The essay below was my response.]

|

"The poet: always *in partibus infidelium*" — Celan in *Microliths*

Here in New York, where I write today, snow is falling heavily, covering the bleak brickwork and paving stones, weighing down the tree branches in the nearby park, but what obtrudes, the contours and softened shapes of buildings and cars, the telltale curves and surfaces of the blowing snow that hint at other structures, these remind me of masks and draperies, remind me of the poet Hayim Nahman Bialik's "revealments and concealments" that for me are the substance of the poet's language. Bialik's words have been at the forefront of my mind for many years, most recently as a focal point in a dialogue/conversation with my friend and fellow poet Norman Finkelstein published in a collection of essays, *Imagining the Jewish God* (2016).

And perhaps it is the faint Judaic aura or hangover of that conversation that has led me to think that in the question the editors of *Paideuma* have formulated I wanted to replace the word "renovation" with the older, more resonant word "repair," repair as the *tikkun olam* of the Lurianic Kabbalah, repair as differentiated from renovation, which seemed too cosmetic, too much like a word out of real estate or fixing up the surface of what exists. Repair, because, from the immediate sense, it seemed that in recent days, some grievous blow had been struck close to home. Some act had locally opened a chasm, knocked down a wall or revealed a new deeper than usual fault line, though anyone who follows such matters will realize it merely as a newly exposed fault-line alongside of which the wretched of the earth still toil in semi-slavery, the polluted earth itself continues to fester, and the more things seem to have changed cosmetically the more of the same disaster things actually continue to be. So repair: because as long as I have lived the world has been in pain, been riven. I was born while the Shoah began, in fear, blackout curtains were pulled across the windows of our Brooklyn home, gold stars for the dead hung in other Pulaski Street windows, an older brother served on a destroyer during the Korean War, I acted out in Angry Arts during the

Vietnam War, global famine and disease, on and on. So while I hadn't intended to be dramatic here—or maybe I do— because deep down, as I think of the course corrections of my own rhetoric and attempts at poetry over the years, I sense that the need for "repair" comes out of what actually is the steady-state condition of the world, its massive destruction and chaos—I guess that *is* being dramatic.

But, in semi-deference to the formulation offered by the editors of *Paideuma*, maybe, what I really want to say is that I fear that the concept of renovation without the deeper added sense of repair strikes me as close to meaningless, useless, perhaps worse, harmful, perhaps tremendously distracting. The editors' question has been posed to poets, to scholars and thinkers concerned with poetry and other literary matters, and I sense in it, especially behind the implications of the word "share," that we are being asked something defensively, almost, if I may coin a term, self-querulous, with an air of hopelessness, or a hope that carries a desire for justification. I also hear in it a faint echo of George Oppen's profoundly anguished rejoinder "we wanted to know if we were any good out there." But this question, despite my suggestion of a necessary edit, struck me as *the* legitimate question during our "destitute time," as Heidegger said, referring to Hölderlin, the time when the poet's utmost task was to ask the question of "why to be a poet?" Being born in 1937, I also ask myself a companion question: when have we not lived in a destitute time?

So I want to invoke the history I lived and in so doing step outside the confines of the poetry world whose current manifestations often invoke zeitgeists and approaches that seem entropic, telling us that everything has been exhausted: that the attempt to translate human suffering into linguistic *techné* appears to be a failure. The poets of feeling had not managed to save the world, and so new poets had to turn to the mechanization of poetry, to its physical structures and to the ambient platforms of materiality that mirrored the culture's turn from politics to novelty to consumerism. Inevitably, the goal of such novelty became the goal of obsolescence and anyone who thinks for a moment will recognize the aggression and commercialism within the urge to make obsolete.

What now seems a truism is that the public's language has been pretty much left untouched. The evolution of language—the speech between people—has always differed greatly from the experiments of poetry, and has always proceeded both more swiftly and more slowly than those experiments, particularly by poets who insist on justifying their inventions in terms of the social good. In this sense, the distance between public speech and individual linguistic invention remains immense, and a problematic and deeply ironic truth is that many experiments with language that did seem to "break through" had already been anticipated by politicians, marketeers, electronic and broadcast media advertisers, and public relations firms. Disjunction and fragmentation had become tools of commercialism and extremism, ultimately of oppression. As Canetti wrote about Fascism, its linguistic power lay "in the adjacency of construction and deconstruction." Such cultural and political effects had already been calculated by Orwell—we note the resurgence of *1984* as a text for our time—, and by Packard's *The Hidden Persuaders* of 1955, McLuhan's "the media is the message," and many others post-war works. They had been practiced by Joseph Goebbels in the 1930s.

What remained to counter the poetry community's deliberative balkanizations around novelty, were the cries of pain, pride and empowering self-awareness among the marginalized, the overlooked and the oppressed. The collectivity of these cries and their awarenesses did not emanate from groups with defined boundaries—in their cumulative power and effect they transcended clique, group, school, doctrine, dogma—their power issued from somewhere else. It lay on a border where language seemed almost the skin of flesh, on the beaten areas of the body and the psyche. And what readers heard or read was the sound of these impingements, whose forms—for which their creators were occasionally criticized—were close to that of ordinary people, people in their homes or on their streets.

Of all the sounds seeming to emanate from individuals, these sounds were the sound of repair, the beginnings or prompts of repair. Because they were a call to arms or conscience, at least, a call to awareness. What could not be established, let alone maintained, is that this restorative power could be traced back to some linguistic sleight of hand, that some technique would liberate, or, to put this phenomenon in a broader, more variable context, would make it remind me or you of your humanity, the depth and breadth and uncanniness of it. And, looking back, one can safely claim that the testimonials of twentieth-century poets I mentioned above were, indeed, part of a repair of society, one that continues today even as it remains unfinished. Similar instances can be noted in the case of the dissident poets of certain societies, and one can go back even to the ancients where poetry, whether by the *scop*, the dramatist, the shaman or even the court poet, had a role, sometimes slight, sometimes dramatic, in the re-inventions of social and political culture. Shelley's "unacknowledged legislators" came from these cohorts.

The question posed by *Paideuma* and my thoughts above reminded me of a resonant question and answer from a conversation I had with the poet and critic Jon Curley published in a critical book on my work. It expands, perhaps somewhat repetitively, on my comments above.

JC: You seem to suggest that the enormity of historical events engenders both compulsion to respond to them and an artistic and personal responsibility to do so. Is there a dual requirement, maybe even more crucially, a commitment on your part—to serve as both witness to history and personal experience but also, just as importantly, as recorder of one's arduous experience in trying to express and respond?

MH: Let me make some distinctions. The poet, at least this poet, is a citizen, and therefore has the political arena before him, with all the possibilities and responsibilities that that entails, voting, participating in causes, being an activist, a donor, an anarchist or whatever one chooses. But these choices are quite different from imagining one's poetry as politically, culturally and socially enacting change or realizing political ends. I'm fond of Shelley's idea of the poet as "unacknowledged legislator," someone whose perceptions—let's say those of certain poets at least—saturate and work slowly through societies and cultures. In the nineteen-sixties, just after I came back from Spain to a U.S. in turmoil, I underlined in Barthes's *Writing Degree Zero* this sentence: "All writing will therefore contain the ambiguity of an object which is both language and coercion," and further down that same page, "for it is power or conflict which produce the purest types of writing." I read this nearly fifty years ago, and it has stayed with me. Barthes seems to speak to me of two things at once, the brutal instrumentality of language and also the need to thoroughly understand this fact for one who takes up language. So I see a responsibility, call it a political responsibility if you wish, for the poet.

In my essay 'Avant-Garde Propellants of the Machine Made of Words,' as part of my critique of "experimental" school poetics, I enlisted Bahktin's ideas about "utterance" as I questioned whether any school's claims for influencing politics or effecting change held up to scrutiny (at that time, you will remember, the

Language poetry group, for instance, was insisting on its Marxist orientation). I concluded that much of their maneuvers with language had already been executed by early twentieth-century Dadaists, Futurists and others, and more to the point, were now being appropriated by contemporary commercial television, the internet and news media. The media jump-cuts, discontinuities and the like were aimed at novelizing news, ads, political problems and sometimes/often with sinister intentions, to befuddle its consumers. It struck me that the poets were working with a hopelessly defanged aesthetic, that the "rhetoric" of the work, especially its coercive aspects, lay not in the work itself but in the polemical theorizing that surrounded it—this is not to condemn the work, some of which I find beautiful and even powerful, but to resist the sociopolitical claims it made for itself. Anyway, history will record that on the current playing-fields of academe, the "experimentalists" have surely won their argument. And they have caught me up too, as in a recent conference in France titled 'Tailor-Made Traditions' where I was billed as an "American experimental poet."

In that essay, I proposed instead a poetry of "counter-continuities," by which I meant, a poetry of responses that met, in a kind of negative symmetry, the continuities and discourses that were the sources of oppression, indifference, confusions and misunderstandings. It is a term for what I think has already been going on in investigative poetry, protest poetry, in the work of the Objectivists, Oppen especially, and in postwar Eastern European poetries, some of which have demonstrated actual political power, altering public perceptions and inducing political activity. To use the cliché, these poetries "speak truth to power," sometimes in a not-so-subtle fashion, one which can make a reader cringe. But let us admit that in some places, among dissidents or oppressed and marginalized groups, such poetry has played a significant role. We are talking about a broadband phenomenon here, from the Social Realism of the 'twenties and 'thirties to poets like Baraka or Zbigniew Herbert or Miłosz, from sentimental and propaganda-driven verse to rather complex, oblique poetry, some of it among the finest of its times. These poetries—I'm using a very broad brush here—seem intended to make it shame rather than make it new. That is their Barthesian "coercion," to disclose or expose, to bring individuals into immediate proximity to what is impelling their lives—that is, from the political perspective, their public lives. This I believe was the goal of Benjamin's "now-times" poetics—its immediate shock value to social consciousness—which he got from his studies of Baudelaire.

The epigraph above by Celan, that the poet is always in territory inhabited by infidels or, to switch the point of view, is always himself/herself a word-infidel embedded in statist language, suggests, as in George Oppen's much quoted lines, that one can use words, "provided one treat them like enemies." Which makes me think that the one legitimacy a poet *qua* poet can claim in the political sphere is that his use of language is always illegitimate, that in a world of cover-ups and disinformation, it heretically seeks truth, transparency and exposure, *and* community, this last even by refusing the embraces of community.

Since I began writing this piece, the snow has come and gone, but for a while, as in Joyce's famous story, "it filled the niches between the living and the dead." Like the snow, poetry comes and goes. When it piles up and lies there against the contours of living and dying, when it makes an image of *what might be out of what is*, then it suggests the nature of the idea of "counter-continuities" that I tried to imagine some years ago. While it lay there, poetry occupied those hollows and gaps that need to be repaired and to be healed; poetry made them visible, they enabled.

I have written elsewhere of how I "blundered" into the writing of poetry, and how the label "poet" has never had the power over me that it may have had for others. And yet, no matter what has been happening in my life or in the world around me—and I guess, the motive of this request by *Paideuma* is related to our current situation—it has never occurred to me that I should stop the activity that I accidentally came into, even as it seemed to be fulfilling a need that I have never quite understood. The closest I came in my understanding was that writing and reading were ways to free myself from myself, from the former construction of myself, whether it were last year's, last week's, last second's. Part of my need was psychological, spiritual, "sacred,"—the correct word eludes me—but it was also always a matter of amplitude and enlarging one's vision, which applied deeply to the cultural, social and political worlds in which I live. It wasn't exactly a faith: it was happening without much willing or even hope, but faith is a word close to one's feeling about it. If I were to wonder about my motives and my commitment to repair and renovation, I would return to that feeling as though it were a faith in poetry which before all else must itself be the faith that poetry generated in oneself, in its power to affect the psyche of oneself and possibly others.

The dialogue with Norman Finkelstein I mention appears under the title 'On the Poetics of the Jewish God' in a volume of essays and poems edited by Leonard Kaplan and Ken Koltun-Fromm, *Imagining The Jewish God* (Lanham, MD: Lexington Books, 2016).

My essay 'Avant-Garde Propellants of the Machine Made of Words' (in *Uncertain Poetries: Selected Essays on Poets, Poetry & Poetics* [Bristol: Shearsman Books, 2012]) refers to "counter-continuities" as responses that meet, in a kind of negative symmetry, the continuities and discourses that are sources of oppression, indifference, confusions, and misunderstandings.

My conversation with Jon Curley appears in *The Poetry and Poetics of Michael Heller: A Nomad Memory*, edited by Jon Curley and Burt Kimmelman (Madison, NJ: Fairleigh Dickinson University Press, 2015).

MICHAEL HELLER
INTERVIEW WITH ANDY FITCH

Andy Fitch: Could we start with you offering a lived history of how *This Constellation Is A Name* came into being? Had you long planned or hoped for this type of full-scale collected volume spanning more than four decades? Did it emerge as a Nightboat-driven initiative? Who made the selections that did occur, and did this happen with any overall project plan in place? I, for instance, would have loved to see the *Beckmann Variations* prose sections included, but I also consider this a lovely, quite generous volume, with its spacious design presumably making some cuts necessary.

Michael Heller: The history of the volume is a bit murky in my mind, but as I remember it, blame for the book must be shared between me and Stephen Motika, Nightboat's editor/publisher. Stephen, as you know, worked at Poets House, and there was a period in 2010 and 2011 when I was there quite a lot, giving a seminar on modern poetry, coming to meetings and events. I had published *Eschaton* in 2009, the Beckmann book in 2010 and I had a fair amount of work published in magazines and online that had not yet been collected in book form, including about 20 pages of my Segalen re-workings, and, despite my general carelessness in thinking about my 'career' and my age, I think it was Stephen who said something like "wouldn't it be nice to have a big book, your collected, come out around your 75th birthday." Which, of course, is exactly what happened. I gathered all the work of my previously published volumes and the new work into a collected poems. The result was a beautiful book, which I feel honors my work and, I hope, honors Nightboat. And naturally, I have the usual ambivalence about publishing a Collected—it's at once very satisfying to feel its heft, its weight of completed ambition, but also, it has that old "intimation of mortality" aspect as well. Indeed, a few times when inscribing a copy for someone, I've written "this book is a tome, but it is not a tomb." Luckily, I've had a bit of a productive run since then, and Nightboat published my new collection, *Dianoia*, in 2016.

AF: The collection's attentions to multiple temporalities intrigued me. As the endnotes, let's say, explained the origins of the phrase "yellow submarine," I wondered precisely whom/when this book is for. I also noted that it privileges biographical over bibliographic chronology (with *A Look at the Door with the Hinges Off*, written early, yet published several decades later, still coming first), even as the ruminative return to certain elegiac preoccupations diverts from any progressive timeline, pushing the eschatological examinations towards new formal possibilities as much as towards any personal or historical resolution. So could you discuss the types of internalized temporalities you see *This Constellation Is A Name* now offering? If, as the poem 'East Hampton Meditations' suggests, we often seek, through writing, to bind ourselves to the dead even as we reach towards those to come in the future, how does this book aim to combine those projects?

MH: Your phrase "multiple temporalities" intrigues me as well, which I place in tandem with your linking of it to the possible *raisons* of an audience. To the extent that I have anything resembling a project, it is not one of specifically defining epochs, but of intervening in the discourses that have lulled or submerged us in regulated time, that have captured our minds in their logic, their cultural, economics and emotional envelopes. As you may sense from any number of poems in the book or from a lot of my critical prose, I'm an acolyte of Benjamin, a student of, as a recent essay of mine seeks to make clear, a "now-time" poetics that hopes to interrupt time and history and to redeem our current moment for new directions and possibilities. So if by temporalities, one means specific segments of time, with their particular characteristics, I'd have to say that my sense has always been that poetry at its best is a matter of interference, including disruptions of those segments (it's why I have little interest in movements and groups that seem to or claim to have figured out what is necessary for any particular zeitgeist). The most profound representations of a culture or milieu are often embedded in those works that critique them. In my 'Notes on Counter-Memory,' the guiding thoughts for my memoir *Living Root*, I find myself enthralled by the sense that the most genuine expression of a religion is found in its heretics—In addition to Benjamin, the "patron saint of this work," I draw on Ernst Bloch, on Gottfried Arnold and Joachim of Fiore— the last believing that autobiography consists of a "theology of crisis". Elsewhere, I've called such works "counter continuities," because they must not only disrupt—that seems all too easy for an artist or poet—but offer a coherent challenge at many points to an existing state of affairs. In this sense, they are never solely about "art" or the practices of art.

That's why your mention of "internalized temporalities" suggests that externalized ones—are we thinking Pound or certain late twentieth century poetic movements that want to flash-freeze certain periods?—are perhaps more "objective," that if one just expunged the self out of the conception, we'd be in truth and light? 'East Hampton Meditations,' with its last section concerns for "memory" and "traceries" expresses the interrelationship of these two themes in terms of errancy (of "having lost your way"), which if one thinks hard on it, is also the condition of our freedom. And which is its redemptive power, "not for *now*/but to remind one/of the dead//or of those yet to come." The thought here is an echo of the last prose entry in my *Living Root*:

> He could not meditate on death, which he did not know. He could think about illness (or dying?), about the decay before one's eyes which is visible and which can be imagined through one's own fevers and flus, through one's injuries and hurts.
>
> He understood his parent's deaths as at least a kind of closure while all other lessons about "death" invoked only false nostalgia, sentimentality, and guilt. He understood that the only logical response to a closure was to evaluate what had come before. The "value" of a death, of a closure, can only be an utterance of sorts.

AF: As other readers have noted, an inclination towards ekphrasis remains one constant across this collection's manifold formal, intellectual, emotional explorations. And you have spoken eloquently, both in your own voice and in ventriloquistic engagements with figures such as Max Beckmann, about how the most meaningful ekphrastic work departs from trying to capture or affix nature or art, from trying to settle into descriptive linguistic rendering, from speaking in words alone for the mute and inarticulate. So I'd love to hear you discuss or parse your engagement with ekphrastic and mimetic tendencies. I think of your preferred typed of ekphrasis as an emulative rather than a descriptive mimesis—an effort, as in certain forms of Chinese painting, to become the growing leaves, rather than to record this phenomenon. Along such lines, I admire not only your empathic/ekphrastic engagements with a diverse range of artists (Piet Mondrian, John Coltrane, Rachel Blau DuPlessis), but also your knack for constructing a syntactical rhythm that operates like a heartbeat, like the subaqueous pacing of coral's growth, like a window's sunlight "without thought," like an egret or heron, like a creek. Of course, as *This Constellation Is a Name* notes, poets long have picked up on Homer's efforts to mimic, through poetic pacing, waves breaking off Hellas. But what do you consider your distinctive contribution or attraction to questions of how ekphrasis, mimesis, radical empathy might play out in a contemporary poetics? Or if we return to the early lines "the human scales the world, the / successive /reminiscences of a thing's / properties," what role have your long-term ekphrastic engagements played in refining your sense, your phenomenology perhaps, of embodied human consciousness, of inter-relationality, of formal arrangements prioritizing the fragment and/or the ongoing, asymptotic, ever-incomplete utterance? What in lived experience and/or adjacent realms of knowledge does your poetics most emulate?

MH: That is one extensive question. If its sentences were not in the interrogative mode, I'd say it pretty well (and generously so) captures manifold aspects of my work, of my concerns. My "engagement" with particular artworks – not only visual ones but, literary ones as well as music and opera – is complicated. As I write in the interview in *The Poetry and Poetics of Michael Heller: A Nomad Memory,* artworks are "nexes of intelligence and experience… arenas, perceptual tests and challenges, sometimes acts of possession in the psychic and spiritual sense, at once disturbing and pleasurable." I have no program for my encounters. Rather, over the years, wandering around galleries or concert halls, or looking in books, certain works have seemed so powerful and seductive to me that I've wanted to respond, to understand my responses, and see where they lead. In the spirit of Picasso's "a picture is a hoard of destructions,"—Wallace Stevens cites this remark in his *The Necessary Angel,* also insisting that "a poem is a horde of destructions"—(*NA* 161) it is this disturbance that I seek to articulate, something which lies neither purely in the artwork nor in the culture in which it is placed but in the intellectual and emotional energy that links the two. How to express that, which seems the territory of poetry and art as opposed to the discourses? As a poet, I've wanted to submit my world view to destruction, something perhaps linked to my studying Buddhist thought and its practice, as I would call it, of a kind of self-destruct. One senses immediately before certain works: they are not pleasant, not confirming, they move and instruct as teachers and parents often do, disabusing as well as instructing. What I want my work to embody is this double energy of construction and deconstruction. Powerful works don't leave one in the desert, in nullity. But can a poetics really "emulate?" Is that a legitimate question to ask a poet, one who has said from the start that his entire "career" constitutes a series of blunders and accidents?

AF: I'd love to discuss fragments more thoroughly, but first I wonder if tracking your long-standing engagement with specific philosophical and scientific world-views might help (we also could address more conspicuously mystical, spiritual, religious preoccupations). A pre-Socratic (later, of course, Keatsian, Emersonian) emphasis upon "hidden harmonies" arrives early in this book, with corresponding formulations of insight's lightning flash—tracing Platonic models of internal and external oblivion ("One dark outlined against a dark"), tracing Walter Benjamin's conception of a text's occasional illuminating bolt followed by its "thunder rolling / long afterwards." And your scientific/engineering training adds autobiographical context for this collection's atomistic depictions of photons, of perception, of Robert Delaunay's attempts to reach "sources of emotion / beyond the limits of all subject matter." Could you talk more about formative poetic, metaphysical, anti-metaphysical influences on your work, either figures or ideas or approaches?

MH: For me, the vocabulary of science is essentially metaphoric. The physical world, its objects and weathers, comes to us without any names or labels. We've constructed the entire thing and, from my perspective, embedded our longing, our hopes and desires in that labelling, an impulse that co-arises I would imagine with the dawning of literacy and orality. The pre-Socratics, whom I read closely when I thought I might get a graduate degree in philosophy, were highly influential, Heraclitus in particular, whose 'Fragments' form a tone poem of the highest order. It's important to remember his divine *Logos* comes to us on top of centuries of animistic and shamanistic activity with all its hope for connection, fear of disconnection, fear of the sun going out, harvests lost, hope, loss, salvation. I think the point for me is that language alone can never quite account for language, that we are always in relation to both words and experience/existence in its broadest terms. My readings and my influences, with few exceptions, are not systematic. I'm much more of a magpie reader. The Notes in the back of my collected, *This Constellation Is A Name*—well, they constitute a constellation of sources I've drawn on, to which one could add the usual suspects, most important what I have taken away from my readings and re-readings of Oppen and Benjamin, from the work of phenomenologists such as Merleau-Ponty, on through

Buddhist texts dealing with Mahamudra and dialectics to all sorts of cultural and historical readings, anything that contains or gives me the mysterious *frisson* of a human working him/herself out via language. My "career" is essentially one of continually going on in this direction.

To give you some early instances: the Delaunay quote comes from '4:21 PM On Saint George's Clock: Film' in my earliest full collection, *Accidental Center* (1972). It is one of a number of poems in which my background in the sciences plays a significant part, not merely in its deployment of technical diction, but in its constant recourse to the something like the inexpressible, as in the ending of '4:21...,' "each frame isolate as our lives are//but a lonely gesture to the next." Other poems, 'Telescope Suite,' 'Incontinence' (about our response to the space program), any number of others, all leading to justifying (if that is the right word) the vision in the last lines in the book from 'Birds At The Alcazaba,' "for the otherness is beautiful/and terror and delight/in the same moment flood the heart." This habit of speculation and observing persists. It has almost nothing to do with audience or fashion. And whatever has evolved in my work orbits around the understandings and consolations—curious word, but it describes the feelings of resolve and momentary completion—which I achieved for myself in that book.

AF: Could we also try to reach this book's ever-evolving, often cosmic conception of love—compared, early on, to "the cold light / Touching stone / Across the distance," then refracted throughout this collected text, which so often suggests that "only love is at the end of it"?

MH: That conception, as you describe is, in the most profound sense, not one I feel comfortable addressing, a fear that anything I might say would only reduce what has led to a resolution that can only come about via poetry. It seems to me that, aside from the conventional uses of the word "love," you are pointing to a place in my work where the term is all that's left of what I am able to say, as though a process of awarenesses and realizations led ultimately to the brink of speechlessness. Oppen talks of an ennobling clarity, and I think it is tactful—even necessary—not to qualify or overdefine such endpoints, such completions made possible by poetry.

AF: I want to address the redemptive force or at least the respite provided by erotic and sexual experience as much as by abstracted conceptions of love. Early on, sex gets tied to restorative forms of silence, darkness, chiaroscuro, to corporeal simplicity amid embodied engagement with others and with the world (if an example helps to clarify: "half-light, half-dark arcings / of pleasure and silence— // so much done together / natural, cloven / yet joined // audacious desire / have you writhe under me/ come so sweetly"). Lyric often has valued the restorative power of the erotic or of nature (or nature's nearest equivalent, as in 'Adulation's' Cheeveresque reappraisal of suburban comforts, alongside a more cynical friend's snide remarks), and you artfully pick up on such traditions. But then later this collection references "the galaxy seemingly drained of that covenant." Or your Baudelairean 'Like Prose Bled Through a City' as it constantly pivots from aesthetic serenity to individual human suffering. No such poetic solace here seems conclusively serviceable. So we could talk about the legacy of erotic, lyric, pastoral tropes offering redemptive tonalities throughout your books. We could also or instead discuss what seemed to me like the emergence of more wary or pessimistic tonalities accruing in later pieces. I remember, from an interview with Jon Curley, you stating that your work seeks to bridge a distance "between what has already been said or written and what a constantly changing world would require." What has and what does your world require of the erotic?

MH: I quarrel with your use of the word "respite," as if some version of the erotic amounted to a longueur. The way you use "redemptive" also is tinged with a kind of use-value, the efforts of self-appointed salvationists. I guess what I'm asking is: can we talk of requiring something from the erotic—isn't it quite the other way around, that the erotic seems to exert demands on us, more broadly, that on every level, the world is a seductive place eliciting our intimacy, our indwelling, our understanding? To go back to your earlier question, isn't this the "cosmic" dimension of the erotic, its all-pervasive energy? I'm speaking of something larger than sexual attraction, though our personal intimacies can almost be seen as metonymies of our other relatedness. The religious responses to such energies range across the whole spectrum of behavior, from the ascetic's attempt to shut out the world to unreflective embracing or dancing with the phenomena. As I've said *ad infinitum*, the world beats on the poet. I'll add for clarity, the erotics of the world beat on the poet—the sound of that drumming, as it is shaped in language by one's psyche and physiology, is his or her poetry. Registering those beats, and how to live with those registrations is what I am about, what drives my seeking and my receptivity to the currents flowing around me.

And naturally, part of that registration is sorting out the signals and so on that one receives, trying to express one's sense of them. I think, in this regard, I'd characterize 'Adulation,' not as Cheeveresque, but as a tongue-in-cheek take on the task, simultaneous desire for and disparagement of the gods of celebrity, patronage, the seductions. The narrator's poet-friend exclaims right at the start of the poem, that "adulation is the structure of the world," and what ensues is a dialectic of hopes and fears—and revulsions—attendant on the tropes of wanting and getting adulation.

If fame is a new religious marker, one of the casualties is the old animism, especially in its updated literary version as nature poem or within the pastoral poem tradition. This is the old "covenant" of spiritual meaning that I'm referring to, which has been drained from the universe ("the galaxy" in that poem).

AF: Of course an elegiac trajectory starts to solidify across this book's arc, shifting the center of gravity away from youthful observations and erotic attractions, to catalyzing concerns for disappeared and disappearing perceptions, individuals, cultures, languages, ecosystems. Most specifically, reflections on your parents' deaths, on the destruction of Eastern European Jewish communities, on September 11th and its aftermath, resound across much of this book's second half. By the time you publish *Knowledge*, your poems implore their readers, their author, themselves not to let meaning nor self-definition perish. And, simultaneously, your poems continue to evolve away from a more elliptical template, towards something more like narrative. 'Through The Binoculars' basically asks how one becomes elegiac: "How does one lose the sense / Of the hymnic and must sing only of what is past." Could you begin to answer that question in terms both of your autobiographical and poetic development, addressing your ongoing dialogues with your parents, with certain literary figures (Baudelaire, Freud, Benjamin, Celan), with certain cityscapes?

MH: I don't plan a trajectory *a priori*, rather I feel like I'm investigating particular situations. I'm looking for a path, sometimes one that seeks to find its way back from loss that can properly be called elegiac, such as in the poems dealing with the deaths of my parents or other figures that are important to me. I don't conceptualize ahead of time, thus what begins in elegiac form, as in 'Through The Binoculars,' where I tried to come to terms with the death of my father, turns out in its last sections to be something of a praise poem: "Beautiful the world the dead have left us to see/Beautiful the shell, thin and delicate in its own right, Yet beautiful as a beautiful woman..." It's as though the poet here turns the corner on grief by transmuting his loss. I can't account for how I got there—all I can think of is something like what Zukofsky says of Shakespeare that he had an "inexpressible trust of expression." I seem to do that kind of trusting.

As to the figures you mentioned, Baudelaire, Celan, etc., I've said elsewhere that I consider my poetry to be a relational act, that my arena is the in-between, that my encounters with the dead are teaching situations. I don't want to imitate them but I would hopelessly hope to approach their depth of intensity, comprehension and lyric beauty. The only way I can go at it is by reading them and by learning what I can about how I use language.

AF: Since you yourself have emphasized, in this book and elsewhere, your departure from an earlier, more self-consciously "experimental style," could you discuss in detail what points of continuity and differentiation you detect between earlier and later parts of *This Constellation Is a Name*? For me at least, early desires to let attention wander, slip (thereby affirming being: "Stopping to let the attentions wander. An absurd elusive sense of self all the more alive because what seemed to slip away was just that attention, the holding of which was proof, at least in words, of the term 'alive'"), doesn't seem so far removed from statements, significantly later, that you have lived long enough to know you love fragment-like "figments," ("thigh turns and orchid boats peeping shyly"). And again, your subsequent depiction of "Life as pointillist" seems a logical step. So I guess I wonder if you have refined early tendencies, more than you have abandoned them. Or what, specifically, has disappeared since the early work? Or for a potentially different microcosmic consideration of your evolving formal process, could you discuss your rewriting and subsequent re-rewriting of Shelley in 'Without Ozymandias' and 'Stanzas Without Ozymandias'? How especially does this latter poem, with its less fragmentary syntax, serve to point readers away from a symbolic realm, toward more "spiritual thought and its ramifications"?

MH: In *This Constellation Is a Name* (which is nearly 600 pages in length), that very self-conscious phase of experimentation, mostly occurring in the mid-60s, is confined to the first 25 pages. It was a time when I was obsessively concerned with what a poem ought to be, and my subsequent disillusion with that period stemmed not from the work, which was very well received (published, anthologized, praised), but from the goal I had set for myself, which seemed narrow, narcissistic and of little use value to anyone. I stopped writing, though I continued to read as deeply as I could in poetry and everything else. Then I met Oppen, read his work and corresponded with him and began to see a way for myself, not in imitation but in seeking for truth and clarity. My little "machines made of words" could be valuable to me—audience was never a big consideration in my thinking—if they were engines of such seeking. Once I crossed what seems now to have been a psychological and even ethical barrier, I began writing again and could see my earlier writing in a better light. My files contain much more work from that period, and now that I've warmed to it again, I may yet publish a book-length collection of those early poems.

AF: I sense many potential questions regarding the form of Stevensian (extended, lightly serialized) meditation that serves you so well across these volumes. But, given what we already have discussed, could you offer further elaboration, from the *Beckmann Variations* prose, on how a poetics, how your poetics, might engage the inexpressible less by capturing and confining it than by immersing oneself in successive streams of words and works? Again how does this trajectory within one multi-part serial poem outline *This Constellation Is a Name*'s more broadly constellated prospects for polyphonic and perhaps perpetual communication?

MH: To repeat Zukofsky's "inexpressible trust in expression" is about as far as I need to go for a "poetics." All else is theme and variation on what any particular nexus of subject, sound, influence, brings up. My interest in using prose—in sensing the poetics of prose—goes back to my readings of Baudelaire, to the figurations and *frissons* I find across all sorts of writing, to my study of the Japanese poetic diary—but I'm describing a tool chest, because ultimately it is a matter of where the activity of writing, of getting down with the material at hand may lead one. My memoir, *Living Root*, for example, led me into a kind of Midrashic structure, prose, poetry, commentary on the poems, what I not so jokingly call "Jewish *haibun*," *haibun* being the prose-plus-poetry form used by Bashō and other Japanese poets. What the form—or multiplicities of form—seemed to enable was an entry into a discussion of personal history, quarrels with tradition and poetics. And though *This Constellation Is a Name* is mostly poetry, I feel it inhabits similar discursive/anti-discursive space. I'm of the school of Valéry, who said he didn't finish a poem but finally abandoned it.

AF: Amid the many elegies and dedications, a sense of aloneness, of isolation, also appears. Sometimes isolation extends an infantile sense of helplessness. Sometimes this book seeks to find within feelings of emptiness a feeling of freedom. Sometimes this sense of isolation gets placed under the sign of death and each individual's unique engagement with death. Sometimes, as in *Eschaton*, personal apocalypse eventually merges with communal apocalypse—as *Eschaton*, say, which closes on the September 11ᵗʰ attacks. Given that *This Constellation Is a Name'* is a celebration both of isolation/silence and of engagement/conversation with others, how would you characterize the place here of the solitary, the singular? Do such solitary sensations, for instance, provide their own form of shared experience?

MH: We're speaking here about solitude, and you'll recall Rilke's formulation of love as "two solitudes saluting each other." Our condition, our solitariness, seems so fundamental, and it is—nothing original here—the essential impetus to communicate, to write poetry. Which is why I have referred to poetry as a relational act, a bridging that begins in recognition of apartness. A physics and metaphysics of poetry stem from and return to that condition. So yes, it is a "shared" experience, an unavoidably shared one. It began on day one of civilization, maybe earlier.

AF: Following from those last topics, I'd again like to pick up one of this book's own lines of inquiry: must a poem always "witness something"; can it ever "simply come to take its place / Beside these lovely things"? And if you would rather not address such questions so directly, does it at least make sense to track, as this collection's elegies begin to accumulate, an emergent emphasis upon individual testimony, individual recollection, as in the deathbed 'St. Francis Hospital' scene of 'Miami Waters,' with its conjecture that "Perhaps the world / which does not cohere in the world, / coheres in one self, in one rememberer"? Or, even more broadly, as you have lived and written across the twentieth-century's second half and beyond, how has your estimation of individual testimony changed?

MH: That phrase "come to take itself beside these lovely things," which comes from my sequence on Paris, 'Fifty-Three Rue Notre-Dame de Nazareth,' could lead us back to your previous question on solitariness. The passage is ironic/semi-confessional in the sense that the poem's narrator attempts to locate himself between some position of pure aesthetics and that need to witness, hence communicate across the solitude to another. It's an attempt to work out our poetic legacy, beginning with the admission that the narrator is "another legatee of Mallarmé,"—let me quote more:

> I have strained against the tongue
> Until the word displaced
> The world's foreign body.
>
> Have played with the exclusionary pun...
> And yet, and yet

Those "yets" constitute a self-demurral as to where one is going. The passage continues with a catalog of pleasurable objects, foods, sights for the eye, etc., before it gets to that question of taking place or witnessing. I think what I've tried to do in that passage and in the other sections of the poem—because as you know it moves from the bourgeois pleasures of daily life, its "tourism," to contemplate clashes of politics, cultures and the modern horrors of our times—is to stage as powerfully as I could the deepest questions of writing poetry, as did Baudelaire and Mallarmé, who are the poem's agons. Which is why the concepts of chance and the depiction of urban horror thread through and populate the main sections of the poem. I will say that if one is looking for *my* ars poetica, my feeling of the relationship between art and life, it probably can be found in reading that poem.

As an answer to your question about "individual testimony," no, it hasn't changed but deepened. The more serious question might be is there any other kind of witnessing? In *Dianoia*, I confess to "falling in with the spirit of the 'I,' the 'I' that lost credibility."

AF: On this individual note, I sensed a slight increase in oppositional tones (at least addressing the literary world) in this book's later stances "for love and against concept," dreading a world of "only irony," mocking "that tepid faculty-room tea" and corresponding "idea/of an impotence authored by others." Could you discuss these emergent tones, again perhaps in terms of your own lived experience with and through poetry?

MH: These observations—maybe you want to call them quips—arise naturally from the subjects I'm dealing with. But perhaps my inner crank is also kicking in. I subscribe to Oppen's resistance to "Art," a realm of pseudo-professionalism, career-hunting and academic self-loathing which has now become nearly all-pervasive, my question being in 'Ordinariness of the Soul': "for whom ought/the muse to be real?" Part of the *via negativa* of any serious poem is the thread through, as Geoffrey Hill calls it, the climate of contexture, the "enemy's country" of received opinion, movements and group-think. Yeah, I am a crank.

AF: To close, this book's concluding 'Tibet' sequence returns us to many preceding concerns. Echoing, for me, Roland Barthes's *Empire of Signs*, your project's pursuit of "non-human Tibet" (as known not from outside, but from within) returns us to the empathic/ekphrastic/mimetic prowess of your poetics. Efforts here to channel the high-altitude, incantatory, exclamatory ecstasies of your own private Tibet recall both Shelley's Mount Blanc and *This Constellation Is a Name*'s ongoing explorations of the Colorado landscape. So could you position this sequence as looking both backwards and forwards across your corpus? We could discuss more specifically the potential you found in Victor Segalen's obscured, proto-Orientalist text 'Essay on Exoticism.' We could discuss how this paean to a timeless, projected Tibet squares with realities from your own lived history and from that nation's, or how/why it elides doing so. But what, for you, for me, makes 'Tibet' such a fitting conclusion to this collection?

MH: Those are very kind words, identifications and comparisons in your question.

Let me say that the 'Tibet' project is by no means over. *Dianoia*, had another six numbers of the sequence, and there will be more to come. But to the broader aspect of your inquiry. Segalen was both a pioneer and supreme strategist of "otherness," writing in French, of course, creating or doubling the otherness for me, a writer in English. He was an exemplary strategist, because the creation and deployment of "a language that never originally existed," as Haun Sussy says of Segalen's *Stèles*, is a statement equally true for Segalen's *Thibet* series and I hope for my own 'made-up' transpositional efforts. It's an unusual stance that enables an approach to the exotic or Other that simultaneously distances and yet honors our fascination. And isn't poetry—when we call upon it to do what we, at the deepest level of ourselves, wish for poetry to do—giving us the world in a "language that never originally existed," one freed from the entrappings and discourses of previous thought? So yes, the 'Tibet Sequence' is part of my personal Archimedean lever to move my sense of the world (in all of its comprehensiveness, as I understand it) that one iota or degree that will give us a momentary grasp on it again. In one new section of the sequence I call this "the bright shard beyond any tangent of being," something beyond our acquisitive psyches, beyond our possessiveness, a revealment that simultaneously restores the world and ourselves in it. Revealment and opening up is what I want my poetry to do for me, and maybe it will do that for others.

WORKS CITED AND REFERRED TO

Adonis. *An Introduction to Arab Poetics*. Translated from the Arabic by Catherine Cobham. Austin, TX: University of Texas Press, 1990.

Alter, Robert. *Necessary Angels: Tradition and Modernity in Kafka, Benjamin, and Scholem*. Cambridge, MA: Harvard University Press, 1991..

Barbour, Susan, 'The Origins of the Prose Captions in H.D.'s *Helen In Egypt*', *The Review of English Studies*, New Series, Vol 63, No 260, pp. 466–490, 2011.

Bashō, Matsuo. *The Narrow Road to the Deep North and Other Travel Sketches*. Translated and Introduced by Nobuyuki Yuasa. Harmondsworth: Penguin Books Ltd., 1966.

Bialik, Haim Nahman. *Revealment and Concealment*. Miscellaneous translators, and with an Afterword by Zali Gurevitch. Jerusalem: Ibis Editions, 2000.

Biale, David, *Gershom Scholem: Kaballah and Counter-History*, Cambridge, MA: Harvard University Press, 1982.

Benjamin, Walter, *Selected Writings, Volume 1 1913–1926*, Edited by Marcus Bullock and Michael W. Jennings, Cambridge, MA: The Belknap Press of Harvard University Press, 1996.

——. *Selected Writings, Volume 2 1927–1934*, Translated by Rodney Livingstone and Others, Edited by Howard Eland and Michael W. Jennings, Cambridge, MA: The Belknap Press of Harvard University Press, 1999.

——. *Selected Writings, Volume 3 1935–1938*, Translated by Edmund Jephcott, Howard Eiland, and Others, Edited by Howard Eland and Michael W. Jennings, Cambridge, MA: The Belknap Press of Harvard University Press, 2002.

——. *Selected Writings, Volume 4 1938–1940*, Translated by Edmund Jephcott and Others, Edited by Howard Eland and Michael W. Jennings, Cambridge, MA: The Belknap Press of Harvard University Press, 2003.

Bush, Ronald, 'Modernism, Fascism, and the Composition of Ezra Pound's *Pisan Cantos*', *Modernism/Modernity* 2.3, 1995, pp. 69–87, 1995.

Cavell, Stanley. 'Thinking of Emerson' in *New Literary History*, 11:1 (1979 Autumn), pp. 167–176.

Celan, Paul. *Breathturn Into Timestead: The Collected Later Poetry*. A Bilingual Edition. Translated and with Commentary by Pierre Joris. New York, NY: Farrar Straus Giroux, 2014.

Cohen, Marcel. 'Notes.' *World Literature Today*. Translated by Steven Jaron. Summer/Autumn 2001. pp. 54–62.

Curley, Jon. *The Poetry and Poetics of Michael Heller: A Nomad Memory*, edited by Jon Curley and Burt Kimmelman (Madison, NT: Fairleigh Dickinson University Press, 2015).

Dembo, L. S., 'Interviews with Four Objectivist Poets,' *Contemporary Literature*, Vol. 10, No. 2, Spring 1969.

Duncan, Robert. *The Collected Later Poems and Plays*. Edited and With an Introduction by Peter Quartermain. Berkeley, CA: University of California Press, 2014.

——. *The H. D. Book*. Edited and with an Introduction by Michael Boughn and Victor Coleman. Berkeley, CA: University of California Press, 2011.

——. *A Selected Prose*. Edited by Robert Bertholf. New York, NY: New Directions Books, 1995.

Elon, Ari. *From Jerusalem to the Edge of Heaven*. Translated from the Hebrew by Tikva Frymer-Kensky. Philadelphia, PA, and Jerusalem: The Jewish Publication Society, 1990.

Frank, Manfred. in *Common Knowledge*. Vol. 1, No. 1, p. 68.

Finkelstein, Norman. *Like A Dark Rabbi: Modern Poetry and the Jewish Literary Imagination*. Cincinnati, OH: Hebrew Union College Press, 2019.

——. *On Mount Vision: Poems of the Sacred in Contemporary American Poetry*. Iowa City, IA: University of Iowa Press, 2010.

——. 'On the Poetics of the Jewish God, a dialogue between Norman Finkelstein and Michael Heller' in *Imagining The Jewish God* (Lanham, MD: Lexington Books, 2016).

——. *Scribe*. Loveland, OH: Dos Madres Press, Inc. 2009. 115 pp.

——. *Track*. Bristol: Shearsman Books, 2012.

Fenollosa, Ernest. *The Chinese Written Character as a Medium for Poetry*. Edited by Ezra Pound. San Francisco, CA: City Lights Books, 1969.

Fields, Rick. *How The Swans Came To The Lake: A Narrative History of Buddhism in America*. Third edition, Revised and Updated. Boston, MA & London: Shambala Publications, 1992.

Gampopa. *The Jewel Ornament of Liberation*. Translated and Annotated by Herbert V. Guenther, and with a Forward by Chögyam Trungpa Rinpoche. Berkeley, CA: Shambhala Publications, 1959, (Foreword by Chögyam Trungpa, 1971).

Grossman, Allen. *Descartes' Loneliness*. New York, NY: New Directions Books, 2007.

——. *The Sighted Singer: Two Works on Poetry for Readers and Writers*. With contributions by Mark Halliday. Baltimore, MD: The Johns Hopkins University Press, 1991.

Guenther, Herbert V. *The Royal Song of Saraha: A Study in the History of Buddhist Thought*. Berkeley, CA: Shambhala Publications, Inc., 1968, revised and reissued, 1973.

——. *The Tantric View of Life*. Berkeley, CA: Shambhala Publications, 1972.

Guest, Barbara, *Herself Defined: The Poet H.D. and Her World*, New York, NY: Doubleday, 1984.

Handelman, Susan A. *Fragments of Redemption*. Bloomington, IN: Indiana University Press, 1991.

H.D., *Collected Poems: 1912–1944,* Edited by Louis L. Martz, New York, NY: New Directions, 1983.

——. *Helen in Egypt,* Introduction by Horace Gregory, New York, NY: Grove Press, 1961.

——. *Magic Mirror, Compassionate Friendship, Thorn Thicket, A Tribute to Erich Heydt,* Edited by Nephie J. Christodoulides, and with a Preface by Demetres P. Tryphonopoulos and Matte Robinson, Victoria, BC: ELS Edition, 2012.

——. *Palimpsest,* with a Preface by Harry T. Moore, Carbondale, IL: Southern Illinois University Press, 1968.

Heidegger, Martin. *An Introduction to Metaphysics.* Translated by Ralph Manheim. New York, NY: Anchor Books. New York: 1961.

——. *On the Way to Language.* Translated by Peter D. Hertz. San Francisco, CA: Harper & Row, 1971.

——. *Poetry, Language, Thought.* Translated by Albert Hofstadter. San Francisco, CA: Harper & Row, 1971.

Heller, Michael. *Accidental Center.* Fremont, MI: Sumac Press, 1972.

——. 'Avant-Garde Propellants of the Machine Made of Words' in *Uncertain Poetries: Selected Essays on Poets, Poetry & Poetics* (Bristol: Shearsman Books, 2012.

——. *Conviction's Net of Branches.* Carbondale, IL: Southern Illinois University Press, 1985.

——. *Living Root: A Memoir.* Albany, NY State University of New York Press, 2000.

——. *Speaking The Estranged: Essays on the Work of George Oppen.* Cambridge: Salt Publishing, 2008. Revised and re-issued, Bristol: Shearsman Books, 2012.

——. 'Mappah.' *Dianoia.* New York, NY: Nightboat Books, 2016. 3, 4.

——. 'Remains of the Diaspora.' *Radical Poetics and Secular Jewish Culture.* Ed. Stephen Paul Miller and Daniel Morris. Tuscaloosa, AL: University of Alabama Press, 2010. 170–183.

——. 'The Uncertainty of the Poet.' *Uncertain Poetries: Selected Essays on Poets, Poetry and Poetics.* Cambridge, UK: Salt Publishing, 2005, reprinted in an expanded edition by Shearsman Books, 2012. 3–14.

Hölderlin, Friedrich. cited in 'The Method of His Madness' by Charles Louth. *Times Literary Supplement.* August 7, 2009. pp. 3–5.

Hollenberg, Donna Krolik, *Between History and Poetry: The Letters of H.D. and Norman Holmes Pearson,* Iowa City, IA: The University of Iowa Press, 1997.

Jamgon Kongtrul. *Creation and Completion: Essential Points of Tantric Meditation.* Translated by Sarah Harding with a commentary by Khenchen Thrangu Rinpoche. Boston: Wisdom Publication, 1996, 2002.

Jaron, Steven. *Edmond Jabès: The Hazard of Exile.* Oxford: Legenda: European Humanities Research Centre, University of Oxford, 2003.

Johnson, Kent and Paulenich, Craig. Editors of *Beneath A Single Moon: Buddhism in Contemporary American Poetry*. Boston, MA: Shambhala Publications, 1991.

Kalck, Xavier, "'Politics is history'": Testing Oppen's "Test of Truth,'" in *RFEA* (*French Review of American Studies*, 2014).

Kenner, Hugh. *A Homemade World*. New York, NY: Murrow, 1975.

Kenner, Hugh, *Motive and Method in the Cantos of Ezra Pound*, New York, NY: Columbia University Press, 1954.

Kisen, Sekito. 'Song of the Grass Root Hermitage' in *Cultivating the Empty Field: The Silent Illumination of Zen Master Hongzhi*. Translated by T. D. Leighton. Boston, MA: Tuttle Press, 2000.

Kochan, Lionel. *Beyond the Graven Image: A Jewish View*. New York, NY: New York University Press, 1997.

Levinas, Emmanuel. *Proper Names*. Stanford, CA: Stanford University Press, 1997.

Lipkind, Lawrence. *The Life of the Poet*. Chicago, IL: University of Chicago Press, 1984.

Löwy, Michael, *Fire Alarm: Reading Walter Benjamin's 'On the Concept of History'*. Translated by Chris Turner. London: Verso, 1995.

Magliola, Robert. *On Deconstructing Life Worlds*. Atlanta, GA: Scholars Press, 1997.

Mandelstam, Osip. *Mandelstam: The Complete Critical Prose and Letters*. Edited by Jane Gary Harris. Translated by Jane Gary Harris and Constance Link. Ann Arbor, MI: Ardis, 1979

Merleau-Ponty, Maurice. *Sense and Non-Sense*. Translated and with an Introduction by Hubert L. Dreyfus and Patricia A. Dreyfus. Evanston, IL: Northwestern University Press, 1964.

——. *The Visible and Invisible*. Translated by Alphonso Lingis and Edited by Claude Lefort. Evanston, IL: Northwestern University Press, 1968.

Morrison, Paul, *The Poetics of Fascism: Ezra Pound, T. S. Eliot and Paul de Man*, New York, NY: Oxford University Press, USA, 1996.

Nishitani, Keiji. *Religion and Nothingness*. Translated with an Introduction by Jan Van Bragt. Forward by Winston L. King. Berkeley, CA: University of California Press, 1982.

Nietzsche, Friedrich. *Friedrich Nietzsche on Rhetoric and Language*. Edited and translated by Sandor L. Gilman. Oxford: Oxford University Press, 1989.

——.*Project Gutenberg's Thoughts Out of Season (Part II)*, Translated by Adrian Collins. http://www.gutenberg.org/files/38226/38226-h/38226-h.htm

——. *The Use and Abuse of History 2nd Revised Edition*, Translated by Adrian Collins, with an Introduction by Julius Kraft, New York, NY: Macmillan for The Library of Liberal Arts, 1957.

Nicholls, Peter. *George Oppen and the Fate of Modernism*. Oxford: Oxford University Press, 2007.

Oppen, George, *New Collected Poems*. Edited by Michael Davidson. New York, NY: New Directions Publishers, 2002.

——. 'The Philosophy of the Astonished' in *Sulfur* 27, Fall, 1990. pp.202–220.

——. *Selected Letters of George Oppen*. Edited by Rachel Blau DuPlessis. Durham, NC: Duke University Press, 1990.

——. *Selected Prose, Daybooks, and Papers*. Edited and with an Introduction by Stephen Cope. New York, NY: New Directions Publishers, 2007.

Owen, Steven. *Traditional Chinese Poetry and Poetics*. Madison, WI: University of Wisconsin Press, 1985.

Pound, Ezra, *The Cantos of Ezra Pound*, New York, NY: New Directions, 1970.

——. *The Literary Essays of Ezra Pound*. Edited by T. S. Eliot. New York, NY: New Directions,1954.

Preminger, Alex and Brogan, T. V. F., Editors, *The New Princeton Encyclopedia of Poetry and Poetics*, Princeton, NJ: Princeton University Press, 1993.

Prochnik, George. *Stranger in a Strange Land: Searching for Gershom Scholem and Jerusalem*. New York, NY: Other Press, 2017.

Revault d'Allonnes, Olivier. *Musical Variations on Jewish Thought*. Translated by Judith Greenberg, and with an Introduction by Harold Bloom. New York, NY: George Braziller, 1984.

Rexroth, Kenneth. *One Hundred Poems from the Japanese*. New York, NY: New Directions, 1964.

Reznikoff, Charles. *The Poems of Charles Reznikoff 1918–1975*. Edited by Seamus Cooney. A Black Sparrow Book. Boston, MA: David R. Godine, 2005

——.*Selected Letters of Charles Reznikoff 1917–1976*. Edited by Milton Hindus. Santa Rosa, CA: Black Sparrow Press, 1997.

Scholem, Gershom. *The Fullness of Time*. Translated by Richard Sieburth, and introduced and annotated by Steven M. Wasserstrom. Jerusalem: Ibis Editions, 2003.

——. *On the Mystical Shape of the Godhead*. Translated by Joachim Neugroschel, edited and revised by Jonathan Chipman, and with a Forward by Joseph Dan. New York, NY: Schocken Books, 1991.

——. "Reflections on Jewish Theology." *On Jews and Judaism in Crisis: Selected Essays*. New York, NY: Schocken Books, 1976. 261–297.

Sieburth, Richard, 'In Pound We Trust: The Economy of Poetry/The Poetry of Economics,'*Critical Inquiry, Vol 14, No. 1, Autumn 1987.*

Stambaugh, Joan. 'Commentary on Takeshi Umehara's "Heidegger and Buddhism"' in *Philosophy East and West*. Vol. 20, No. 3, (July 1970) pp. 283–286

Stern, David. 'Midrash and Indeterminacy.' in *Critical Inquiry*, Vol 15, No 1, Autumn 1988 pp 132–161.

Stevens, Wallace. *The Necessary Angel*. New York, NY: Vintage Press, 1965.

——. *Opus Posthumous*. New York, NY: Alfred A. Knopf, 1989.

——. *Stevens*. Edited by Helen Vendler. New York, NY: Everyman's Library Pocket Poets, 1993.

Suzuki, DT. *Zen and Japanese Culture*. New York, NY: Bollingen Foundation. Pantheon Books, 1971.

Tarn, Nathaniel. *Views from the Weaving Mountain: Selected Essays in Poetics and Anthropology.* Albuquerque, NM: *An* American Poetry *Book.* University of New Mexico Press, 1991.

Trungpa, Chögyam. *Cutting Through Spiritual Materialism*. Boston, MA: Shambhala Publications, 1987.

——. *Garuda III: Dharmas Without Blame*. Berkeley, CA: Shambhala Publications, Inc., 1973.

——. *Meditation in Action*. Boston, MA: Shambhala Publications, Inc., 1996.

——. *The Myth of Freedom*. Berkeley, CA, & London: Shambhala Publications, Inc. 1976.

——. *The Sādhana of Mahāmudrā*. Halifax, NS: Nālandā Translation Committee, 1990.

Waldrop, Rosmarie. *Lavish Absence: Recalling and Rereading Edmond Jabès*. Forward by Richard Stamelman. Middletown, CT: Wesleyan University Press, 2003.

Wasserstrom, Steven M. *Religion After Religion: Gershom Scholem, Mircea Eliade, and Henry Corbin at Eranos*. Princeton, NJ: Princeton UP, 1999.

Whalen-Bridge, John and Gary Storhoff. Editors of *The Emergence of Buddhist American Literature*. Albany, NY: State University of New York Press, 2009.

Whitman, Walt. *Walt Whitman: Complete Poetry and Collected Prose*. New York, NY: Library of America, 1982.

Wittgenstein, Ludwig. *Notebooks, 1914–1916*. Edited by G. H. von Wright and G. E. M. Anscombe and with an English translation by G .E. M. Anscombe. New York, NY: Harper & Row, 1961.

Wilson, A. N. 'A Kind of Poetry.' *Times Literary Supplement* No. 5857 (July 3, 2015): 22.

Wohlfarth, Irving, 'The Measure of the Possible, The Weight of the Real and the Heat of the Moment: Benjamin's Actuality Today,' *New Formations*, No. 20, Summer 1993, 1–20.

Wolin, Richard, *Walter Benjamin: An Aesthetics of Redemption*, Berkeley, CA: University of California Press, 1982.

Ziarek, Krzysztof. 'The Reception of Heidegger's Thought in American Literary Criticism' in *Diacritics*, 19.3–4 (1989) pp. 114–126.

Zukofsky, Louis, *Complete Short Poetry*, With a forward by Robert Creeley, Baltimore, MD: The Johns Hopkins University Press, 1991.

——. *Prepositions +*, Forward by Charles Bernstein, Additional Prose Edited and Introduced by Mark Scroggins, Hanover, NH: Wesleyan University Press, 2000.

www.ingramcontent.com/pod-product-compliance
Lightning Source LLC
Chambersburg PA
CBHW030543030726
47495CB00004B/1110